THE MARK

OF THE

NEW WORLD ORDER

D1403155

Unless otherwise specified, all Scriptures are taken from the King James Version of the Holy Bible.

The Mark of the New World Order
© 1996, 2009 by Terry L. Cook

Printed in the United States of America

ISBN 1-933641-30-4

THE MARK

OF THE
NEW WORLD ORDER

Terry L. Cook

TABLE OF CONTENTS

About the Author

Terry L. Cook is a fundamentalist Christian intelligence analyst and a retired Los Angeles County Deputy Sheriff. He also is a former State of California Deputy Real Estate Commissioner/fraud investigator. He holds A.A., A.S., B.A., and B.S. degrees. He also holds California State teaching credentials in a variety of subjects and has completed some postgraduate study in theology. He is a licensed real estate broker in three Western states and is licensed by the FAA as an Airline Transport Pilot (ATP commercial jet) and flight instructor as well.

For the past eighteen years, Mr. Cook, an ordained minister of the gospel, has been investigating current geopolitical events as they relate to the fulfillment of "last–days" or "end–times" Bible prophecies, with an emphasis on biometric identification technology, including smart cards and biochip transponder implants. He is accepted widely as an authority in the field. He is much in demand as a speaker in churches and other lecture forums, including appearances and interviews on radio and television.

If your organization would like to invite to your area for a speaking engagement, you may contact him directly by mail at 12402 N. Division Street, #277, Spokane, Washington 99218. Mr. Cook's email address is: tlkmcook@gmail.com

Terry L. Cook is a man called by God for this particular mission at this particular time . . . to educate and alert the church, so they won't be caught sleeping or unaware in these last days and overtaken as by a "thief in the night." Remember the admonition in the Word of God, "I would not have you ignorant." Mr. Cook's desire is that you would not be "ignorant" of what is happening around us and the importance of the message it foretells.

Indeed, Mr. Cook hopes to convey to everyone who reads this book that Jesus is coming back soon, and we need to get serious about God and get prepare for what's coming!

FOREWORD

There are some books that have been written before their time. George Orwell's *1984* was such a book; H. G. Well's *The Time Machine* (1895) and *War of the Worlds* (1898); and Jules Verne's *Twenty Thousand Leagues Under the Sea* (1869) and *From the Earth to the Moon* (1865). And, we could reference others like the Book of Revelation as received from God by the Apostle John.

When the preceding books were first written, they received little notice, but as their projections came into view with the passing of time, the readership increased exponentially. I believe *The Mark of the New World Order* by Terry Cook is such a book. When published in 1995, it received only modest circulation, because it was written before its time. What Terry Cook projected in 1995 has now become reality. There is only part of this book that has yet to be completely realized, and that is the actual receiving of the mark by every one on earth under the threat of execution by beheading (Rev. 20).

The Bibles tells us that the Antichrist, along with his mark, will not be revealed until certain things come to pass as follows:

1. Exponential increase in travel and speed of communication (Dan. 12).
2. Exponential increase in knowledge (Dan. 12).
3. Babylon fall to Medo–Persia; Medo–Persia fall to Greece; Greece fall to Rome; Rome break up into multiple empires (happened in A.D. 500); breakup of a divided Roman Empire into many small nations (happened after WWII); global government out of all nations to produce the Antichrist (happening now). All prophesied in Daniel 2.

4. Jesus said that we would see and hear of all these things which He prophesied, including the image of Antichrist (probably on TV), and the bodies of the two witnesses lying dead in the streets of Jerusalem. This would not be possible without radio and television.

5. The days of Noah again, with the population increasing over the face of the earth with violence and wars. From eight souls after the flood, the world's population did not reach one billion until 1804, forty-five hundred years later. The last billion was added in just twelve years, making the population approximately what it was at the time of the flood.

6. Jesus said that when the Antichrist appeared it would be as in the days of Sodom. Homosexuals are now legally being married in many states already, and in April 2009 the United Nations passed a resolution making homosexuality morally acceptable in every nation in the world.

7. Jesus and the prophets said that the Jews would be scattered into all the world for two thousand years (Hos. 3:4–5; 5:15; 6:1–2; Luke 21:24). Zechariah also prophesied that even after Israel was restored, Jerusalem would be a burdensome stone to ALL NATIONS (Zech. 12:3). Jerusalem is the only capital city of any nation in the world today where no other nation will have an embassy.

Even after Israel became a nation again, the prophet Daniel said that the Antichrist will divide the nation for gain. The United Nations, including the United States, is now trying to divide Israel into two nations with East Jerusalem and the temple belonging to the Muslim majority. What kind of a person will the Islamic army on the Temple Mount permit to stand upon it and declare to the world that he is God and demand that everyone take his mark and number?

I could reference dozens of other pre–Antichrist prophecies being fulfilled right before our eyes, yet the Bible says that the world's masses will be asleep concerning what they mean, and the reign of Antichrist to the end of the Second Coming of Jesus will come as a thief in the night upon the nations.

We are informed that the Antichrist will have control over the gold, silver, and the riches of all nations. The recent economic upheaval that shook the world indicates this time is near. Henry Kissinger said in December 2008 that we must have a world government and President Obama would be the right man to be the president of the global government.

There are hundreds of other social, political, and technical entities regarding the "mark of the beast" in this book by Terry Cook that warn us how very near it is. This book that was written before its time is now updated and ready for everyone who wants to be prepared for the coming of the Lord.

An Overview

> Some even believe we [the Rockefeller family] are part of a secret
> cabal working against the best interests of the United States, char-
> acterizing my family and me as "internationalists" and of conspir-
> ing with others around the world to build a more integrated global
> political and economic structure—one world, if you will. If that's
> the charge, I stand guilty, and I am proud of it.
> —David Rockefeller, *Memoirs,* p. 405

Clichés . . . clichés . . . clichés! Some people speak in nothing else,
but sometime they seem to serve better than anything to illustrate a point or make a difficult message more easily understood. I
imagine throughout this book I'll probably use my share . . . and perhaps more. For example, there's the old "love and marriage . . . you
can't have one without the other" cliché. It makes the point exactly
that I wish to convey when telling you about the thrust of this book.
Just substitute the words "surveillance and control" for the words
"love and marriage," and you'll get the appropriate image.

The world is in the process of a great shaking, and not just physically (although in fulfillment of prophecy we can expect much more
of that than we presently are experiencing). We are being shaken together in order to "even out the playing field," as it were (see, there's
another of those clichés)—both socially and economically. The only
way to accomplish that is if each nation surrenders its individual
sovereignty to the leadership of a world governing body or leader,
who will in turn see to it that all nations will capitulate, either vol-

untarily or by force. Naturally, all of this will be "for our own good and/or convenience." What will finally "shake out" will be that about which we have heard so much lately, the *New World Order* (or some other agreed-upon name with the same goals and methods).

Many nations would benefit greatly from this "evening out" of the playing field, which, of course, would be at the expense of many others. For them it will cost *everything*—economy, military, health, education, natural resources, self-rule, in other words, all personal liberty/freedom and possessions.

However, many are not deceived by the old line that they are "doing it for our own good," and are refusing to "roll over and play dead." Exactly what can you do about all these rabble-rousers and troublemakers? The only way for such a turnover of power to occur successfully is if everyone complies and cooperates. The "powers that be" have been planning this scenario for centuries. Now that the plan is about to see fruition they are not going to look kindly upon dissenters or uncooperative types. (In a speech, Rockefeller stated that there was too little time left to get the plan accomplished gradually because the fundamentalists were waking up, so they are stepping up their speed.)

The first thing they must accomplish is to remove as many as possible of our constitutionally-protected rights and freedoms— legislatively and judicially—in effect, making all dissenters "outlaws." Once they have succeeded in declaring their opposition to be the "bad guys," then they have all the power of the police, military, and judiciary behind them. You will either join the system or oppose it. Of course, if you refuse to join, you are automatically in opposition and one of the above-described rabble-rousers and troublemakers.

The only way those who enforce the new regulations (for lack of a better word) will be able to achieve their goal of bringing everyone into the New World Order is through surveillance and control. They can't control you if they can't find you and keep track of your movements, activities, communications, purchases, *et al.* In other words, there must be a grand and global scheme for the *surveillance* of everyone before you can hope to *control* everyone.

An article by Richard Falk states, "It is evident that the new world

order as conceived in Washington is about control and surveillance.
. . ." Lest you be misled, do not mistake Mr. Falk for a right–wing conservative; on the contrary, he believes that their motives are anything but "pure" toward equality in the New World Order. In fact, he continues, " . . . not about values or a better life for the peoples of the world." He believes the wealthy nations are using their technology as an advantage to keep the poorer nations from being a threat to them.

Although the major thrust of *The Mark of the New World Order* is identification and tracking systems, a certain amount of foundation needs to be laid first. Therefore, I will cover a number of subjects in addition to tracking technology.

Some people find this subject matter to be "science fiction," some consider it fulfillment of Bible prophecy, and still others consider it the raving of some lunatic who sees a conspiracy under every rock; but the ones who study it carefully see it as the next logical step toward establishing the New World Order. Most all of the people, however, are somewhat staggered by the pervasiveness of the proposed systems, and its seeming inevitability lurking just on the horizon. In other words, they are experiencing what has come to be known as "future shock." So I will touch on future shock and its effect on the masses, as well as on the individual.

I will address the New World Order: What is it? When is it? How will it take over? Who's in charge? Where did the idea originate, and how old is this plan for a one–world government?

Other subjects will include loss of privacy and electronic bondage, the United Nations Resolution 666, the new constitution, the Illuminati, biometrics, barcoding, GPS (Global Positioning System), the cashless society . . . let's pause here for a minute. There are other subjects to mention, but I want to address this subject before I proceed, because we are so far down the road toward a cashless society . . . further than most of us recognize!

This is one of the first few steps that must be enacted to get us ready for biochip implants, and it is one of those "we're doing it for your own good" type of actions. If studied fairly, without consideration for the prophetic implications, it really is for our own good; however, the end result of the drawbacks far outweighs any temporary convenience or good it will accomplish. Some of the good things about which you will be hearing more and more as the time draws closer and closer are: it will stop theft, robberies, and muggings; it will stop international drug dealing; it will stop income tax "cheaters"; it will stop "deadbeat dads"; it will give you access to your funds anywhere; you won't have to carry money to shop or travel, just your identity card; your earnings could be deposited directly into your account; you could pay bills at home by PC. Think of the convenience and safety!

But what are those drawbacks I mentioned? To start with, everything you have, owe, or own is in a machine (including your health records, family history, religious affiliations, job history, credit history, political leanings—all this comes later, but not as much later as you might imagine), which gives everybody with the authorization all the information about your personal business . . . no more privacy—except from you (it is not intended for the holder to have access to the information on the card). The identification system (SMART cards, MARC cards, or whatever) must be tied unalterably to you in order to prevent theft of the card and fraudulent use thereof. The card must be used in conjunction with some other source of positive identification, such as retina scan or fingerprint match. Can you already see the direction this path is taking you? What if your card were lost or stolen? We can fix that! This tiny little biochip no bigger than a grain of rice (and maybe smaller as technology progresses) can be slipped under your skin and give you lifetime access to everything the New World Order will afford its happy members.

This is the first time in history when the technology has been available to fulfill the prophecy in Revelation 13:16–18, which tells us that no one can buy or sell without a mark in their right hand or forehead. Naturally, the manufacturers of this technology try to assure us that it wasn't designed for that purpose, but even as they speak, plans are being discussed to implant the "difficult" cases, i.e. the prison population, runaway teens, the elderly who have a tendency to wander off and become lost, and even implanting babies before they leave the hospital to put an end to kidnapping and child-stealing. Doesn't that sound like a *really GOOD thing?* (Excuse me for being facetious!) Don't assume it will never happen. At the moment, the method is used widely in pet identification and agricultural animals, but just recently there were reports of tracking and punishing poachers of salmon with implants, and the government ruled that all surgically implanted body parts will henceforth contain a biochip (of course, that's also for your *good,* as it retains the information about its manufacturer, your surgeon, how and why it was implanted, etc.), and breast implants are some of the first to be manufactured with the biochip. Another recent use of radio transponder identification (biochips) was in permanently riveted vinyl bracelets applied to over fifty thousand Haitian and Cuban refugees at the Guantanamo Bay U.S. military base. (They are now investigating the possibility of producing them with a metal strip in the band, as it seems that some people resent this type of "numbering" and have been trying to remove them.) Since children's wrists are too small, they are applied to the child's ankle.

Have you noticed lately how everything on television is *smart?* Pay close attention to the current rash of commercials—AT&T actually calls theirs the Smart Card, but the term *smart* is used in so many different advertisements that it will amaze you—once you start taking notice of the use of that one word. That's because they want you to become so acquainted with the term (read that "desensitized") it will seem like second nature to you. I'll be telling you how a SMART card is constructed, what its features are, and its intended purpose in this unstoppable chain of events. The credit card companies and banks are already offering to exchange—free of charge, mind you— your old credit card with a brand new one with your digitized photo on the front. Of course, they don't tell you what else will be contained (or have the capability to be contained) on this fancy new card.

There also will be chapters on the MARC military identification card, and the national and state identification cards. Of course, one of the largest chapters will discuss biochip technology—its origination, manufacture, current uses, proposed uses, and unlimited possible future uses. Finally, I will summarize these facts, and introduce the prophetic connections as described in the Bible. I hope by reading this book you will be informed and awakened from your slumber—

if, indeed, you have been blissfully, but ignorantly, slumbering along, enjoying all this new "Star Trek" technology without being cognizant of the dire consequences.

—Terry L. Cook

THE COVERT MEANING OF THIS OCCULTIC SYMBOL IS:

ANNUIT: ANNOUNCING
COEPTIS: THE BIRTH OF
NOVUS: THE NEW
SECLORUM: WORLD WITHOUT GOD
ORDO: ORDER
Under the ALL-SEEING EYE of the Antichrist!

CHAPTER ONE

FUTURE SHOCK IS HERE!

D on't reach for your wallet at the checkout counter. After your items have been priced, totaled, and bagged, *simply pass your RIGHT HAND* over the scanner and the amount will be deducted from your bank account.

Impossible? The plot of a science fiction novel? Hardly! The technology to accomplish such futuristic feats is already here, and nearly every type of store is using either a stationary or hand–held laser scanner to read the barcodes and enter your purchases into the computer. Long gone are the days of the old–fashioned cash register.

"But just suggest something like an implant in human beings and the social outcry is tremendous," says Tim Willard, executive officer of the World Future Society, a Washington, D.C.–based organization that claims 27,000 members worldwide, including *Future Shock* author Alvin Toffler. "While people over the years have grown accustomed to artificial body parts, there is definitely a strong aversion to things being implanted. It's the '*BIG BROTHER is watching*' syndrome. People would be afraid that all of their thoughts and movements were being monitored. It wouldn't matter if the technology were there or not. People would still worry."

But wait, we're getting a bit ahead of ourselves here. First we need to define the term *future shock* and how it came into our vocabulary. According to *Webster's New Collegiate Dictionary*, Ninth Edition, *future shock* is defined as: "The physical and psychological distress suffered by one who is unable to cope with the rapidity of social and technological changes." As words in the dictionary go, this one is of fairly recent origin. The dictionary tells us that it first came into common usage about 1970.

I don't know if Toffler can be credited with originating the term, but using it as the title of his book certainly promulgated its wide acceptance, and the definition is one with which most people of this decade are familiar, to at least some degree.

Future shock has come to be considered a negative term which bridges the age gap from children (who feel they are being propelled into the future before they are ready, and that adults have pretty much messed it up for them anyway) to senior citizens (who are befuddled by all this electronic computer technology and long for the "good old days"). It also bridges all areas of life, from banking, economics, and industry to education, social sciences, art, music, communications, databases, *et al.* We are being hurled ever forward by knowledge that is expanding exponentially.

And the most distressing symptom of future shock is the dehumanizing feeling we experience that we are all becoming nothing more than numbers . . . and in fact, that is the truth. With the world shrinking because of travel and communication technology and the pressure by the "powers that be" to merge us all into a one–world government (spell that, New World Order), the only way to "organize" us and keep track of us (for our own good, of course), is to give us all a single identification method that can be recognized worldwide. And if you think that's not where we are headed, you're just kidding yourself.

So, future shock is real . . . it's just not very much in the *future* anymore. Future shock is here . . . future shock is now! Perhaps "Big Brother" wasn't watching us by the year *1984,* as Orwell's book title speculates, but he wasn't all that far off target. The technology is here now via fiber optics, satellites, and other modern marvels for Big Brother to sit on the Information Superhighway, right in your living room. The only difference is that during the time from 1984 to 2009, we have been brainwashed into believing that this is a wonderful thing, so Big Brother didn't have to force his way in, as Orwell postulated; he is with us by our own invitation.

BIOCHIP—RFID TECHNOLOGY

The *very IDEA* of implanting *even our pets* with identifying microchip transponders is a concept that for years was approached very slowly. "We wanted to make sure it's right for the animals, and that the *community is willing to accept* this new technology," said Diane Allevato, director of the Novato, California, animal shelter. Now, however, such high-tech "tagging" is on "fast-forward" since people have grown accustomed—by successful *conditioning*—to what once was considered offensive technology. For example, if people are now willing to have such devices injected into their pets, why would they not put them into their own bodies? Or, to soften the blow just a little, into old folks who wander away from home, children (to prevent kidnapping), prison inmates, and runaway teens, because all that would be for the good of society as a whole . . . it's always for your own good! Once you have edged your way into accepting these logical implant choices, it's no great leap to accept the fact that a non-removable implant would be terribly convenient and much safer for us than carrying around cards for all our needs (economic, health, passports, travel, etc.)—cards that could be lost or stolen.

BIOCHIP THE SIZE OF A GRAIN OF RICE

For household pets, the transponder chip implant is about the size of a grain of rice. It is permanently imprinted with an identifying number that corresponds to the name, address, and phone number of the pet's owner. This information pops up on a viewing screen when the animal is scanned externally (up to three± inches from the skin) by the antenna of a scanner wand.

A Novato, California, animal shelter earlier was the first shelter in the country to use the biochips. One lady phoned them to say she felt the implants were "unnatural and weird." "And there is no doubt about it, injecting an animal with such a chip is a pretty unnatural thing to do," Allevato said. "But it's also unnatural, obscene really, that about 15 million stray animals are destroyed in this country each year because their owners cannot be found," she continued.

As of the writing of this manuscript, animal implants are no longer considered "unnatural and weird." In fact, the system is in common usage worldwide, and the "service" is readily available to pet owners at many veterinarians and animal hospitals. In addition, implant identification has gone from being *advocated* to being *mandated* by the animal control departments of most metropolitan areas.

The transponder chips being implanted into most animals today are manufactured by four major companies: American Veterinary ID (AVID) of Norco, California; Infopet Corporation of Minnesota; Hughes Aircraft in Southern California; and Texas Instruments of Attleboro, Massachusetts. Originally, Destron IDI Corporation of Boulder, Colorado, began the concept, but they now serve primarily as a research and development company for both Hughes and Texas Instruments, through various joint ventures.

RFID IMPLANTS

Many more companies have now entered the RFID manufacturing field, but few have decided to enter the implantable biochip field. As yet, this is a fairly exclusive technology. It seems, however, that RFID identification has become the wave of the future for both animate and inanimate object identification.

Biochip usage now has surpassed the "personal pet" stage and is being used in many different areas of farming, ranching, racing, and wildlife identification and monitoring. In conjunction with computer technology, RFID biochips are used to track and monitor the health histories, bloodlines, etc. of various farm animals, race horses, breeding stock, and more.

In the ranching business, it eliminates the need for branding your cattle and serves as a deterrent to rustlers. It is used to identify and track the health and performance of prize breeding stock.

In the modern dairy business, good ole' Bossie can come into the barn, pass under a scanner, be directed to her stall, and find her own specially prepared diet in place, just awaiting her arrival—all based upon her identification combined with the computer–stored information about what the handlers want her to eat. Her health records, milk production, and other pertinent factors are all considered, and the optimum diet assigned to her.

Wildlife has been tagged and tracked manually/visually for many years, but now it is possible to track even life as small as a honeybee by attaching an RFID to its back. Of course, this is a real stroke of genius, according to the ecologists, for monitoring all types of wildlife, especially the endangered species.

According to Destron director Jim Seiler, implantable RFID biochips are even being used to track fish. In some fishery applications, salmon are injected with these biochips, then scanned and tracked as they pass through specially equipped dam sites "to assure environmentalists that they are not being chewed up in the dam's power turbines," Seiler said.

[NOTE: At the writing of this manuscript, reports were coming out of Europe that poachers were being caught and fined because the biochip implants in the fish led the authorities to the poacher. The implications of this announcement are staggering. It means that the biochip no longer has to be scanned at a close distance of three to twelve inches. It would indicate that technology has been developed and actually put into service that could scan for detection of biochips at great distances, possibly even by satellite. This is the ultimate direction biochip technology is heading, as surveillance and control of humans is of far more importance to the leaders of the New World Order than the tracking of animals.]

While there are at least "10,000 application ideas to explore when it comes to the chip's potential," Seiler insisted Destron is concerned only with animal identification and *is not considering HUMAN application.* "There is no need to apply the technology to humans because the human fingerprint is unique enough to identify them," he said. "Animals don't have such a unique identifier." All present manufacturers deny that they are considering any form of human application; however, latest info indicates to the contrary.

But Tim Willard, managing editor of the World Future Society's bimonthly magazine, *FUTURISTS,* said the technology behind such a *human microchip* is "fairly uncomplicated and with a little refinement, *could be used in a variety of human applications.* ... Conceivably, *a number could be assigned at birth* and go with a person throughout life," Willard said.

THE ID CHIP WILL BE IMPLANTED IN THE HAND!

"Most likely," Willard added, "it would be *implanted in the back of the right* or left *hand* for convenience, so that it would be *easy to scan* at stores. . . . It could be used as a *universal identification card* that would replace credit cards, passports, that sort of thing. . . . At the supermarket checkout stand, you would simply *pass your hand over the scanner* and your bank account would be automatically debited. . . . It could be programmed to replace a medical alert bracelet. For example, at the scene of an accident, a medic could *scan the victim's hand* to find out his recent medical history, allergies, a relative to contact, etc. This would be especially valuable if the person were unconscious."

In another very logical application, such microchips could replace the need for keys to home, car, and workplace locks, since *the chip in one's hand* would serve as a *universal key* for all such locks. One would simply scan the back of his or her right hand over a high-tech microreader device designed into future locks to gain access. Security would be enhanced tremendously, since, allegedly, no one would be able to "pick" the locks. Doesn't that make you feel really safe? Not if you understand that any burglar worth his salt has always found a way around locks and security devices, no matter how complex. It might serve as a deterrent to an inept low-life, but a serious crook would manage to get in somehow. The bigger the target, the cagier the crooks!

NEW BIOCHIPS OF LIVING PROTEINS

If you really want to go into future shock, or jump right into Star Trek, consider the probability that down the road a few years today's microchips will be outclassed by new biochips made of *living proteins.* According to Willard, "a powerful biochip that, once surgically implanted in the brain, could make it possible to *program or upload an unlimited amount of information into the mind, without ever having cracked a book!*" Compared with the microchips of today, "it will be infinitely smaller and have the capacity to carry much more information. It will have a wide range of functions that will simply boggle our minds," Willard said.

LOSS OF FREEDOM AND PRIVACY

Chapter two of this book will discuss extensively the loss of our privacy and electronic bondage, but I should at least address it briefly here, as it contributes greatly to the condition called future shock.

The capabilities described above carry with them the inherent risk of abuse by government and other organizations, particularly over the issue of privacy. How would—or could—access to such information be limited and controlled? And if (read that "when") it is passed around (usually without our knowledge, much less our consent) to a variety of entities, both private and governmental, how will we know of errors that occur when someone is updating information? No system is foolproof . . . errors will *always* occur somehow. Recipients of the error will not make any adjustments to *their* records/databases. You must determine the origination of the error and try your best to get them to correct the mistake (not likely to occur, I might warn you, since admitting such a blunder would make them financially liable for any injury you might have suffered because of their negligence). And getting them to pass such a correction on to everyone who received the erroneous data from them is practically hopeless.

It would be very difficult to impose enforceable limitations on the availability of such information in today's sophisticated environment of internationally–linked databases. There would be no guarantees that confidential information might not inadvertently "leak" out to someone not authorized to have it . . . except YOU, of course! You are not authorized. There is no plan to give you access to the information that all the various businesses, governments, insurance companies, credit bureaus, etc., have collected on you. Regardless of restrictions that are alleged to have been implemented, information on you regularly changes hands between these entities.

A HUMAN BIOCHIP ID SYSTEM

A human microchip identification system, Willard said, "would work best with a *highly CENTRALIZED computer system* where *only one ID number* would be needed to gain access to medical, credit, academic, home security, and other kinds of data. But under this arrangement, as you can imagine, *security risks are somewhat intense.*

"People tend to be *idealistic* about their independence and privacy, *but the reality is that most information pertaining to education, credit history, whatever, is readily available to just about anyone who asks.* Anyone who has ever experienced a simple credit check knows this," Willard said.

One futurist found the concept of microchip implantation in *humans* offensive. "It reminds me of tattooing concentration camp victims during World War II," said Robert Mittman of the Institute for the Future, a nonprofit research and consulting firm in California. He said there were better methods of identifying people than "violating the integrity of their skin." He continued, "Personally, I have problems with it. . . . People would *end up sacrificing some civil rights.*"

Another concerned individual is the associate director of the ACLU for Northern California, Martha Kegal. Kegal expressed concern over how private records would be kept from "inquiring minds" *if* such a system existed.

THE SYSTEM IS ALREADY IN PLACE

But the question is not whether or not such a system exists, because we all know it does. It is already in place and obvious to all but the most naïve. Rather, the question most troubling any intelligent mind would seem to be the system's final destination, as it were. Whenever we get to wherever it ultimately is taking us . . . will it have proven to be good or evil? For an answer to this question, we must turn to our Creator's operations manual, the Bible, for only God knows how all things will end.

ONLY THE BIBLE HAS THE ANSWERS

According to God's holy Word, the end result of all our present circumstances is quite clear. Our generation is apparently the one that has been appointed to be alive at the time of the conclusion of all ages, better known as the *end of the world.* For the first time in history, the technology is available (and nearly in place) to accomplish the things prophesied in the Bible. Precisely which technology will be used is immaterial—the fact is, never prior to this generation has *any* technology been available to permit the conduct of commerce in the manner described in Revelation 13:16–17.

Such an end–times scenario necessarily involves the implantable biochip technology (or something comparable) around which this book has been written, for without it the final worldwide system of satanic government, as outlined in the books of Daniel and Revelation, simply would not be feasible.

Current technological and political circumstances soon will lead to a system of universal totalitarian enslavement by means of a global economic network of computerized bartering. This system will be led by a global dictator whom the Bible calls the *Antichrist.* This Antichrist, Satan's personal representative on the scene—the final "Hitler"—will successfully orchestrate the affairs of the entire globe via a one–world government. This man will be the very epitome of evil. The Bible tells us about the number **666** of which Hollywood has made such a big deal in horror films. Of course, as is typical with Hollywood, the number *really is* a "big deal," even though they treat it as fiction or a myth. Consider the following: "That no man might buy or sell, save he that had the mark, or the name of the beast, or the number of his name. Here is wisdom. Let him that hath understanding count the number of the beast: for it is the number of a man; and his number is Six hundred threescore and six" (Rev. 13:17–18).

As we are admonished to seek understanding and wisdom, for generations Bible scholars have been studying this mystery in an attempt to identify who would become this world leader, this Antichrist. It is not such an impossible task as it may seem, because the New Testament was written in Greek, and Greek characters not only comprise their alphabet, but each character carries a numerical value as well. If you were a good student of Greek and knew your scriptures well, you could become very intrigued with checking the names of world leaders who are volleying for position on the international horizon today. However, even though it seems impossible that this future dictator is not somewhere on the scene today, the Bible says that he will not be revealed for sure until about halfway through the Great Tribulation. If, indeed, we are the generation who will witness the return of Jesus Christ, then he surely is born at this time and working his way up through the ranks—although whoever it is may come out of seeming obscurity and rise quickly to power because of the abilities given to him by Satan.

I have a personal theory that bears indirectly on the relevance of this book. We are told in the Bible by Jesus that no one knows the exact day and hour of His return (Matt. 24:36), but we will know when it is very near, even at the door. Only the Father knows when He will send Jesus back again, although the Bible implies that it will be at the end of the age. Now consider this: If even *Jesus* does not know, it is certain that *Satan* cannot know. Therefore, in order for him to be in a position to fulfill the prophecy about the Antichrist given in Revelation, he would have had to have someone of the right age and a name that equaled "666" waiting in the wings, as it were, at all times throughout history, since Jesus' ascension. Not engraved in Scripture, but interesting food for thought.

The Bible is very clear on one thing, however—that even the very elect will be deceived if they are not alert and do not exercise discernment.

THE 666 "MARK" ECONOMIC SYSTEM

In the Antichrist's global economic system, *no one* will be able to work, eat, own property, or "buy and sell" anything without accepting a world-government "mark" (probably a biochip) in their RIGHT hand or forehead. This New World Order biochip "mark" will be the means by which all financial transactions are consummated. Without it, no one will be able to transact any business anywhere in this forthcoming *CASHLESS, debit, computerized, bartering system.*

This sounds very sinister, doesn't it? Like science fiction? *Like your worst nightmare?!?* Well, it is, but the worst is yet to come. If one refuses to cooperate with this global program of electronic bondage by refusing the mark, *he will be killed!* (In Revelation, the method is beheading, and the relevance of the method will become apparent in future chapters.) On the other hand, if one *does* accept the mark, he will burn in Hell forever, according to Scripture (Rev. 14:9-11).

We are told in the book of Revelation that whoever resists taking the mark will be *coerced into compliance under the threat of death!*

For rejecting it, he will lose his head. How horrible! Could this be true? Yes, God tells us that this will be a classic "do or die" situation that will be the final test of all ages. Will you worship Jesus Christ or the Antichrist? There is no middle ground—either you are *for* Jesus Christ or *against* Him. If you are not *for* Him, by virtue of that decision, you automatically are *against* Him. It's that simple!

THE SATANIC NEW WORLD ORDER

Such an evil scenario certainly does not sound like the "kinder, gentler, democratic New World Order of peace and safety," that George Bush, Bill Clinton, Barack Obama, and other globalists worldwide have been selling us, does it? But according to Scripture, that's exactly what's on the immediate horizon! Now you know why I have devoted all of the next chapter to the New World Order.

In any event, let me just make this clear to you . . . *please do not be deceived* by all the confusing rhetoric you are hearing presently regarding how beautiful and glorious this new system of global government will be. Such propaganda and communistic disinformation is nothing more than a smoke screen—an evil satanic lie. The New World Order will be the most horrible form of totalitarian government the world has ever known. In fact, it will enslave us all.

Yes, the "Big Brother" world government system that has been dreaded for years is nearly upon us. There are many attempts being made by "influential" people to allay our fears about "Big Brother"-style government. It is being defined and touted by many as the wonderful New World Order (there's nothing *new* about it—this plan has been on the drawing board in some form since Adam and Eve were kicked out of the garden!). This diabolical global agenda has finally become public—George Bush brought it out of the occultic closet and because of the diligence of many astute, alert Christian scholars and researchers, this information is now available to all who will listen and learn. For the past two hundred years, this plan for global unification and control has been gaining momentum . . . and gaining ground. It is a demonic "spiritual" plan that transcends generations. It appears this is the generation that will witness and experience the culmination of Satan's efforts in this regard. And as usual, the majority of this nation has been lulled into a stupor by the gradual desensitizing of our mental faculties about our hard–won liberties.

However, due to the efforts of the above–mentioned scholars and researchers, the "sleeping giant" is beginning to awaken (a fulfillment of prophecy, of course, as we approach the time of our Lord's return), which is exactly what Rockefeller stated as the reason for speeding up their agenda, as we conservatives and Christians are beginning to "muck up the works."

THE OCCULTIC SKULL & BONES SOCIETY

Former president George H. W. Bush, a member of the highly secret cult located in New Haven, Connecticut, called the "Skull & Bones Brotherhood of Death," began conditioning America for this "New World Order of peace and security" as he involved us in the Gulf War. Remember the scripture that says when men cry peace and safety, sudden destruction will come upon them? Well, maybe I used that a little bit out of context, but it doesn't seem too far off, does it?

THE CFR AND TRILATERAL COMMISSION

In fact, Bush vocalized this occultic, global government "New World Order" phrase *more than two hundred times* in public appearances since 1990. It is no mistake that he continues to advocate publicly such a United Nations–controlled world government system with this evil Masonic, Illuminist, communist, globalist terminology, for he has been associated with many socialist, occultic, globalist organizations for years. Two of the most notable of such organizations are known as the *Trilateral Commission* and the *Council on Foreign Relations* in New York.

THE SECRET "BILDERBERGER" CULT

Bush has not only been a member of the above two socialist world-government organizations for some time, but he also served as an officer and director of the CFR in 1979. Additionally, Bush is a member of the very powerful secret Bilderberger Club in Europe. The Bilderbergers control all the money in the world!

U.N. RESOLUTION 666

When Bush started his New World Order Gulf War in 1990, the U.N. Security Council voted approval of it under United Nations Resolution 666, the biblical number of the Antichrist, the man who is called the *Beast* of the apocalypse in Revelation 13! Coincidental? Hardly!

President Bill Clinton, though not a member of the Skull & Bones Brotherhood of Death, is also a member of the Council on Foreign Relations, the Trilateral Commission, and the Bilderbergers. As indicated, these "clubs" are dedicated to bringing forth a satanic New World Order global government of communism/fascism whereby the national sovereignty and Constitution of the United States, as well as other nations, will be eliminated. Soon America will be subjugated to the dominion of the evil United Nations communistic system of world government. In other words, shortly the United States will cease being a sovereign, independent, free nation. But I'm sure this isn't news to most of you. Unfortunately, you can see your liberties eroding on a daily basis . . . headed toward the ultimate loss of individual and national independence.

CLINTON'S "NEW WORLD ORDER" AGENDA

You might ask if there is any other evidence that would indicate that Bill Clinton's agenda is identical to George Bush's regarding the imposition of this New World Order plan on America? Yes, there most certainly is! The day after President Clinton's inauguration, January 21, 1993, the *Los Angeles Times* carried a front–page article about him entitled "Clinton Must Now Choose Big Gambles or Safe Bets." In the first and second paragraphs of this article the following statements were made: "The Great Seal of the United States [as seen on the back left side of every dollar bill—the pyramid with the eye over it] and with it a motto . . . *Novus ordo seclorum* [Latin for New World Order]—A New Age Now Begins. . . . And President Clinton, like many of his predecessors, invoked that spirit . . . [at his] inaugural address."

AMERICA'S GOVERNMENT IS CONTROLLED BY OCCULTISTS AND SOCIALISTS

To the informed, astute citizen, it is quite obvious that our government has been taken over secretly and quietly from within by satanic conspirators. Indeed, America is presently under the control of a very powerful, elite, occultic group of people pulling the strings like we are a bunch of puppets. And if this doesn't send you into future shock, you already must be too numb to notice! This secret group is called the Illuminati, and they control not only our government, but all the governments of the world. The evil men who belong to this group orchestrate world affairs from their European base of operations by issuing marching orders to all the nations on earth.

What gives them the power and ability to do this? It sounds like science fiction again . . . just too big for our ordinary, finite brains to comprehend on such a global scale. And for years there have been people who see a conspiracy "under every rock." But remember the old adage that the one who controls the purse strings rules the world? Well, *they control the purse strings* . . . in fact, they *own* the whole purse! They control all the money on this planet via international centralized world banks, including the Federal Reserve Bank, a private banking corporation here in America. ("The Fed," as it is commonly known, is a privately–owned and controlled institution, even though our government has granted them the authority to control the rise and fall of our total economy through the raising and lowering of interest rates . . . whatever they say goes, and EVERY bank, mortgage company, savings and loan, etc., in the United States immediately capitulates to their almost daily fluctuations.)

This is why the near–simultaneous occurrence of numerous earth–shaking global events is accelerating at such an unprecedented exponential rate. Such rapidly occurring global events are rushing to usher in this satanic "global village" community of nations called (presently) the New World Order. *Future Shock, here we come!*

THE POPE CLAIMED HE WOULD CONTROL THE NEW WORLD ORDER

Even Pope John Paul II expressed a similar New World Order view in Malachi Martin's book, *The Keys of This Blood*, a 700–page volume detailing "the grand design's" intricacies. According to Martin, John Paul II claimed that he himself would lead this New World Order world government system by the year 2000. Although Pope John Paul II died in April of 2005 without this dream becoming reality, the intent of the Catholic Church to lead this New World Order is still in place.

THE CASHLESS 666 ECONOMIC SYSTEM

Before proceeding further, first we need to acquire a basic understanding of the concepts behind the coming universal cashless financial system. Such insight and knowledge will help us fully appreciate how the New World Order's system of servitude fits together. And since this is such an important issue, we are going to spend considerable time discussing it in chapter six, for the coming cashless society will be the financial means by which we all will be enslaved.

666 BARCODE AND BIOCHIP IMPLANTS

In chapter five, I will discuss the *666 barcode* versus biochip transponder systems and why biochip implants are the ultimate breakthrough in ID technology. In fact, we will learn that, unlike barcodes, biochips are a foolproof, unalterable system of identification—a system of absolute certainty, if you will. As I pointed out previously, such a "Big Brother" system of positive identification is needed in the coming satanic New World Order; otherwise, it would be impossible to totally control, track, monitor, and enslave people. This is a time unlike any other time in the history of the world!

ELECTRONIC BONDAGE

Once this satanic, global, computerized Big–Brother financial network is fully in place, you will have lost all your privacy and freedom. You will have become enslaved to the global, electronically-controlled New World Order dictatorship!

Are you now able to visualize how all of this might materialize? And how soon? Good! Now that you all are thoroughly *future shocked*, let's move right on in to chapter two and the loss of your privacy.

LOSS OF PRIVACY AND
ELECTRONIC BONDAGE

E ven as I write this chapter, I am reminded of the horrendous events that unfolded in Oklahoma City in April 1995, where terrorists bombed a nine–story federal building, allegedly with a single truck–bomb parked in front of the structure. Supposedly, they just parked it, drove away in another vehicle, and detonated the massive bomb from a remote location, or perhaps with a timing device. (Currently, the feasibility of this method is being challenged by some who are experts on the construction of this particular building. Their feeling is that additional internal explosives would have been required, placed on certain crucial supports, to have rendered the kind of damage that resulted.)

This terrorist act affected the federal building, which housed primarily what would be referred to as civilian activities, i.e., Social Security offices, federal assistance offices, and a sizable daycare center, as well as a few such as FBI, CIA, and Secret Service, but the devastation was not limited to that one building. The shock was felt as far away as fifty miles, and the glass in buildings as far away as four to five blocks was blown out, injuring many unsuspecting pedestrians and office workers, as well as a number of other children in the YMCA facility across the street.

The fatalities surpassed one hundred fifty, with a few bodies never located. The medical personnel ran out of body bags and requested that people donate sheets. Dogs with high–tech, extremely sensitive microphones were sent through the rubble in an attempt to locate any remaining survivors. One victim had a leg amputated on the spot in order to extricate her from the debris and permit her life to be saved.

The nine floors "pancaked" down on top of one another and landed in a crater created by the bomb. Despite all the efforts of the engineers to shore up the wreckage, and the extreme care taken by the rescue workers, one was killed and two others were injured in the heroic rescue attempts. The devastation has been compared in magnitude with the earthquake of two years earlier in Northridge, California.

However, there is a big difference . . . and the resulting effect on the population, both in Oklahoma and across our nation, is much more explosive. This act of violence was committed by radical people with a religious or political agenda . . . hardline fanatics who practice the principle that the end justifies the means—regardless of the innocent victims who were in no way involved in their cause, either pro or con.

Since this has been hashed and rehashed on every TV station, newspaper, magazine, talk show, and in books, you may be asking yourself why I'm bothering to include it here. As time passes, it will become readily apparent to most of you. When this kind of terrorism strikes the heartland of America, rather than its big cities or Washington, D.C. (where people assume such actions may occur), fear grips the hearts of everyone, and *prevention* becomes the top priority in our minds. A groundswell of cries for justice and protection starts to rise from the grassroots.

Why did this happen? *It could be for any reason in any distorted mind.* Will it happen again? *Undoubtedly!* Can we stop it? *Probably not.* What are we willing to do to *try* to stop it? *Bingo! You are willing to give up some more of your freedoms and willing to submit to more covert surveillance and more control of your lives . . . because how else can we protect the safety of all those innocent victims?*

The subject has been discussed, and the conclusion has been reached that we need to increase our surveillance techniques and strengthen our laws to aid law enforcement units in the tracking and capturing of dangerous dissidents. It has already been pointed out that the CIA, the FBI, and the Secret Service should have better information-gathering abilities, so they can know about these *before they happen* and arrest the culprits on some kind of conspiracy charge *before a criminal act has actually been committed.*

Everything that's in me wants to shout, "Yes!" But that brings me back to the situation of how much liberty and freedom I'm willing to forego. Am I going to *invite* "Big Brother" to turn this country into an armed camp (someone on the news referred to it as "bunker mentality"), with all rights of privacy tossed out the window in the process? If we give them that kind of power, will it stop the terrorism? *No!* Did it stop the IRA from bombing London on a regular basis? Has it stopped the Islamic terrorists from bombing Israel on a regular basis? Did it protect our Marine base from a terrorist bombing? *No! to all of the above.* The very nature of terrorism means that you can't stop it. They don't operate by the rules and they are willing, if necessary, to die to deliver the explosives to the target . . . and they don't care who dies with them!

We might succeed in making them go a little further under cover, and their actions may become more covert, but if they are crazy enough, and determined enough, they'll find a way.

[NOTE: Since the original writing of this book in 1996, the World Trade Center was destroyed by terrorists on September 11, 2001, as well as many other terrorist acts abroad.]

So what will be accomplished by forfeiting our liberties? We will give the government the right to meddle even further into our businesses and lives . . . for our own good, of course, as with all the other things they are doing to us for "our benefit."

President Clinton introduced a five-point piece of legislation to Congress that even the senator from Oklahoma declined to endorse in its original form, because he was opposed to infringing on the constitutional liberties of the great majority in this country in an attempt to protect us from the violent radicals. Of course, he stated his willingness to cooperate fully once sufficient constitutional safeguards to our rights to privacy were incorporated into the proposal.

In addition to adding personnel to law enforcement investigative agencies, they want to enhance the ability of these agencies in their electronic eavesdropping, via our local phones, cell phones, fax transmissions, etc. Also, they want the government to help the telecommunications companies pay for the mandated purchase and installation of new software and equipment to provide access to their digital systems, which would allow the government to intercept and monitor *all* telecommunications, in many cases without a warrant. Because prior to the Oklahoma City bombing, the government was trying to force the telecommunications companies to pay for all these expensive conversions themselves, the companies were trying to avoid cooperating.

There is a particularly enlightening article titled "Privacy in the Digital Age" written by Bill Machrone. It appeared in the June 14, 1994, edition of *PC Magazine*. In it the writer points out, among other hair–raising information, that the "pending legislation provides for fines up to $10,000 a day against telecommunications companies who don't give the Feds the access they want to the decoded data streams." It is difficult to believe what is happening. The article also contains an easy–to–understand explanation of the "clipper chip" technology and its effect on digital "everything" systems.

Further, it would authorize this alphabet soup of agencies to infiltrate and spy on any organization *that it would deem a possible danger,* at its own discretion. That doesn't mean only Arab militants; it could mean anyone, especially anyone the government might see as radical, fanatical, right–wing extremists (I wonder why they never consider the left–wing to be extremists?) . . . in other words, anyone who is vocal and who disagrees with the way things are being run.

Another option that has been suggested is bringing in the military to help us monitor and control the civilian population. The final conclusion of such an action would be devastating and would result in total loss of freedom—a police state. But when things get bad enough, even that won't suffice and those "helpful" U.N. troops—that are just waiting for the right opportunity—will be on your doorstep before you can wake up and smell the coffee.

The loss of our privacy and electronic bondage go hand in hand. Once you are in the system, it is impossible to extricate yourself from it. And now the various agencies, i.e., social services, health care, insurance systems, medical groups, retail sales, credit bureaus, Social Security, IRS, vehicle/driver's license, registration, voter registration, etc., are sharing the information in their files about you.

As much as you might like to avoid it, there are plenty of places you probably already exist in Big Brother's "big brain." One of the biggest cracks in the security of your privacy is the rampant use of your Social Security number to currently identify you just about everywhere. The fact that many of the people who use it to identify you freely print it in public view—or make it easily accessible to anyone who seeks it—makes it relatively easy to obtain information on your most personal activities, and even to make changes in your file.

A particularly good article by Robert S. Boyd appeared in the February 24, 1994, edition of the *Phoenix Gazette.* It is titled "Social Security privacy gap grows."

It seems a 30–year–old lawyer lost his right to vote when he refused to give the registrar his Social Security number (it was their practice to publish the number with his name as a matter of public record, and anyone could have access). He explained his reasons for refusing, to no avail.

"As a test, Greidinger [the attorney] had a friend dial an 800 number, the government–sponsored Student Loan Marketing Association (Sallie Mae) in Washington. 'He entered my Social Security number into the telephone and was able to get access to my files. He found out how much I owed, and when I made my last payment. He even changed some data in my file.'"

Now, what else would you expect an attorney to do? He sued the county, and a federal appeals court ruled unanimously in his favor.

"'The harm that can be inflicted from the disclosure of a Social Security number to an unscrupulous individual is alarming and potentially financially ruinous,' the court said. The Greidinger case was another round in a 50–year struggle between those who want to use Social Security numbers as a personal identifier for everything from law enforcement to check cashing—and those who view its widespread use as a serious threat to privacy."

Rutgers University (until stopped by a lawsuit in 1992) posted the students' names and numbers on a bulletin board, along with their grades. Talk about your loss of privacy!

"Social Security numbers are easy to fake and hard to authenticate. 'There is no way to verify the accuracy of existing numbers or that the number holder is who he or she claims to be,' the ACLU's Goldman said."

Then there's the IRS. We've all felt for quite some time that they knew more about us than they needed to know (certainly more than we wanted them to know!). Well, hold on to your seats . . . it's about to get better—or worse—depending on which side of the computer you're sitting. I quote from a couple of articles.

The *Los Angeles Times* on February 12, 1995, reported:

> If you have a back tax bill with the Internal Revenue Service, watch out. In the midst of a program called economic reality, the federal tax agency is going on line, searching for signs of noncompliance as well as electronic records of cars, credit and real estate it can seize from delinquent taxpayers. . . . A cadre of IRS agents with computers and modems now will be searching records filed with Department of Motor Vehicles, county tax assessor's offices, credit-reporting companies and the U.S. Bureau of the Census in an effort to find people who are underreporting their business sales, overestimating their deductions or trying to hide assets—or themselves—from federal tax collectors. IRS officials say . . . 'We will be using information from various [electronic] sources as part of our economic–reality approach.' . . . The IRS will begin compiling a host of demographic information about people in each district. . . . This information will include currency and banking reports, license information, construction contact information and census data. . . . The IRS will get current addresses for taxpayers who have apparently dropped off the rolls by buying them from credit–reporting companies. . . . It can get your full credit file to determine whether you have enough credit to pay the bill. . . . DMV records will be tapped . . . to see if you have a car to sell to pay taxes—and to help determine whether a taxpayer is lying about income or deductions. The IRS will be suspicious, for example, of a waiter who reports $20,000 in total income but drives a new Porsche. Property

records will be used in the same way.... A few credit experts warn that it also puts a burden on individuals who are under IRS scrutiny. Why? The records are not always right. And *the tax agency does not need to inform you that it is searching these records, nor is it required to allow you to correct records that are in error*... it cannot correct somebody else's database.... If you're under IRS scrutiny, it may behoove you to check your own records for accuracy.

A helpful article appeared in *Business Week* on May 25, 1992, entitled "Getting the Kinks Out of Your Credit Report." It gives some very good information about how to check on your records, and some suggestions for attempted correction if they contain errors. But the bottom line on this shared database situation is that if there is an error, you might correct it at that point, but you have no way of knowing how many people have picked up that misinformation and now stored it in their own files, freely sharing it with anyone else who asks. In other words, it's an endless trail that you will *never* win.

Another article on the IRS appeared in the March 18, 1995, *Reno Gazette-Journal.* The thrust of this article, entitled "IRS auditors become gumshoes," is that under the new strategy, dubbed "Compliance 2000," they are training the auditors—formerly accountants, for the most part—to be detectives, using all databases at their disposal to compile a composite of YOU—what you should be driving and where you should be living (based on the income you reported), weddings of your children, your cultural background, vacations, home furnishings, etc. They want to develop a complete profile on you. And these techniques have now become standard practice for *all audits.*

"Well, aside from my W-2, this intrusion can't reach me on my job," you say. Wrong again! *U.S. News & World Report,* August 8, 1994, reports: "Employers are finding more ways to watch workers. Some use cameras. Some eavesdrop on phones. Some read email. As a result, the International Labor Organization reports this week in a three-volume study, workers in industrialized nations have steadily lost privacy. American employees, the ILO concludes, are among the most closely watched. One survey indicates that perhaps 80 percent of U.S. workers in telecommunications, insurance, and banking are subject to telephone or computer-based monitoring."

An excellent article appeared in the May 18, 1994, edition of the *Los Angeles Times*. Titled "Someone May Be Watching," it points out the surveillance scrutiny of our workplace, home, and habits. It begins: "Everywhere we go, we're increasingly under surveillance. Employers, marketers, even private detectives use high-tech tools and scan mostly unregulated databases to pry into our daily lives."

The article was accompanied by a graphic with a caption:

Always Under Watch: A Day in the Life . . . Whether by video camera or computer, surveillance techniques may threaten your privacy. Here are some of the ways: (1) The Commute: Cameras on freeways catch a driver speeding to work. (2) At Work: Parking garage video camera can note a worker's arrival time, companions in auto. (3) Workstation: Employers can monitor computer messages and other electronic work. (4) At Lunch: A diner's credit card scan shows restaurant and bill. (5) After-Work Errand: ATM camera and computer records transaction. Credit card used at store shows where consumer shopped, what was bought. (6) Drive Home: Toll-booth scanner records when auto passed.

And naturally, law enforcement will get in on the act: ". . . Prepare for the Federal Bureau of Investigation's NCIC 2000 program. This is a set of computer standards the FBI has mandated that enable state and local law enforcement agencies to share information nationwide, including digitized images of fingerprints and mugshots. . . ."

And what could infringe on your privacy more than being shackled to a biochip in a vinyl bracelet. We will address this issue fully in chapter ten when we get into an in-depth discussion on biochip technology. But for now, I want to tell you about all the Haitian refugees that were given RFID wristbands for identification while interned at the naval base at Guantanamo Bay, Cuba. This project is abbreviated DMPITS, so whenever you see that acronym, you'll know what they are talking about. Of course, the extended use of this technology is to keep track of prisoners who—for whatever reason—are housed at their homes, or to locate runaway teens, or to keep track of grandpa who has a tendency to wander off and get lost, or to find kidnapped kids, etc., and ultimately to keep track of you!

Then there's the high–tech matters affecting your automobile (and its driver). A lot of different things are being combined on your driver's license, which we will address in detail in a later chapter. According to one article there will be a 2–D barcode on your driver's license, title, and car registration. Another article (*The Advocate*, Baton Rouge, LA, August 13, 1994) tells about the "Auto Arrester" which targets high–speed evaders and electronically overloads the ignition systems, disabling fleeing cars. The activator switches are kept by law enforcement personnel. The device itself can be used three different ways. It can be embedded in the road permanently and activated by police when needed; it can be set on a road ahead of a fleeing vehicle (in other words, a patrol car from another area could intercept the escape route before the fleeing vehicle arrives at that point); if the vehicle had been pulled over for some reason, then tries to race off, the officer could actually throw the device on top of the car and then activate it.

From the October 17, 1994, issue of *Forbes 400*, editor's column, "Fact and Comment," here are a few of the comments by Malcolm S. Forbes, Jr., editor–in–chief: "A cry for a national identification card is rising again. . . . We should resist the temptation. Such a card will rapidly be used for far more than employment. The loss of privacy outweighs any gains. . . . Assurances that laws would protect our privacy rightly ring hollow. With a national ID card your whole life could end up on a government central computer file. . . . Do we as a nation of individualists really want that?"

Below are some crucial excerpts from an article that appeared on page 16 of *Spotlight* magazine, June 13, 1994. It's in the section called "Technology & Liberty" and is titled "Danger in the Mail . . . Now that I have free access to your bank records . . . Your House is Next! Nibbling away your freedom bit by bit."

Don't look now, but Uncle Sam has some shiny new shackles with your name on them. Indeed, sources in the U.S. Postal Service recently revealed that they're all set to deliver your very own personalized federal ball and chain directly to your mailbox.

... [The Postal Service] told several people that they were prepared to mail 100 million of the cards in a matter of months.

... The Clinton administration, which says it's determined to "break the cycle of dependency" among welfare recipients, is preparing to reduce every American to total dependence—and near-total surveillance—through these infamous cards.

... The Postal Service's proposal (which was echoed by the IRS—what a coincidence!) calls for the card to "mediate" the information about you in every government database. It will be like a magic key, which opens every government database with information about you.

And here's another troubling fact. If federal computer systems are already integrated to this extent—where one card can "unlock" every piece of information about you—then what makes you think you have the only key?

Of course you won't have the only key. And potentially everything you own and all your assets, benefits and entitlements can be "withheld" from you with the push of a few buttons at the Treasury Department, IRS, or who–knows–where.

... The databases are ready to be integrated under the card.

To me, that means the databases are integrated now. It can take well over a year to integrate a couple of big databases. If the Postal Service is ready to start mailing 100 million of these cards within months, then the databases are integrated now. They work together—for Big Brother—now. They are being used now.

... People at the conference expressed reservations about the U.S. Card. Not technical reservations, mind you. They know the U.S. Card will work as advertised.

They expressed political reservations.

These people buy and sell folks' privacy for a living. I guess it's one thing to sell branding irons, but quite another think to accept a brand yourself. It's up to you.

The only way Big Brother (in George Orwell's *1984*) was able to successfully maintain control over the lives of the people was to abolish all personal privacy. They were under total surveillance, stripped not only of their privacy, but of their freedom, worth, and dignity, as well. Orwell describes the scene this way:

> The telescreen received and transmitted simultaneously [Author's note: Check out the capabilities of today's fiber optics systems coming into your homes via television, computer, modem, cable, telephone, fax, *et al*]. Any sound that Winston made, above the level of a very low whisper, would be picked up by it; moreover, as long as he remained within the field of vision which the metal plaque commanded, he could be seen as well as heard. There was, of course, no way of knowing whether you were being watched at any given moment.
>
> How often, or on what system, the Thought Police plugged in on any individual was just guesswork. It was even conceivable that they watched everybody all the time. But, at any rate, they could plug in your wire whenever they wanted to. You had to live—did live, from habit that became instinct, with the assumption that every sound you made was heard, and except in darkness, every move was scrutinized.

The Clinton administration consistently pushed for a number of new high-tech systems to enhance their "people control and monitoring" activities. Among their favorites: the national ID card, the Information Superhighway, and installation of a "clipper chip" in our telephones, computers/modems, fax machines, and other electronic devices, to allow the government easy access for the purpose of tapping and monitoring *all* of our communications via those systems.

Don McAlvany informs us that even though the clipper chip project was pushed hard by Clinton, Janet Reno, and former FBI director Louis Freeh, it actually was launched by George Bush in 1991 and developed by the National Security Agency (NSA), a supersecret organization. The August 1994 issue of *The McAlvany Intelligence Advisor* reports as follows:

Reno and Freeh are presently pushing Congress to enact requirements that telecommunications providers (i.e., local telephone services, cellular phone companies, wireless services, long distance networks, etc.) be mandated to develop and install software and equipment that allows the government to intercept and monitor *all* telecommunications in America. Freeh and Reno argue that *"to stop terrorism and organized crime, the American people must give up some of their personal freedom and privacy."* [Author's note: You can see from the date of this newsletter that this plan was on their agenda long before the Oklahoma City bombing occurred. This just gave them the excuse they needed to push such legislation through the Congress. Kind of makes you wonder whose "plans" benefited most from that act of terrorism.]

The FBI has reintroduced its 1992 proposal to require that communications service providers redesign their equipment to facilitate electronic surveillance. The Digital Telephony and Communications Privacy Improvement Act of 1994 [Ed. Note: That title is Orwellian "doublespeak," because the act will *destroy all privacy.*] mandates that phones, cable, and computer network companies modify their switches and computers *to ensure that surveillance can be conducted concurrently from a remote government facility. All transactions and phone calls (in and out) will be monitored and recorded. Companies who refuse to comply will be fined $10,000 per day.*

The Electronic Frontier Foundation has warned: *"The FBI scheme would turn the data superhighway into a national surveillance network of staggering proportions."*

The Clintonistas have said that within a few years they plan to link every home, business, lab, classroom, and library via their high-tech computerized information superhighway. The *Wall Street Journal* warned in an editorial (7/10/94) that even if the Congress blocked the government-backed installation of the "Clipper Chip" that the bureaucracy would make an end run and install it anyway.

The *Wall Street Journal* pointed out that *sophisticated terrorists and organized crime syndicates could easily evade the "Clipper Chip" surveillance, but that it would enable the Big Brother bureau-*

cracy to monitor every phone call, every credit card purchase, every bank transaction, and every telecommunication of every private citizen in America. The *Wall Street Journal* concluded that: *"The potential for government manipulation and intimidation of the citizenry is enormous."*

USA Today (7/20/94) carried a front-page story entitled "Privacy Abuse Confirms the Worst Fear," which discussed how IRS officials had admitted at a Senate hearing that more than 1,300 IRS agents have been investigated over the past five years on suspicion of improperly snooping through taxpayers' files. About 56,000 IRS employees (nearly half of the agency's 115,000 work force) have access to the Integrated Data Retrieval System (IDRS), the computer system that handles collection and storage of taxpayer information.

Evidence of IRS privacy abuses was revealed by the Senate Governmental Affairs Committee in August 1993. Committee member Senator David Pryor (D–AR) said: "The IRS' disregard of taxpayer (privacy) rights confirms the worst fears that the American people have about the IRS. This illegal and offensive activity must stop, and it's clear that Congress must act." *But the major problem with the IRS violation of taxpayer privacy rights is not just IRS snooping of taxpayer returns. It is the sharing of that information with dozens of other government agencies—a practice which until recently was strictly forbidden.*

The most ominous part of the *USA Today* article was the revelation that "the IRS is in the middle of an **$8 billion** computer systems upgrade. Eventually, optical character readers will be used to scan and direct tax returns into three main computers hooked together in a national network that links the ten IRS service centers, eight regional offices, and sixty–five district offices."

Because of grassroots pressure and their success in enlightening the populace as to the true meaning and end results of some of these measures, many of the "control" elements of the New World Order will not be passed by the Congress. But that doesn't seem to be hindering the progress of the current administration as they move us ever forward toward the New World Order.

No problem! They'll just enact what they want via an "executive order." Executive orders give a president the ability to declare a state of emergency, martial law, and a suspension of all constitutional rights, in essence converting our democratic form of government into a total dictatorship with merely the stroke of a pen. Congress can subsequently accept these executive orders, publish them in the *Federal Register*, and establish them as laws of the land. These can be implemented at the whim of the current president on a moment's notice just by declaring a state of emergency.

Clinton used this method to move U.S. troops under U.N. command (PDD–25 signed May 5, 1994). Whether allowing foreign (Russian and U.N.) troops onto U.S. soil, implementing the national ID card, or a host of other measures, if they can't get it through Congress, they simply write an executive order and use unconstitutional, dictatorial powers to accomplish their goals.

Executive orders date back as far as Franklin Delano Roosevelt. President Carter signed No. 12148 delegating the power to run the entire country to FEMA, then on June 3, 1994, Clinton signed a new executive order transferring control of the country in an emergency from FEMA to the National Security Council and the national security advisor. Some of the executive orders which subsequently have made their way into the *Federal Register* (and are now laws) are reported by McAlvany as follows:

10995—All communications media seized by the federal government. 10997—Seizure of all electrical power, fuels, including gasoline and minerals. 10998—Seizure of all food resources, farms and farm equipment. 10999—Seizure of all kinds of transportation, including your personal car, and control of all highways and seaports. 11000—Seizure of all civilians for work under federal supervision. 11001—Federal takeover of all health, education, and welfare. 11002—Postmaster General empowered to register every man, woman and child in the U.S.A. 11003—Seizure of all aircraft and airports by the federal government. 11004—Housing and Finance Authority may shift population from one locality to another. Complete integration. **11005**—Seizure of railroads, inland waterways, and storage facilities. **11051**—The director of the Office of Emergency Planning authorized to put Executive Orders into effect in "times of increased international tension or financial crisis." He is also to perform such additional functions as the president may direct.

In short, if there should be nationwide riots (*a la* Los Angeles in '92) for any reason; a national financial crisis; massive social upheaval (i.e., a huge quantum jump in crime); major resistance to national gun confiscation or to the installation of the New World Order or other socialist/police state measures; etc., *[the president] . . . and his "comrades" have the power and machinery to instantly suspend the Constitution and declare a total dictatorship.*

On April 19, 1995, an article appeared in the Clifton, New Jersey, *Herald & News.* Writer Rich Calder titled the article "Clifton group OKs listing of residents; City council urged to register everyone." This city called for a computer database with which it could *track all residents.*

A 26–member committee . . . recommended last night that the city council approve an ordinance requiring all residents to register with the city. This proposal would obligate all renters and homeowners to fill out a dwelling certificate . . . listing all occupants in their household. The certificate would require residents to list their names and ages, along with the names and ages of their children. This measure . . . may raise constitutional issues. Members of the ACLU have said that this procedure will threaten residents' privacy. Committee members who support the proposal said that people with nothing to hide shouldn't have anything to worry about. . . . Mayor James Anzaldi hailed the plan at last night's meeting, saying the council should implement an ordinance right away. . . . The dwelling certificate would be supplied by several city agencies. . . . The proposal also calls for a centralized computer database to be created that would help track . . . violations.

Finally, I recommend that you acquire a copy of the June 1986 edition of *The Gospel Truth* (for reprints write to Southwest Radio Ministries, P.O. Box 100, Bethany, OK 73008, or call 1-800-652-1144). Written by Noah Hutchings, it is titled "Liberty or Electronic Bondage: How Near the Choice?" Even though he was a few years ahead of much of the commentary on this situation, he was seeing the "handwriting on the wall" where this subject was concerned. It is an excellent piece with much research reported.

Have we lost our privacy? For sure! But as one lady put it earlier, "You ain't seen nothin' yet!" Are we in electronic bondage? You bet! and probably already too far into the system to ever get out. All we can do is sound the warning and get prepared for the battle cry, because for most of us, it's too late to pull a "disappearing act" from the system, unless it's the disappearing act described in the Bible when the Lord returns to snatch us away. However, we don't know exactly when that will be, so we *must be prepared* to survive (victoriously, I hope) in the troubled times that lie ahead, as Scripture is emphatic about one thing: in the end times (and we're there, folks), things are going to get *worse* before they get better.

But we are not to despair—we have a blessed hope and lots of promises in the Word from our heavenly Father, such as He "will never leave us nor forsake us," His "strength is made perfect in our weakness," "I've never seen the righteous forsaken, or their seed out begging for bread," and, finally His instruction to "comfort one another with these words": "When you see these things begin to come to pass, look up for your redemption draweth nigh."

Chapter Three

NWO Organizations
The Illuminati / Skull & Bones /
Freemasonry
Council on Foreign Relations
Trilateral Commission / Bilderbergers

This is going to be a difficult chapter to write because it addresses so many different topics of importance. Many writers have covered these subjects in depth, and it is not my intent to duplicate their efforts. On the contrary, I only want to give you a brief background. And I want to forewarn you that as you study these groups and their activities, be especially alert for the recurring presence of the Rockefellers and the Rothschilds throughout this integrated maze of secret organizations (even though said organizations vehemently deny that they are doing things in secret).

The Council on Foreign Relations, Trilateral Commission, and Bilderbergers (with covert assistance from others) run the world through manipulation of the banking systems. In the United States it is the Federal Reserve, a private organization which most Americans *incorrectly assume* is owned, run, and/or controlled by our government. In other countries the World Bank is in control of international finance.

The Illuminati
Webster's Illustrated Encyclopedic Dictionary gives the following definition under the word "illuminati," and it couldn't be more accurate if it had been written by your traditional right–wing conservative.

1) Persons claiming to be unusually enlightened with regard to some subject. 2) a. The members of a secret society of freethinkers and republicans that flourished in Germany during the late 18th century. Also called "Illuminaten." b. Persons regarded as atheists, libertines, or radical republicans during the 18th century (such as French Encyclopedists, the Freemasons, or the freethinkers). 3) The members of a heretical sect of 16th–century Spain, who claimed special religious enlightenment.

Consider the *first* definition: "Persons *claiming* to be unusually enlightened with regard to some subject." The Illuminati consider themselves to be the only ones qualified and sufficiently enlightened to run the world, and they are power–hungry enough to scheme until they actually control it ... and us! The *second* definition (part "a") refers to a "secret society going back to Germany as far as the eighteenth century; part "b" says they were regarded as atheists, libertines, and radicals, and further adds a reference to the Freemasons; the *third* brings in the religious aspect of the Illuminati, calling them a heretical sect claiming special religious enlightenment. They're enlightened, all right! But exactly what is the source of their light? Reminds me of the scriptures telling about Satan coming as an "angel of light" for the express purpose of deceiving us.

Where the CFR, Trilateral Commission, and the Bilderbergers emphasize control of the world through control of world finances, the Illuminati/Freemasons, Skull & Bones, and similar secret societies found on university campuses around the world focus on education, or the control of the minds of our future leaders. Of course, they all adhere heavily on the "old boy" network, where anyone who belongs to the organization is assured successful placement in a position of power and prominence. In personnel or other selection, priority is always given to candidates who are brothers of this elite group over applicants or candidates who are not.

Antony Sutton, former research Fellow at the Hoover Institution, Stanford University, as well as professor at California State University, Los Angeles, has authored a book entitled *America's Secret Establishment: An Introduction to the Order of Skull & Bones.* It details as much as you will ever find on the Order of the Skull & Bone (without becoming an initiate), gives a brief background on the origin of the Illuminati, and makes the case for a plausible link between the two groups, though the author is careful to point out that his documentation is inconclusive as yet.

The Illuminati was a group of Bavarian conspirators dedicated to the overthrow of government. The society was founded on May 1, 1776, by Adam Weishaupt of the University of Igolstadt (while in America we were busy drafting the Declaration of Independence). It was a secret society, but the Order of the Illuminati presumably ceased to exist when it was raided by the Bavarian police in 1786. The Order was dissolved and its papers seized and published. Because the Bavarian state ordered the papers to be published, we have authentic information about the organization and its methods of operation. Subsequent investigation of those documents determined that the aim of the Illuminati was world domination, using any methods to advance the objective, i.e., the end always justifies the means. It was anti–Christian (although clergymen were found in the organization), and each member had a pseudonym to disguise his identity . . . a truly secret society in every sense of the term.

The Illuminati's concept of education can be traced to the influence of early nineteenth century German philosophers. These concepts were introduced in the United States by postgraduate students studying in Europe, bringing their ideas back home with them, then instigating the Illuminati plan to educate our youngsters according to their goals and philosophies.

Antony Sutton states (quoting John Robinson in *Proofs of a Conspiracy*): "So far as education is concerned, the Illuminati objective was as follows: 'We must win the common people in every corner. This will be obtained chiefly by means of the schools, and by open, hearty behaviour, show, condescension, popularity, and toleration of their prejudices *which we shall at leisure root out and dispel.'"*

Johann Friedrich Herbart was a major German philosopher when the Yale postgraduate students were studying there. Herbart adhered to the Hegelian philosophy (the State is superior to the individual) and thoroughly indoctrinated his protegés in this teaching.

Therefore, for Herbart, education had to be presented in a scientifi-
cally correct manner, and the chief purpose of education, in his opinion, was to prepare the child to live properly in the social order, of
which he is an integral part. The individual is not important. The
mere development of individual talent, of individual fitness, mental
power, and knowledge is *not* the purpose of education. The purpose
is to develop personal character and social morality, and the most
important task of the educator is to analyze the activities and duties
of men within society.

The function of instruction, according to Herbart, is to fulfill
these aims and impart to the individual *socially desirable ideas.* In
today's vernacular, we would call this being "PC" (politically correct!). All these ideas in today's American educational philosophy
can be recognized as originating and being transmitted by members
(knights and patriarchs) of Skull & Bones, having been learned at
the feet of Illuminati educators. This link may not have been proven
beyond doubt at this point, but it looks pretty obvious to me.

As we progress further into this chapter, you will become increasingly aware of the difficulty I am experiencing trying to keep
these organizations separated for study purposes, as many people
are members of two or more. For example, former president George
H. W. Bush is a member of the Order of Skull & Bones (as was his father before him), as well as a member of both the Council on Foreign
Relations (CFR) and the Trilateral Commission (TLC). Other prominent contemporary members of Skull & Bones include Winston Lord,
former ambassador to China, U.S. senators David Boren of Oklahoma
and John Chaffe of Rhode Island, as well as William F. Buckley (allegedly conservative publisher of *The National Review*), among others.

Another good book written on the bizarre cultic society of Skull
& Bones is by researchers Walter Isacsson and Evan Thomas, entitled *The Wise Men.*

But I'm getting ahead of myself again! Let's discuss the questions, "What is the Order of Skull and Bones?" and "How did it begin?" According to Sutton, those on the "inside" know it simply as
"The Order." Others have known it for more than one hundred and
fifty years as "Chapter 322" of a German secret society. For legal

purposes it was incorporated in 1956 as the Russell Trust. It was also once known as the "Brotherhood of Death." The casual name (or sometimes used derogatorily) is "Skull & Bones," or just plain "Bones."

The Order is not just another Greek letter campus fraternity, with passwords and secret handshakes. It is far more insidious. Chapter 322 is a *secret* society whose members are sworn to silence (they are supposed to actually leave the room if someone outside the Order even mentions the name Skull & Bones). So far as we can determine, it exists only on the campus of Yale University, though rumors are beginning to surface indicating there may be a select number of other locations and possible links to a couple of other secret societies on the Yale campus, the Scroll & Key and Wolf's Head, both founded in the mid–nineteenth century. Allegedly, these are competitive societies; however, Sutton believes them to be part of the same network. It has rules and rituals . . . ceremonial rites which I will mention briefly a little later.

Sutton states that its members always deny membership, and in checking hundreds of autobiographical listings for members, he found only half a dozen who cited an affiliation with Skull & Bones. He is concerned about whether the many members of the various administrations (either elected or appointed) have declared their membership in the biographical data supplied to the FBI for their obligatory "background checks," implying that it is not likely.

Further, Sutton asserts, then documents, that the Order is unbelievably powerful.

Skull & Bones is an organization of only senior students at Yale University. Each year only fifteen initiates are selected in their junior year (all males prior to 1995, when they proposed inducting women into the formerly all–male group—at present Buckley has an injunction in place to stop this). Therefore, the organization is oriented primarily to the postgraduate outside world. The Patriarchs only meet annually on Deer Island in the St. Lawrence River.

Admission to Skull & Bones is by invitation only; there is no lobbying, electioneering, or applying for membership. During commencement week, the juniors are privately "tapped." The junior is given an option: "Skull & Bones. Accept or reject?" This method has not changed since the Order's inception in 1832. Those who accept (presumably the greater number) are invited to attend the Bones Temple on campus to undergo an initiation ceremony (described briefly below). For the ambitious, "tapping" is the magic password to a future success–guaranteed career. Potential candidates are apparently selected based on their school and extracurricular activities, their support of Yale, and particularly their sports ability—teamwork is held in very high esteem. The most unlikely choice would be a loner, an iconoclast, or an individualist—a person who goes their own way in the world. They want people who put the Order first, without question, and who will abide by the rules at all costs. Sutton states:

> The most likely potential member is from a Bones family, is energetic, resourceful, political, and probably an amoral team player. A man who understands that to get along you have to go along. A man who will sacrifice himself for the good of the team. A moment's reflection illustrates why this is so. In real life, the thrust of the Order is to bring about certain objectives. Honors and financial rewards are guaranteed by the power of the Order. But the price of these honors and rewards is sacrifice to the common goal, the goal of the Order. Some, perhaps many, have not been willing to pay this price.

Initiates undergo bizarre rituals and initiation ceremonies with sexual overtones, conducted on the order of brainwashing techniques, designed to strip the initiate of all pride and sense of self, then being "reprogrammed" to embrace only the philosophies and goals of the Order. (Sutton describes these rituals in great detail in his book.)

At any given time about five to six hundred are alive and active. Roughly about one–quarter of these take an active role in furthering the objectives of the Order; the others either change their minds or just lose interest and become silent dropouts.

It has been postulated concerning the number "322" under the skull and crossed bones of the Order's logo or official emblem. Since the organization was imported from Germany in 1832 as the second chapter of a German order, it has been speculated that the "32" denotes the year of origination and the next "2" indicates that it is the second chapter of the organization. A much more likely theory is that this order descended from a fraternal society dating back to Damascus in 322 B.C., as Bones records are dated by adding 322 years to the current year, i.e., records originating in 1950 are dated Anno Demostheni 2272.

Inside the Order there are many other numbers and symbols which appear beside the names of the members in the "Catalogue" (or membership list). Although we don't know for sure, Sutton makes some interesting speculations regarding their possible meaning. The Catalogue contains the birth names of the members, but Sutton tells us: "Entry into the Order is accompanied by an elaborate ritual and no doubt psychological conditioning. For example: Immediately on entering Bones the neophyte's name is changed. He is no longer known by his name as it appears in the college catalogue but like a monk or Knight of Malta or St. John, becomes Knight so–and–so. The old Knights are then known as Patriarch so–and–so. The outside world are known as Gentiles and vandals."

In the century and a half years since the Order was founded, active membership has evolved into a core group of perhaps twenty to thirty families, according to Sutton:

It seems that active members have enough influence to push their sons and relatives into the Order, and there is significant intermarriage among the families. These families fall into two major groups.

First we find the old line American families who arrived on the East Coast in the 1600s, e.g., Whitney, Lord, Phelps, Wadsworth, Allen, Bundy, Adams, and so on.

Second, we find families who acquired wealth in the last 100 years, sent their sons to Yale, and in time became almost old line families, e.g., Harriman, Rockefeller, Payne, Davison. . . . In the last 150 years a few families in the Order have gained enormous influence in society and the world.

Although the "old line" families used to look down their blueblood noses at the *nouveau riche,* that is not so much the case anymore. They have discovered it takes money to maintain their power—not just the name—so if they couldn't make it on their own, they "married" it into the family. But whatever it takes, you maintain the power at all costs.

The Order has penetrated every segment of American society, e.g., the White House, legislatures, political parties, foundations (charitable and otherwise), "think tanks," policy groups, education, media, publishing, banking, business, industry, commerce, and even churches. In many cases the Order is the founder of these organizations. They determine the goals and objectives, as well as the methods for achieving them, then usually installs the first president, chairman, or CEO and/or CFO. This explains why so many such organizations are based on the premise of secular humanism. Their roots can be traced directly back to active members of the Order.

Since it seems the most unlikely, let's first take a look at the connection of the Order to the church. Although the percentage has declined in recent years, about two percent of the Order is in the church—all Protestant denominations. Again quoting Sutton:

> A key penetration is the Union Theological Seminary, affiliated with Columbia University in New York. This Seminary, a past subject of investigation for Communist infiltration, has close links to the Order. Henry Sloane Coffin (1897) as Professor of Practical Theology at Union from 1904 to 1926 and President of Union Theological Seminary, also known as the "Red Seminary," from 1926 to 1945. Union has such a wide interpretation of religious activity that it has, or used to have, an Atheists Club for its students.
>
> Henry Sloane Coffin, Jr. (1949) was one of the Boston Five indicted on federal conspiracy charges.
>
> And this is only **part** of the Order's penetration into the church.

I will let Mr. Sutton expand on the connection between the Order and the other areas, i.e., the law, communications, industry, the Federal Reserve/banking, and the White House/politics/government.

The Law

The major establishment law firms in New York are saturated with the Order.

In particular, Lord, Day, and Lord, dominated by the Lord family already discussed; also, Simpson, Thatcher, and Bartlett, especially the Thatcher family; David, Polk, Wardwell, and Debevoise, Plimpton, the Rockefeller family law firm.

Communications

There has been a significant penetration into communications. Some examples:

» Henry Luce of *Time–Life* is in the Order.
» So is William Buckley ('50) of *National Review.*
» And Alfred Cowles ('31), president of Cowles Communications, *Des Moines Register, Minneapolis Star*
» And Emmert Bates ('32) of Litton Educational Systems, plus
» Richard Ely Danielson ('07) of *Atlantic Monthly*
» Russell Wheeler Davenport ('23), *Fortune*
» John Chipman Farrar ('18) of Farrar, Strauss, the publishers.

The most prestigious award in journalism is a Nieman Fellowship at Harvard University. Over 300 were granted from 1937 to 1968. The FIRST director of the Nieman Fund was member Archibald McLeash.

Industry

The oil companies have their links to the Order. Members Percy, Rockefeller, the Paynes, the Pratts, all link to Standard Oil. Shell Oil, Creole Petroleum, and Socony Vacuum also link. A wide variety of manufacturing firms have members in the Order, from the Donnelly family in Chicago (printers of *The Official Airline Guide* and other references); lumber companies like Weyerhauser, who is also a Trilateralist; Dresser Industries, and so on.

The Federal Reserve System

A dozen members can be linked to the Federal Reserve, but one appointment is noteworthy, Pierre Jay ('92), whose only claim to fame in 1913 was to run a private school and be an obscure vice president of Manhattan Bank, yet he became FIRST chairman of the New York Federal Reserve, the really significant Federal Reserve.

The White House, Politics, and Government
This is the area where the Order has made headway, with names like Taft, Bush, Stimson, Chafee, Lovett, Whitney, Bundy, and so on.

I have done my best to give you "skeletal" information (no pun intended) on the Illuminati and the Order of Skull & Bones. Before I move on, I want to address the matter of the extreme secrecy in both movements (which Sutton believes is further evidence of a link between the two). I have already mentioned the fact that Bonesmen are supposed to refuse any comment regarding the Order or their membership therein. The same unquestionably applied to the Illuminati (if, indeed, you can relegate the Illuminati to the past tense). Secrecy can be used to conceal illegal activities, among other things. *Obviously, secrecy is needed if there is something to conceal.* Secrecy is superfluous if you have nothing to hide. A private letter between members of the Illuminati, which was published by the Elector of Bavaria, contained the following statement: "The great strength of our Order lies in its concealment; let it never appear in any place in its own name, but always covered by another name and another occupation." And just as the Order works, so does/did the Illuminati, as this excerpt from an Illuminati letter reveals: "The power of the Order must surely be turned to the advantage of its members. All must be assisted. They must be preferred to all persons otherwise of equal merit."

Although we are not yet to our discussion of the CFR and TLC, I briefly will address them here, as they relate to Skull & Bones Chapter 322.

CFR and TLC, though not looking for a spotlight on their discussions and activities, are not secret organizations in the sense that the Illuminati and Skull & Bones are secret. Their membership rosters are available to anyone who asks, and they are making the dates and locations of their meetings available to the media, though the media is not permitted inside to witness the activities, nor are their members permitted to give interviews revealing what has occurred at their meetings (as spelled out in their bylaws).

The Order is represented in these organizations, but does not always dominate. David Rockefeller, former chairman of the CFR, is not a member of the Order, but the family was represented in the Order by Percy Rockefeller; however, a later CFR chairman, Winston Lord, is a member of Bones.

Visualize three concentric circles, consisting of the inner core, the inner circle, and the outer circle. The outer circle is made up of large, open organizations (e.g., CFR or TLC) some of whose membership is made up of Bones members. The inner circle is made up of one or more secret societies, such as Chapter 322. The inner core is believed to be a secret society within the Order, a decision–making core. As yet the existence of this inner core cannot be documented, but evidence points to its existence. Sutton even believes that he could identify the chairman.

The CFR is the largest organization in the outer circle, with about 2,900 members at any one time (as many as the Order in its entire history). The TLC has 325 members worldwide, but only about 80 in the United States. Other groups in the outer circle include the Pilgrim Society, the Atlantic Council, the Bilderbergers, and the Bohemian Club (of San Francisco). As an example of the number of Bones members who are also members of the CFR, following are just the Bones members whose last names begin with the letter "B": Jonathan Bingham (congressman); William F. Buckley (editor, *National Review* and the Order's house conservative); McGeorge Bundy (foundation executive); William Bundy (CIA); George H. W. Bush (former president of the United States).

The Trilateral Commission was founded in 1973 by David Rockefeller, who was not a member of the Order. The same appears to be true of many TLC members; however, if you investigate the family tree, you will find members of the Order sometimes as close as one generation removed, and in other cases in the family line in great numbers, though not the current TLC member. Sutton points out that the TLC is not a conspiracy, it just doesn't publish its activities too widely, as the general populace probably wouldn't appreciate what they are planning for us behind closed doors.

Sutton reports that he "has openly debated with George Franklin, Jr., coordinator of the Trilateral Commission, on the radio. Mr. Franklin did show a rather ill-concealed dislike for the assault on his pet global New World Order—and made the mistake of attempting to disguise this objective." Where the TLC is concerned, even though David Rockefeller is not a Bones member, keep these facts in mind: J. Richardson Dilworth, chief financial and administrative officer for the Rockefeller Family Associates, is a member of the Order, as was Percy Rockefeller (1900). And TLC purposes, as portrayed in their own literature, are almost identical to those of the Order.

So far as Sutton can determine, William F. Buckley is the only member of both the Order and the Bilderbergers. The Pilgrim Society has no current Bones members, but the family names of past members are found, i.e., Aldrich and Pratt.

I have discussed the guarantees of success for Bones members, as well as the intermarriages to consolidate the power, wealth, and influence of the families. Now, we will look at the chain of influence.

A chain of influence that is spread over many years guarantees continuity and must be extraordinarily impressive to any new initiate who doubts the power of the Order. Members of the Order are to be found in every segment of our existence: education, foundations, politics, government, industry, law, and finance. Consequently, *at any time the Order can tap influence in any area of society.* The major occupations, however, are in law, education, business, finance, and industry. Percentage of Bones members in each area follows: 18 percent, law; 16 percent, education; 16 percent, business; 15 percent, finance; 12 percent, industry. The remaining 23 percent are scattered among all remaining occupations.

Sutton makes a good case for the interference of the Order in promoting wars and conflict in order to maintain and increase their world control: "If we can show that the Order has artificially encouraged and developed **both** revolutionary Marxism **and** national socialism while retaining some control over the nature and degree of the conflict, then it follows *the Order will be able to determine the evolution and nature of the New World Order."*

He makes the above statement while documenting a link between the Union Bank and support for the Nazis during World War II. He traced the flow of money through a long trail that attempted to hide its ultimate destination, and proved the involvement of at least eight men, four of whom were members of the Order (including Prescott Bush, father of President George H. W. Bush) and two of whom were Nazis.

As I conclude this section on the Skull & Bones, Brotherhood of Death, I want to discuss the spiritual aspects of the Order. Sutton tells us: "What happens in the initiation process is essentially a variation of brainwashing or encounter group processes. Knights, through heavy peer pressure, become Patriarchs prepared for a life of the exercise of power and continuation of this process into future generations. In brief, the ritual is designed to mold establishment zombies, to ensure continuation of power in the hands of a small select group from one generation to another. But beyond this ritual are aspects notably satanic."

We can make at least three definite statements about links between the Order and satanic beliefs. First, photographic evidence documents the satanic device (as well as the name) of the skull and crossed bones. Second, there is a link to satanic symbolism. Third, the link between the Order and the New World Order is well documented in the book *Hidden Dangers of the Rainbow* by Constance Cumbey.

The skull and crossed bones is not just a logo or printed artwork; photographs exist that show the use of actual skulls and bones in the ceremonies of the Order. According to other evidence, at least three sets of skulls and other assorted human bones are kept within the Bones Temple on the Yale campus. At best, that makes the members grave robbers. But using these bones for ceremonial purposes shows absolutely no respect for the dead, and is a blatantly satanic activity.

Author Constance Cumbey identified and linked several organizations to the Order and its objectives. She identified Benjamin

Creme and the Tara Center as a New Age phenomenon, then linked Creme to the Unity and Unitarian churches. Sutton continued the chain by pointing out the Order's longstanding and significant link to these churches. Former president William Taft, whose father co-founded the Order, was president of the Unitarian Association in his time.

Cumbey identifies the link between Hitler and the New Age movement and previous research by Sutton linked the Order to the founding and growth of Naziism. Cumbey states that the New Age movement plans to bring about a New World Order "which will be a synthesis between the U.S.S.R., Great Britain, and the United States." Later information indicates that it will come closer to encompassing the entire world, i.e. both industrialized nations and third–world countries.

Finally, Cumbey points out that the anti–Christ and satanic aspects are woven into the cult of the New Age movement. I don't think there is any doubt about it! The goals and activities of the Skull & Bones and their leaders' plans for our future are undoubtedly satanically inspired.

As we move on to investigate the groups who endeavor to control world governments, wars, *et al,* through control of finances, I am going to discuss our money and its emblems. That means going back into the discussion of the Illuminati and Freemasonry, as they are at the root of most of these satanic symbols.

At right you will find the pyramid that is shown on the back of our money. Note that the Latin translates: "Announcing the birth of the New World Order."

Although the pyramid on the American dollar with its thirteen levels ties in with the thirteen colonies, the original association was with ancient Egyptian and Babylonian mysticism. Note also that the cornerstone or capstone is missing from the top of the pyramid. In its place is the All–Seeing Eye. The Illuminati's mutual spying system was an integral part of the program to keep its associates in line. The eye symbolized the "Big Brother" concept for controlling its domain. Some dismiss the idea, claiming the eye in the illustration is the "all–seeing" eye of God. However, the literal translation of the Latin, *Annuit Coeptis* and *Novus Ordo Seclorum*, indicates quite the contrary, i.e., "Announcing the Birth of the New Secular Order," commonly known today as the New World Order.

Before we progress (if you can call that progress) to a cashless society, many changes will take place in our currency. In fact, some have already taken place (under the guise of inhibiting counterfeiting, of course). Former congressman Ron Paul had this to say about the U.S. Mint facility in Fort Worth (note particularly his comments about the pyramid shape of the building):

> The government is crowing, the greenback will be produced on U.S.–made presses for the first time in more than a century. Only it won't be green.
>
> The Stevens Graphics Corporation is producing an ominously named Alexander Hamilton press for the Bureau of Engraving and Printing. (Hamilton was—appropriately enough—a proponent of fiat–paper money, big deficits, and big government). . . .
>
> The new press can embed plastic or other strips in the bills, do the microprinting the Treasury has talked about, and—oh, yes—print in three colors.
>
> The feds say not to worry. The greenback will remain green. But then why pay for this extra capacity? It can only be to print the New Money.
>
> In an effort to find out more about where the New Money will be printed, I went on an investigative visit to Fort Worth, Texas, to survey a new BEP currency plant. This is no normal federal building. It is one of several places in the country where the New Money is in preparation.
>
> The new BEP building is a monstrosity that perfectly symbolizes unconstitutional abuse of power. A giant windowless blockhouse [circular], it sits on an enormous piece of land, surrounded by a prison–style cyclone fence topped with barbed wire.

The appropriately evil-looking New Money plant went up fast. On my last visit, I noted a new addition to the administrative end of the building: a pyramid. Two interpretations are possible: one, that it copies the Masonic–Illuminatist symbol that also, unfortunately, made it on the back of our one dollar bill; or two, that it symbolizes the kind of society the politicians and bankers have in mind for us: they're the pharaohs and we're the enslaved workers. Or maybe it's both.

Paul pointed out also that former House Speaker Jim Wright and H. Ross Perot were instrumental in the selection of Fort Worth, with the enthusiastic backing of Senator Phil Gramm. He also calls it "a 'public–private partnership' not unlike the Federal Reserve itself."

The Council on Foreign Relations is undoubtedly tied in to all this monetary control through the Federal Reserve and the World Bank, as well as through government influence and other sources of control. In this "time line" we learn a bit about the history of the CFR as it relates to the promotion of the New World Order.

» **May 30, 1919**—Originally founded by prominent British and Americans as two separate organizations: the Royal Institute of International Affairs (in England) and the Institute of International Affairs (in the U.S.). Two years later Colonel House reorganized the Institute of International Affairs as the CFR.

» **December 15, 1922**—CFR endorses world government. Philip Kerr, writing for CFR's magazine *Foreign Affairs,* states: "Obviously there is going to be no peace or prosperity for mankind as long as [the earth] remains divided into 50 or 60 independent states. . . . Until some kind of international system is created which will put an end to the diplomatic struggles incident to the attempt of every nation to make itself secure. . . . The real problem today is that of the world government."

» **February 17, 1950**—CFR member James P. Warburg, co–founder of the United World Federalists and son of Federal Reserve banker Paul Warburg, tells the [Senate Foreign Relations] subcommittee that "studies led me, ten years ago, to the conclusion that the great question of our time is not whether or not one world can be achieved, but whether or not one world can be achieved by peaceful means. We shall have world government, whether or not we like it. The question is only whether world government will be achieved by consent or by conquest."

» **November 25, 1959**—CFR calls for new international order. "Study Number 7" advocated "a new international order [which] must be responsive to world aspirations for peace, for social and economic change . . . an international order . . . including states labeling themselves as 'socialist' [communist]."

» **1975**—In the *New York Times,* CFR member and *Times* editor James Reston writes that President Ford and Soviet leader Leonid Brezhnev should "forget the past and work together for a new world order."

» **1975**—Retired Navy admiral Chester Ward, former Judge Advocate General of the U.S. Navy and former CFR member, in a critique, writes that the goal of the CFR is the "submergence of U.S. sovereignty and national independence into an all-powerful one-world government. . . . Once the ruling members of the CFR have decided that the U.S. government should adopt a particular policy, the very substantial research facilities of the CFR are put to work to develop arguments, intellectual and emotional, to support the new policy, and to confound and discredit, intellectually and politically, any opposition."

» **1977**—*Imperial Brain Trust* by Laurence Shoup and William Minter is published. The book takes a critical look at the CFR with chapters titled "Shaping a New World Order: The Council's Blueprint for Global Hegemony, 1939–1944" and "Toward the 1980s: The Council's Plans for a New World Order."

We are going to "back our way" into this discussion by telling about the CFR, then getting into the Federal Reserve and world financial control . . . and who controls it! The current membership list for the CFR reads like a *Who's Who* of American leaders in every walk of life, i.e., government, private industry, education, the media, military, and high finance.

In 1921, Edward Mandell House founded the CFR (from an organization begun two years earlier, the Institute of International Affairs). He was a close friend and advisor of President Woodrow Wilson. House persuaded the president to support and sign the Federal Reserve Act and to support the League of Nations, forerunner of the U.N. and other globalist groups. Finances to found the CFR came from the same crowd who formed the Federal Reserve, namely J. P. Morgan, Bernard Baruch, Otto Kahn, Paul Warburg, and John D. Rockefeller, among others.

The CFR shares a close cross–membership with other globalist organizations, which we shall disclose in the course of this section. At the time of the first publication of this book, the CFR had over 2,900 members, most of whom resided in just three cities: New York, Boston, and Washington, D.C. The CFR had thirty–eight affiliated organizations located in major U.S. cities.

As I reported earlier, Rear Admiral Ward said they planned to bring about the surrender of the sovereignty and national independence of the U.S., and in 1950 member James Warburg testified before the Senate Foreign Relations subcommittee that, "We shall have world government whether or not you like it—by conquest or consent." Presently, their plan is to erode national sovereignty piece by piece. The New World Order came "out of the closet" at the time of the Gulf War when former CFR director George Bush publicly used the term.

Pay attention here: At the beginning of World War II, the CFR (with the help of Franklin Roosevelt) gained control of the U.S. State Department, and after the war helped to establish the United Nations in 1945. *The U.S. delegation for the U.N.'s founding conference contained 47 CFR members.* Those members included **John Foster Dulles, Adlai Stevenson, Nelson Rockefeller,** and Soviet spy, **Alger Hiss,** who served as secretary–general of the founding conference.

Many prominent people have served as director of the CFR, including Walter Lippmann, Adlai Stevenson, Cyrus Vance, Zbigniew Brzezinski, Paul Volcker, Lane Kirkland, George H. W. Bush, Henry Kissinger, David Rockefeller, George Schultz, Alan Greenspan, Brent Scowcroft, Jeane Kirkpatrick, and Dick Cheney.

I told you it reads like *Who's Who!* And you "ain't seen nothin' yet." Private industry financially supported and/or controlled by the CFR includes (because of space I have abbreviated the company names): ARCO, BP, Mercedes–Benz, Seagram, *Newsweek, Reader's Digest, Washington Post,* American Express, Carnegie Corp., Ford Fdn., GE Fdn., General Motors, Mellon Fdn., Sloane Fdn., Xerox Fdn., IBM, AT&T, Ford, Chrysler, Macy, Federated Dept. Stores, Gimbels, Sears, JC Penney, May Dept. Stores, Allied Stores, and various Rockefeller concerns.

The CFR shares many cross–memberships with the Bilderbergers, which we will address last in this study. I will share some of their names with you at that time.

The Club of Rome draws many members from the CFR. It was founded in 1968 and consists of scientists, educators, economists, humanists, industrialists, and government officials who see it as this organization's task to oversee the regionalization and unification of the entire world. It has divided the world into ten political/economic regions or "kingdoms."

In the Club of Rome we glimpse the dark, spiritual side of the globalist movement. Aurelio Peccei, the Club's founder, revealed *Mankind at the Turning Point* his pantheist/New Age beliefs, writing about man's communion with nature, the need for a "world consciousness" and "a new and enlightened humanism." He was a student of Pierre Teilhard de Chardin, one of the New Age occultists' most frequently quoted authors.

Club members include the late **Norman Cousins** (former honorary chairman of Planetary Citizens), **John Naisbitt** (author of *Megatrends*), **Betty Friedan** (founding president of the National Organization for Women), **Robert Anderson, Harlan Cleveland,** as well as many other New Age speakers and authors. Members also include U.S. congressmen, Planned Parenthood representatives, U.N. officials, and Carnegie and Rockefeller foundation people.

The CFR has a stranglehold on America. The CFR effectively controls the four most powerful positions (after the presidency) in our government, i.e., secretaries of state, treasury, and defense, and the national security advisor.

At the time of the original writing of this book, 15 of the 21 treasury secretaries since 1920 had been CFR members; plus 12 of the last 14 secretaries of state; 10 of 13 national security advisors (since Eisenhower); and 11 of 12 defense secretaries (since Eisenhower). Of the 60 people who held these strategic positions during the years specified, 48 were CFR members—that's 80 percent!

By the Nixon administration, 115 CFR members held positions in the executive branch. Carter appointed scores of TLC and/or CFR members. All of his National Security Council were or had been members: Mondale, Brzezinski, Vance, Brown, Jones, and Turner. Ronald Reagan appointed 76 CFR and TLC members to key posts, but George Bush broke records with 354 [recognizable names in highest levels of government]. . . . The State Department is saturated with CFR/TLC members. Almost every prominent ambassador or diplomat is a globalist.

As for the Treasury Department, Brady and Regan are members, and Federal Reserve chairmen Greenspan, Anderson, Vance, and Volcker are all insiders.

Every U.S. secretary of defense for the past 35 years, except Clark Clifford, belonged to either [the CFR or the TLC]. Every Supreme Allied Commander in Europe and every U.S. ambassador to NATO have been insiders, as well as 9 of 13 CIA directors.

Except for John F. Kennedy and Ronald Reagan, almost every U.S. president was either a CFR or TLC member. JFK may have been a member of the Boston affiliate of the CFR. Ted Kennedy is definitely a member of the affiliate, though his name is not listed in the general CFR membership.

The bottom line is: **The same one–world agenda moves forward, despite who wins our elections!**

The media is well represented in the membership of the CFR, including such familiar names as Paley, Rather, Moyers, Brokaw, Chancellor, Levine, Brinkley, Scali, Walters, Schorr, McNeil, Lehrer, and Carter III. Not surprisingly, Rockefellers' Chase Manhattan Bank has minority control of all three major networks (CBS, ABC, and NBC).

AP, UPI, and Reuters wire services all have CFR members in major positions. Other CFR members in the media include William F.

Buckley (also a Bones member), Diane Sawyer, Rowland Evans, and David Gergen.

Most major newspapers today have a strong CFR influence, including the *New York Times, Washington Post, Wall Street Journal, Boston Globe, Baltimore Sun, Chicago Sun–Times, LA Times, Houston Post, Minneapolis Star–Tribune, Arkansas Gazette, Des Moines Register & Tribune,* the Gannett Co. (which publishes *USA Today* and newspapers in more than forty cities), *Denver Post,* and *Louisville Courier.* This is just a partial listing of papers staffed by CFR affiliates.

Magazines with CFR connections include *Fortune, Time, Life, Money, People, Sports Illustrated, Newsweek, Business Week, U.S. News & World Report, Saturday Review, Reader's Digest, Atlantic Monthly, McCall's,* and *Harper's Magazine.*

Book publishers include MacMillan, Random House, Simon & Schuster, McGraw–Hill, Harper, IBM, Xerox, Yale University Press, Little Brown, Viking, Cowles Publishing, and Harper & Row. Many of these publish school textbooks, which brings us to just how far the tentacles of CFR influence reach into the education of our children.

CFR foundations, primarily Carnegie and Rockefeller, provided two–thirds of the gifts to all American universities during the first third of this century. And the man who is considered the "father of progressive education," John Dewey, was an atheist who taught four of the five Rockefeller brothers. He spent most of his life educating teachers, including those in the U.S.S.R. This man's influence extends not just through years, but throughout generations. Today, 20 percent of all American school superintendents and 40 percent of all education department heads have advanced degrees from Columbia where Dewey headed the education department for many years.

The National Education Association (NEA) adopted his philosophy of humanism, socialism, and globalism, then put them into our classrooms. CFR members head the teaching departments at Columbia, Cornell, NYU, Sarah Lawrence College, Stanford, Yale, University of Chicago, Johns Hopkins University, Brown University, University of Wisconsin, Washington University, and Lee University.

As I have emphasized since the beginning of this book, this New World Order plan has its roots in the spiritual, rather than a material or physical basis, as its proponents would have you believe. Tying the CFR leaders and members directly to the New Age movement ultimately includes the radical ecology groups, Lucis Trust, nominal churches, the U.N., and others.

So, how does the New Age fit into the one-world movement? The New Age is pantheistic—the belief that God is the sum total of all that exists. No personal God exists; rather "God" is a god-force which flows through all living things—and which supposedly makes humans "gods." New Agers believes that since global unity is essential to the proper flow of the god-force, when unity occurs in a one-world government a new age of enlightenment will emerge. Occult practices (and eastern mysticism) accompany pantheism.

The Theosophical Society (TS) is at the forefront of New Age globalism. Lucis Press (offspring of Lucis Trust, formerly headquartered at the U.N.) was established by TS leader Alice Bailey. Lucis Press promotes the preeminence of Satan (Lucifer) and is well connected with the one-world political societies and the World Constitution and Parliament Association. Past and present members include TLC and CFR cross-memberships: **Robert McNamara, Donald Regan, Henry Kissinger, David Rockefeller, Paul Volcker,** and **George Shultz.**

The World Constitution and Parliament Association (WCPA) has already written a world constitution, the Constitution for the Federation of Earth, and has submitted it to world leaders for ratification. Dominated by environmentalists, U.S. personnel, Nobel Laureates, leftist churches (i.e., the WCC), educators, financial leaders, and eastern mystics (pantheists), it calls for an international monetary system; administration of oceans, seabeds, and atmosphere as the common heritage of all humanity; elimination of fossil fuels; redistribution of the world's wealth; complete and rapid disarmament (including confiscation of privately owned weapons); an end to national sovereignty; a global environmental organization; world justice system; and world tax agency.

Many of its members embrace eastern mysticism. U.S. members include **Jesse Jackson** (also CFR) and former attorney general **Ramsey Clark.** Its director, Philip Iseley, belongs to Amnesty

International, the ACLU, Global Education Associates, Friends of the Earth, Sierra Club, Audubon Society, American Humanist Association, SANE (nuclear freeze group), Planetary Citizens, and the Global Futures Network, among many other organizations.

The U.N. is the chosen agency that is moving us toward world government; but the U.N. charter is not a *constitution*. Plus, it is an organization of *sovereign* nations, which is anathema to globalists. So the WCPA's world constitution is ready for acceptance at the proper time.

In the November 2, 1994, edition of the *Los Angeles Times*, Doyle McManus writes an article titled "U.S. Leadership Is More Diverse, Less Influential." "Almost half a century ago, when Harry S Truman needed help running the foreign policy of the United States at the dawn of the Cold War, the remedy was simple: 'Whenever we needed a man,' one of his aides recalled, 'we thumbed through the roll of Council [on Foreign Relations] members and put in a call to New York.'"

He tells about the expanding of the so–called "elite" to include every area of influence, from academics, scientists, and religious leaders to rock stars and others. Leslie H. Gelb, president emeritus of the CFR, says, "This is the largest foreign policy elite this country has ever enjoyed," and adds that he plans to expand and diversify the "august" organization's membership to embrace new areas such as sports and the arts. Ironically, says McManus, just as the elite is growing in size and diversity, it may also be diminishing in power.

Recent surveys, including the *Times Mirror* polls, suggest that the general public is less willing than in the past to accept the advice of the foreign policy elite—at least on issues that come close to home, like free trade with Mexico or the use of American troops in peacekeeping missions overseas.

"There's more information going straight to the general public now," said Brent Scowcroft [CFR and TLC member], who served as national security advisor to President George Bush. "That tends to reduce the influence [of the elite]. It makes it more difficult to get support for a potentially unpopular policy."

There are currently (in 2009) around 4,300 CFR members (you'll be amazed at some of the names you find there).

Now for the Federal Reserve, a.k.a. the FED! This entity is closely tied to the policies and policymakers of the CFR. As I told you earlier, it is not a federal agency, just because the word appears in its name. It's just another profit–making banking corporation, which has been given unconstitutional control over U.S. finances and the printing/recalling of currency, as well as determining the interest we pay. . . all duties that were constitutionally assigned to Congress. We all are familiar with the term "prime rate." That is the lowest interest rate set by the Fed (the rate paid by large banks who borrow from them and then increase the interest rate as they lend the money to you, i.e., "prime–plus"). The prime rate fluctuates frequently and regularly, with interest rates determined by the Fed in an attempt to manipulate inflation and recession, followed by immediate reaction by the stock market in response to whichever direction the variable interest takes. In a brochure by Thomas D. Schauf, a CPA, the Fed is exposed totally. He encourages reprinting his brochure freely, so I have quoted some of his information below:

> The Federal Reserve Bank (Fed) can write a check for an unlimited amount of money to buy government bonds and the U.S. Treasury prints the money to back up the check. UNBELIEVABLE . . . IT'S TRUE! Read *National Geographic,* January 1993, pg. 84. Go to the library and read the books exposing this SCAM! The Fed is a private bank for profit . . . just like any business! Check the *Encyclopaedia Britannica* or, easier yet, look in the *1992 Yellow Pages.* The Fed is listed under COMMERCIAL BANKS, not GOVERNMENT. The Fed is no more a *Federal* agency than *Federal* Express.

Schauf goes on to explain some of the intricacies of how the Fed prints currency, then sells it to the government in exchange for government bonds, on which we pay interest, and which becomes part of the national debt which we, the taxpayers, are obligated to repay. Then the Fed sells these instruments to others, including foreign agencies, spreading around, as it were, our debtors. It seems they don't want to keep all their eggs in one basket, or to put it another way, if they spread around the debt, they also spread around the risks. Just remember, as they sell off this debt and receive funds or obligations for funds in exchange, they haven't yet done anything to earn this money but authorize the printing of the currency. A pretty good scam, isn't it? For a more detailed account of how all this works, I recommend reading Wright Patman's *A Primer on Money*.

This system can be bypassed; we can print our own money, as the Constitution requires. On June 4, 1963, President John F. Kennedy issued Executive Order 11110 (one of the rare instances where this executive power was used for something worthwhile) and printed *real* U.S. dollars with no debt or interest attached, because he bypassed the Fed bank! However, upon his death the printing ceased and the currency was withdrawn. For proof, ask any coin dealer to show you a 1963 Kennedy dollar. You'll find that it says "United States Note," NOT "Federal Reserve Note"!

Today the government prints dollars and forwards the cash interest free to the Fed. The Fed exchanges this cash to buy newly issued Federal Bonds and collects the interest. Much of the government debt is owned by the Fed banking system.

If Kennedy had lived and continued to print U.S. dollars, interest free, debt free, there would be no $4 trillion of debt. Why give the Fed dollars interest free and allow the Fed to use these dollars to buy new government bonds, paying them interest? Kennedy's solution (Exec. Order. 11110) made this seem ridiculous. Why didn't the media tell the truth. We need to force Congress to make the change. [Schauf tells below why the media is silent.]

Article I, Section 8, of the Constitution states that only Congress coin [create] money. In 1935, the Supreme Court ruled that Congress cannot constitutionally delegate its power to another group and the Fed illegally controls the printing of money through its 12 banks. Rockefeller and Rothschild are two of the original 300 owners of the Fed!

Rothschild, a London banker who dreamed up the Fed, wrote a letter saying: "It (Central Bank [Fed]) gives the National Bank almost complete control of national finance. The few who understand the system will either be so interested in its profits, or so dependent on its favors, that there will be no opposition from that class. . . . The great body of the people, mentally incapable of comprehending, will bear its burden without complaint, and perhaps without even suspecting that the system is inimical [harmful] to their interests." The Fed profits from our stupidity and apathy! OUR FOREFATHERS TRIED TO PREVENT THIS!!! . . .

Congressmen McFadden and Patman, chairmen of a Banking Committee, plus others, attempted to abolish the Fed. The problem was that the media remained silent, so citizens remained ignorant. . . .

Why has the media remained silent? [Author's note: At the lower levels of writing and reporting, I'm sure that the people don't understand the situation any better than most of us. Let's face it, they have concocted a very complex system that even the would-be experts have difficulty comprehending. However, in the upper echelons of management, it's a different story. They understand, all right, but to them it's a matter of personal and business financial interest . . . read on!] Rockefeller is one of the original 300 shareholders of the Fed. In July 1968, the House Banking Subcommittee reported that Rockefeller, through Chase Manhattan Bank, controlled 5.9% of the stock in CBS, and the bank had gained interlocking directorates with ABC. In 1974, Congress issued a report stating that the Chase Manhattan Bank's stake in CBS rose to 14.1% and in NBC to 4.5% (through RCA, the parent company of NBC). The same report said that the Chase Manhattan Bank held stock in 28 broadcasting firms. After this report, the Chase Manhattan Bank obtained 6.7% of ABC, and today the percentage could be much greater. It only required 5% ownership to significantly influence the media. The Fed knows if people become informed, they will demand change. . . . The Fed can control the media by withdrawing loans! Ask any CPA!

Rockefeller also controls the Council on Foreign Relations (CFR). Nearly every major newscaster belongs to this Council. The CFR controls many major newspapers and magazines. Additionally, major corporations owned by Fed shareholders are the source of huge advertising revenues that surely would influence the media. By controlling the media, you control the population, the elections, and public opinion. . . .

How did [Fed control] happen? In 1913, Senator Nelson Aldrich, maternal grandfather to the Rockefellers, pushed a bill through Congress just before Christmas when many of its members were on vacation. Private bankers funded and staffed President Wilson's campaign. When elected, Wilson passed the Fed. Later Wilson remorsefully replied (referring to the Fed), "I have unwittingly ruined my country."

The media misled the public, and sponsors of the Fed made 10 promises, none of which were kept. Now the banks fund both Democratic and Republican candidates. The bankers employ members of Congress on weekends (nicknamed T&T Club) as consultants with lucrative salaries (supporting documentation can be provided). Within months of starting the Fed, income tax was created to pay for this new interest expense. The same 1913 law said the Fed will pay no IRS tax! Our taxes pay interest on all new currency issued! Note: The bankers created this new legislation (law), not Congress! Now the Fed wants the New World Order (NWO) and Cashless Society (CS)! People, oppose it! The Fed's CS would absolutely control you!

. . . Thomas Jefferson said this about a Fed–type banking system: "If the American people ever allow private banks to control the issue of their currency, first by inflation then by deflation, the banks and the corporations will grow up around them, will deprive the people of all property until their children wake up homeless on the continent their fathers conquered." Experts believe the Fed created the Great Depression and inflation, and profits from people's misfortune. Below Congress, Fed Chairman Eccles admitted the Fed creates new money from thin air (printing press) and loans it back to us at interest. Before the U.S. had huge deficits, we printed new money interest–free, without paying bankers interest. Today, the Fed profits from huge deficits . . . and they're getting BIGGER ever day!

Schauf adds that the U.S. government can **buy back** the Fed at any time for $450 million, according to the *Congressional Record,* and tells some of the ramifications of doing so. I'm sure by now you are beginning to see how the tentacles of these various occultic organizations are all intertwined.

Another major faction involved in world control through economics and trade is the Trilateral Commission. It was founded in 1973 by banker David Rockefeller to promote world government by encouraging economic interdependence among the three superpowers: North America, Japan, and Europe. Rockefeller selected Zbigniew Brzezinski (later to become Carter's national security advisor) as the commission's first director and invited President Carter to become a founding member. In his book *Between Two Ages,* Brzezinski calls for a new international monetary system and a global taxation system. He praised Marxism as a "creative stage in the maturing of man's universal vision" and quoted New Ager de Chardin.

By 1979, just six years after the TLC was founded, its activities were already known well enough to be addressed by retiring Arizona senator Barry Goldwater in his autobiography, *With No Apologies.* Goldwater writes:

> In my view the Trilateral Commission represents a skillful, coordinated effort to seize control and consolidate four centers of power—political, monetary, intellectual, and ecclesiastical. All this is to be done in the interest of creating a more peaceful, more productive world community. What the Trilateralists truly intend is the creation of a worldwide economic power superior to the political governments of the nation–states involved. They believe the abundant materialism they propose to create will overwhelm existing differences. As managers and creators of the system, they will rule the future.

The European Community, North America (U.S. and Canada), and Japan—the three main democratic industrialized areas of the world—are the three sides of the Trilateral Commission. The Commission's members comprise about 325 prominent figures with a variety of leadership responsibilities from the three regions.

When the first triennium of the Trilateral Commission was launched in 1973, the most immediate purpose, allegedly, was to draw together—at a time of considerable friction among governments—the highest level unofficial group possible, supposedly for the purpose of examining the common problems facing the three areas.

At a deeper level, there was a sense that the United States was no longer in such a singular international leadership position, and founders of the TLC felt that a more shared form of leadership—including Europe and Japan, in particular—would be needed for the international system to successfully navigate the major challenges of the coming years. They still purport to have these needs as their goal.

The rise of Japan and the emergence of the European Community (EC) dramatizes the importance of such shared leadership, in the eyes of TLC members. And instead of seeing the breakup of the Soviet Union as beneficial, the TLC viewed it as "the receding Soviet threat dissolving the 'glue' holding the regions together" as it began its 1991–94 triennium. They claim that "handling economic tensions among our countries and maintaining the benefits of a global economy will require even more effort than in the past."

From the 325± membership, an executive committee is selected, including the chairmen (one from each side of the triangle), deputy chairmen, and thirty–five others. Once each year the full commission gathers in one of the regions; recent meeting locations have included Paris, Washington, D.C., and Tokyo. They insist these are not secret meetings, and as mentioned earlier, Henry Kissinger was interviewed by the media when entering a hotel conference room at a one meeting, where he pointed out that they were not a secret organization; their meeting times and locations were in plain view for all to see. Of course, he failed to mention that the media representatives were not welcome at the meeting, nor would information discussed behind closed doors be made available for public consumption.

According to the TLC *Organization and Policy Program* publication, a substantial portion of each annual meeting is devoted to consideration of draft task force reports to the commission. These reports are generally the joint products of authors from each of the three regions who draw on a range of consultants in the course of their work. Publication follows discussion in the commissions's annual meeting. Although a number of changes are usually made after discussion, the authors are solely responsible for their final text.

In addition to task force reports, the commission considers other issues in seminars or topical sessions at its meetings. A wide range of subjects have been covered, including the social and political implications of inflation, prospects for peace in the Middle East, macroeconomic policy coordination, nuclear weapons proliferation, China and the international community, employment/unemployment trends and their implications, and the uses of space. Relations with developing countries have been a particular concern of the commission, and speakers from developing countries have addressed each annual meeting since 1980.

Task force reports are distributed only "to interested persons inside and outside government." The same is true for the publication issued on each annual meeting.

Finally, the Bilderbergs! "Last, but not least" is a phrase that definitely fits this group. They are power brokers of the world, and that is no exaggeration!

The Bilderbergers were established in 1954 by Prince Bernhard of The Netherlands, husband of Queen Juliana. She was among the first endorsers of "Planetary Citizens" in the 1970s. Numerous leading Americans have been "Bilderbergers," including **Dean Acheson, Christian Herter, Dean Rusk, Robert McNamara, George Ball, Henry Kissinger,** and **Gerald Ford** (be observant for cross-membership names with CFR, TLC, Skull & Bones, etc.).

The Bilderbergers, funded by major one–world institutions, was created to regionalize Europe. The Treaty of Rome which established the Common Market—today's European Community—was produced at Bilderberger secret meetings. Cross-membership with the CFR includes **David Rockefeller, Winston Lord** (State Department official and Bones family tree), **Henry Kissinger, Zbigniew Brzezinski, Cyrus Vance, Robert McNamara** (former World Bank president), **George Ball** (State Department and director of Lehman Brothers), **Robert Anderson** (ARCO president), **Gerald Ford, Henry Grunwald** (managing editor, *Time*), **Henry J. Heinz II, Theodore Hesburgh** (former Notre Dame president), and others.

Some reliable unnamed sources have provided a pipeline into the secret organization's meetings and furnished copies of the "not for circulation" agenda and roster of attendees to reporters from the *Spotlight*. Again, the names read like a *Who's Who* from around the world. In a report on the Bilderberg meeting at Baden–Baden, Germany, June 6–9, 1991, reporter James P. Tucker, Jr., writes in the September 1991 reprint of *Spotlight* an article titled "World Shadow Government Planning for Another War":

> The Bilderberg group plans another war within five years.
>
> This grim news came from a "main pipeline"—a high-ranking Bilderberg staffer who secretly cooperated with our investigation—behind the guarded walls of the Badischer Hof, who was operating from inside with colleagues serving as "connecting pipelines." . . .
>
> While war plans were being outlined in "Bilderbergese," the air traffic controller at Baden–Baden's private airport reported numerous incoming flights from Brussels, where NATO headquarters are based. . . .
>
> Aboard one of those planes, *en route* to the Bilderberg meeting, was Manfred Woerner, NATO's general secretary.
>
> It was repeatedly stated at the Bilderberg meeting that there will be "other Saddams" in the years head who must be dealt with swiftly and efficiently.
>
> What the Bilderberg group intends is a global army at the disposal of the United Nations, which is to become the world government to which all nations will be subservient by the year 2000.
>
> Crucial to making the U.N. a strong world government . . . is to bestow it with "enforcement powers." "A U.N. army must be able to act immediately, anywhere in the world, without the delays involved in each country making its own decision whether to participate, based on parochial considerations," said Henry Kissinger . . .

[who] expressed pleasure over the conduct of the Persian Gulf war, stressing that it had been sanctioned by the U.N., at the request of President George Bush, himself a Trilateral luminary, before the issue was laid before the U.S. Congress.

The fact that the president would make his case to the U.N. first, when the Constitution empowers only Congress to declare war, was viewed as a significant step in "leading Americans away from nationalism." ...

It was "good psychology" for Bush to allow congressional and other leaders to express their fear of losing 20,000 to 40,000 American lives [in the Gulf War] ... when Bush knew the loss of life would be much lower.

When the allied casualty toll reached "only 378" and Americans read and heard of "only four" Americans dying in a week of ground war, it "was like nobody had died at all," one said, "and Americans enjoyed it like an international sporting match."

Such an adventure was essential to getting Americans into "the right frame of mind for the years ahead," said another. ... They promised each other, there will be "more incidents" for the U.N. to deal with in the years ahead. The Bilderberg group and its little brother, the Trilateral Commission, can set up "incidents" on schedule, they said, but in less direct words. The words "within five years" were heard repeatedly.

Another important step toward a strong, recognized, and accepted world government is taxing power. ...

At its April meeting in Tokyo, the Trilateralists called for a U.N. levy of 10 cents per barrel of oil coming from the Persian Gulf. It would be as "temporary," lasting only long enough to rebuild Kuwait and feed the Kurds until they are back on their feet.

The Bilderbergers approved of the move by their brother group, in which Rockefeller and Kissinger ... serve as leaders. Once people get used to a tax, it never is repealed ... it could be extended worldwide "with appropriate increases" in the years ahead.

From the sum total of all things said, the Bilderberg strategy emerged: Start the tax by imposing it on a newly established "bad guy" who must suffer, and use the revenue for such humanitarian purposes as feeding the Kurds. Keep the initial tax so low that the public is unaware that it is levied. Then kick it up.

Also discussed was the dividing of the world into major regions, eliminating individual countries' borders, "for convenience of administration." Yeah, right! Then they were to apply pressure to the U.S. to pass the free trade treaty with Mexico, another step toward establishing the Western Hemisphere as another region—first free trade with Canada, then Mexico, followed by all other Latin American nations.

Their plan was to have a single currency for all of Europe by 1996, with a one–currency movement for the Western Hemisphere to follow, and ultimately a world government with world currency. They expressed their pleasure with the progress of the trade agreements/treaties which were under way.

How can I close a chapter containing as much information about so many as does this chapter? I can only point out that, according to Scripture, we don't wrestle against "flesh and blood." Our warfare is spiritual, and given the roots of these ungodly organizations, I strongly suggest that you yield your soul to the Lord Jesus Christ, submit yourself to God, and put on the whole armor which Paul describes to us in Ephesians . . . not just to protect yourself from our enemy and adversary, Satan, but so we can go on the spiritual offensive and drive him out of our lives, our government, and our land. You will notice in the description of the armor that there is nothing provided to protect your backside—from which I think we may safely assume that God intended us to go forward in His victory, rather than let the devil put us on the run.

Finally, my brethren, be strong in the Lord, and in the power of his might. Put on the whole armour of God, that ye may be able to stand against the wiles of the devil. For we wrestle not against flesh and blood, but against principalities, against powers, against the rulers of the darkness of this world, against spiritual wickedness in high places. Wherefore take unto you the whole armour of God, that ye may be able to withstand in the evil day, and having done all, to stand. Stand therefore, having your loins girt about with truth, and having on the breastplate of righteousness; And your feet shod with the preparation of the gospel of peace; Above all, taking the shield of faith, wherewith ye shall be able to quench all the fiery darts of the wicked. And take the helmet of salvation, and the sword of the Spirit, which is the word of God: Praying always with all prayer and supplication in the Spirit....

—Ephesians 6:10–18

CHAPTER FOUR

BARCODES

Because of its technical nature, this could easily become one of those "You're telling me more than I want to know!" chapters. I'll try not to bore you, but it is an important part of the control and surveillance going on globally, and I must give the details so you will recognize what it is when you look at some of the variations of the standard barcode.

I think by now you are convinced that the time is rapidly approaching when *everything* on this planet will be marked, controlled, tracked, or monitored. If it *moves,* it will have a UPC (Universal Product Code) number in the form of a barcode of some variety.

You will laugh at the following report, which is fine because it is funny, but it illustrates how far barcodes have progressed, and how commonplace they have become. Cathy Smith of Houston, Texas, submitted these two paragraphs, which were printed by *Reader's Digest* in their August 1994 edition, "Life in These United States" section.

I take my husband's shirts to a laundry that has recently instituted a new identification system. Inside the collar of each shirt, they place labels bearing a bar code and the customer's name. Since I started our account, the words "Smith, Cathy" have appeared on my husband's collars.

Because he did not want a woman's name on his shirts, he made a special trip to the cleaners to have the account changed to Marshall Smith. Unfortunately, only the first six letters of each name are used. Now his collars read, "Smith, Marsha."

Such limitations are quickly disappearing with the newer technology, and I'm sure that before long "Marsha" will once again be "Marshall."

The Global 666 Barcode

In and of itself, there is nothing inherently evil about a barcode—it is just another, more efficient way of keeping track of your inventory and movement of freight, laundry, etc.—chores formerly accomplished with painstaking manual labor. The problem lies in placing this technology at the disposal of a New World Order–minded government who not only wants to meddle in our affairs . . . they want to control them (and us)!

A barcode is simply a mathematically arranged symbol of vertical lines. It is a parallel arrangement of varying width BARS and SPACES. The structural arrangement or spacing of these lines, relative to a given set of parameters, can be made to represent a product's identification number. The UPC, better known simply as "barcode," has been put to this use since 1973, having been adopted by the retail industry in 1972. The UPC barcode is considered to be the "mother" of all microchip transponder technology.

The code is not really as complicated as it may first seem. A typical UPC *Version A* barcode symbol contains thirty black vertical lines (called "bars"). A *pair* of these lines equals only *one digit* or number. In other words, this coding system *requires two lines to equal one number.*

Details of the UPC Version A Code Construction

As depicted herein, the actual UPC code is a ten–digit code: the first five digits represent the manufacturer of the labeled item, and the next five digits are a unique product identifier code. This ten–digit code is then preceded with a "number system digit" and followed by a "transpositional check digit" (TCD), to verify if any of the preceding eleven digits have been transposed.

On each side and in the center of this series of carefully spaced lines are three pairs of longer lines that extend slightly below the

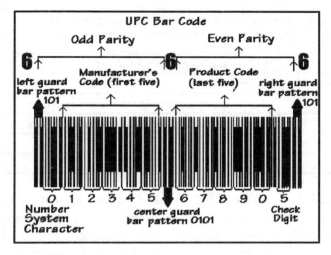

others. These longer pairs of lines are special—they are called "guard bars."

Guard bars provide reference points for store computer scanners (barcode reading machines) by segregating the left half of the code lines from the right half. This is needed because the left lines have a different message on them than the right lines and must, therefore, be read by the scanner differently. The center pair of guard bars in the UPC barcode are used to both divide the code in half and tell the scanner/computer what it needs to know in order to readjust its program to interpret the remaining half of the code. Note again the diagram—the left half represents the manufacturer's code and the right half represents the product code. The following chart defines the numerical values:

UPC VERSION A NUMBER SYSTEMS ASSIGNMENTS	
Number System Digit	Application
0	92,000 manufacturer identification numbers; 8,000 locally assigned numbers
1	Reserved
2	Random weight consumer packages

UPC VERSION A NUMBER SYSTEMS ASSIGNMENTS	
3	Drug product
4	In–store marking without format
5	UPC coupons
6	100,000 manufacturer identification numbers
7	100,000 manufacturer identification numbers
8	Reserved
9	Reserved

In summation, a typical UPC *Version A* barcode symbol consists of two halves, representing a total of twelve numeric digits. These two six–digit halves are surrounded by left, center, and right guard bar patterns. Together, the black and white line produce a series of electronic "dits" and "dahs," similar to the old Morse code telegraph key "dots and dashes." The scanner reads these electronic messages as a series of "zeroes" and "ones." These zeroes and ones represent what are called *binary numbers,* in computer language.

Binary numbers are a "machine language" which is the basic internal language of computers. This is how the computer thinks and gives itself orders. All computers operate on the basis of this two–digit mathematical binary system.

The barcode industry informs us that the UPC system is a binary system. Can we believe that? Is the UPC code, indeed, a true binary configuration as the barcode industry suggests? No, not really. As you can see, the entire system is very deceptively designed around an infamous numerical configuration, biblically known as **666**, the **mark** of the Antichrist or devil (Revelation 13:16–18).

Now, please do not jump to hasty conclusions—it is not likely that the barcode will be the actual technology used to *mark* a person, but in all likelihood, it is the forerunner of that technology.

THE 666 BARCODE CONFIGURATION

Time and space do not permit a thorough examination and discussion of this "666" UPC configuration. However, somehow it was surreptitiously designed around this satanic number described in the

Bible. And these "coincidences" just keep adding up. It's kind of like circumstantial evidence . . . if you collect enough of it, you can convict someone. Doesn't it seem just a little strange that out of over 121 million billions of possible mathematical combinations of code numbers, someone would have just randomly arrived at this very unique numerical configuration? I don't believe this was something consciously planned by the developers of barcode technology, but that the spiritual powers have contrived with the circumstances to make it work out that way. I think we can rule out coincidence. Fulfillment of biblical prophecy? Possibly. What do you think?

Before we get into some of the more technical aspects of the many variations of barcodes, let's review this coding system a final time to ensure clarity. The code's designers inform us in their books that the code was designed as a "coding system," as well as a "symbology." They tell us that the UPC was a fixed-length, numeric, continuous symbology design employing four element widths. In addition, they tell us that there are three different versions of the UPC symbol: (1) Version A—encodes twelve digits (6 + 6); (2) Version E—encodes six digits; (3) Version D—encodes various lengths of digits, but is seldom used.

Of these three codes, however, the primary one in use today in the retail industry is Version A. As we have explained above, it is designed and configured primarily around the satanic number 666, no matter how inadvertently it may have occurred.

The actual data in this coding system is encoded as two bars and two spaces within seven modules. The UPC Version A system is also called a "7,2" code that has twenty unique patterns.

I am not going to spend much more time on this subject, as having more than a superficial knowledge of barcodes is really not necessary in our study here since these applications do not specifically relate to "buying or selling" as indicated in Revelation. However, let me briefly familiarize you with the existence of a few other barcode systems currently in use globally, as they indirectly are a part of the comprehensive global system that will track, trace, monitor, and electronically control and enslave us all by means of computers (remember, don't personify a computer as *evil*—it is just a machine/

tool, no more or less evil than the individual operating it). Such encoding systems include but are not limited to the following:

EAN System—European Article Number System (similar to the UPC)
Interleaved "2 of 5" CodeThe "Code 93" Code
The Codabar CodeThe "Code 49" Code
The "Code 39" CodeThe "Code 16K" Code
The "Code 128" Code

Most present-day general applications make use of the UPC, EAN, Code 39, Codabar, Interleaved 2 of 5, Code 128, Code 93, Code 49, and Code 16K barcode systems. They are the established industry standards. However, several additional symbologies exist and need to be mentioned for the sake of completeness in this overview of global barcoding systems. I'm sure you all will recognize the familiar postal barcode shown here which is now being printed across the bottom of your mail.

The "2 of 5" CodeThe Vericode Code
The "Code 11" CodeThe Data Code
The Postnet/Postal CodeThe UPS Code
The Codablock CodeThe PDF-417 Code
The USA-5 Code

2-D BARCODES

I could not in good conscience close this chapter without including one of the latest innovations in barcode technology. It is referred to as 2-D technology (and with the use of holograms, etc., 3-D barcodes are currently in development). Once you switch to 2-D barcodes, you have greatly expanded your capacity to retain information. In an April 1995 edition of *Traffic Management* magazine, an article titled "2-D or not 2-D?" The article began: "Imagine fitting all the information found in a shipping document into a space the size of a postage stamp. Two-dimensional or '2-D' bar codes promise to do just that. Unlike conventional bar codes—the familiar black and white strips found on grocery-store packages—which essentially string data along a horizontal axis, 2-D codes use both the vertical and the horizontal axes to encode data, hence the name two-dimensional. As a result, hundreds of characters can fit into the space occupied by 30 characters on a linear bar code."

Two-dimensional barcodes were featured in the August 1994 edition of *Automatic ID News,* in the sections "Case Study of the Month" and "Industry Focus."

Since 2-D barcodes bring this technology much closer to home from an ID standpoint (of both objects, i.e., cars and buildings, and people, i.e., firefighters in this article), I briefly have quoted portions from both articles below.

In the Line of Fire: 2-D bar codes track whose [sic] battling fires and provide rescue workers with firefighter's medical history. State accountability OSHA requirements met with 2-D coded Velcro ID tags; eventually, firemen will know a building's layout, gas main shut-offs, and contents by scanning a 2-D code.

Every fire department at one time or another has wrestled with the problem of accounting for its personnel on the fireground. This includes the problem of *having an accurate and readily accessible medical history for any personnel* that are injured and need to be transported to a hospital. And every firefighter, at some time in his/her career, has said, "I sure wish we knew what was in that building BEFORE we arrived on scene and went in." These are the same problems that the Grand Traverse Fire Department has been facing, until now.

Automotive Industry recommends 2-D standards
One of the more amazing technical innovations in Auto. ID to evolve during the latter 1980s and early 1990s is the creation of a whole new generation of high-tech bar codes called two-dimensional bar codes or 2-D symbols. 2-D symbols are designed to hold enough information within the symbol itself to be a small database.

These very unfamiliar-looking bar codes can contain a whole

lot more data than a regular bar code. In fact, many 2–D symbols can carry 2,000 characters of data in a single symbol, as compared with a regular or linear bar code capacity of 15 to 22 characters. 2–D symbols can also carry binary data, which can be made to run a computer program or generate photographs and drawings. In addition to carrying a lot more information, 2–D symbols can be made very thin and shaped in unusual ways.

Probably the most fascinating thing about these symbologies is that, in some cases, you can actually destroy or damage 50% or more of the label and still get 100% of the data contained in the symbol when it is read or scanned! Most 2–D symbol types have "error correction"; that is, there are mathematical formulas embedded in the code that will "reconstruct" any missing portion of the symbol and recreate the missing data.

As you can see, this new technology has enormous possibilities. However, the problem occurs when they start applying it to us. Again, let me warn against a premature conclusion that the barcode is the "mark" of the beast.

Hopefully by now you are getting the picture that it is a very sinister plan. In fact, it should be apparent to anyone at this point that very soon nearly everything in the world—both animate and inanimate—will be marked, tagged, coded, numbered, implanted, and identified with some type of ID system that will allow the dictatorial New World Order global government to label, trace, track, monitor, and control everything and everybody on earth! Indeed, the coming New World **Dis**order will be the most evil system the world has ever known.

I have long warned people that RFID biochip implants—and *not* barcodes—will be the technology the New World Order Antichrist will use to mark and control humans globally, but some insist otherwise. Even after all my warnings, there are still Christians who vehemently insist that the barcode is going to be the mark to which we find reference in Revelation 13. Please consider all the facts. There is no doubt that this system is conditioning us for more advanced technologies which, in fact, do have the capability to fulfill the biblical prophecies of Revelation, but my research of both the technology and the Scriptures has convinced me that the barcode likely *will not* be used for the mark of the Beast.

Now, let's move on to another aspect of this demonic, global system of deception and enslavement . . . tracking our movements via global positioning systems.

United States
GPS Satellite System

Russian GPS–type
GLONASS Satellite System

The U.S. has a 24–satellite GPS system (this is exclusive of the hundreds of other satellites in space serving other functions); Russia also will have 24 satellites when their system is complete. Work is currently in progress to merge the two systems. When fully linked, it will create a very tightly-knit, extremely precise international navigation system which can be used for virtually any application, not the least of which is tracking you. Presently, individual tracking is limited to those carrying a receiver for the proper triangulation for calculation of location. However, they have already been reduced to "hand–held" size, so reducing it further to biochip size is not an unreasonable engineering expectation.

CHAPTER FIVE

GLOBAL POSITIONING
SYSTEMS

This chapter just as well could be called "The Crowded Skies." That's because without all those satellites up there, a Global Positioning System (GPS) would not be possible. But they are, indeed, up there—in abundance. In fact, they seem to be proliferating like little rabbits.

A simplified definition of GPS could be: the ability to locate and track people or things on a global scale, to know the almost exact position of anything, utilizing a battery-powered GPS receiver or other similar telecommunications device.

How does it operate and why is it needed? The answer to the first part of that question is very technical, and the second part is very obvious. Simply stated, signals are sent from a series of satellites from space to earth. Receivers on earth triangulate the signals and calculate latitude/longitude position. The information may then be fed into a computer controlled by the entity or organization doing the "locating."

The possibilities for commercial use of this technology appear to be limitless ... which means the possibilities for abuse of this technology likewise appear limited only to the imagination of the powers who control it. With Big Brother gaining more control and power every day, what do *you* think will be the eventual use of this kind of technology?

Winn Schwartau, in his book *Information Wars*, states:

The question "Where are you?" will be answered at the push of a button. Global positioning satellites will know, to within a few feet, your exact location. Lives will be saved as personal digital assistants broadcast the location of lost or injured or kidnapped people. But what about employees? Will their every step be tracked to enhance security or to evaluate their performances for promotions? To the dismay of the unions who say the practice is an invasion of privacy, we already track the routes and times of trucks to increase shipping efficiency. Computers already know almost everything about us; will we also decide to add our every location to this list?

The May 8, 1994, edition of *The Bulletin,* Bend, Oregon, carried an article by writer Ralph Vartabedian, entitled "Defense Satellite Technology Ready for Commercial Boom." According to Vartabedian, "The Pentagon is awash in obsolete nuclear bombs, mothballed battleships, and surplus military bases [Author's note: Although FEMA apparently has plans to make use of these deserted bases], but out of the scrap heaps left by the Cold War has come a technology with a promising payoff." Below are some excerpts.

When the Defense Department laid plans in the 1970s for its Global Position System, a network of 24 satellites that broadcasts navigation signals to users on Earth, it was intended to help soldiers fight anywhere, from jungles to deserts.

Along the way, though, commercial interests saw a potentially lucrative concept that could revolutionize industries such as land surveying, trucking, environmental protection, and farming.

The technology [is] now poised to leap into virtually every facet of the American economy. . . .

With a special receiver that taps the satellite signals, civilian users can determine their position by latitude and longitude within 100 meters (328 feet) anywhere in the world. Once as big as a file cabinet, the receivers are now the size of a paperback book and still shrinking. . . .

Some visionaries anticipate the day when virtually everything that moves in U.S. society—every shipping container, aircraft, car,

truck, train, bus, farm tractor, and bulldozer—will contain a micro-
chip that will track and, in many cases report its location. [Note:
This is no longer just the dream of some visionaries—it's actually
occurring now, and he forgot to mention they'll be tracking your
garbage, as well.] Massive computer systems, they say, will tie together the movement of assets in the economy, providing a sophisticated information system for the status and location of goods.

"Communications satellites were the first great success in
space, but GPS is going to dwarf that," said . . . a former Hughes
Aircraft chairman. . . . "GPS is going to pervade everything we do."

. . . Eventually the price will drop below $50. . . . At that point,
GPS would be inserted into a lot of other electronic gear . . . that
could instantly alert police [or others!] to an individual's location. . . .

Computerized maps are being used to track the spread of disease, pollution, and crime, based on data collected from GPS systems. Hamburger chains pore over these kinds of computer–generated maps to determine the best sites for new franchises.

Interstate truckers use the system to keep tabs of their road
taxes. . . . Cities use the satellite system to dispatch emergency vehicles and track the location of passenger buses. Railroads are finally able to figure out where their trains are.

Orbiting 11,000 miles above Earth, the 24 satellites are the
heart of the system. . . .

It's true, surveying and mapping are fast becoming a major function
of the GPS because of its incredible accuracy. An article appearing
in ENR entitled "Surveying's Brave New Digital World," included the
following preface:

Surveying and mapping tools have progressed significantly from
the days of meticulously entering transit readings in survey note-
books. From the latest in survey marker technology to the latest in
computer–enhanced technologies, surveyors and engineers can do
their jobs faster, better, and with more precision than ever before.

Recent hardware advances, declining prices of hardware and

software, and the greater availability of pre–packaged data are making geographic information system (GIS) technology an affordable and appealing technology for even the smallest firms. In some instances, state legislatures are funding new initiatives or enacting legislation requiring GIS use throughout the state, and Public Utility Commissions are mandating that utilities use GIS to ensure efficient and low–cost public services. Consultants hoping to contract services to these organizations will have to move into the "all digital" world or risk obsolescence. Many private sector clients—such as large engineering firms or developers—are also requesting surveying firms use computer–aided design (CAD) or GIS on projects and deliver digital products.

In this year's special section on surveying and mapping, we'll look at what's new today and what lies just ahead in products and services—including some exciting trends for users of GIS technology, *global positioning systems (GPS)*, and satellite imagery/aerial photography.

The application of GPS technology can run from the mundane to the "Indiana Jones" adventure project. For example, one company was contracted to map a Caribbean island about ten thousand feet off the coast of St. Thomas. Since it was used for jungle warfare training during and following World War II, there was a real possibility of unexploded ordinance remaining behind. "Lowe [the engineering firm] used the latest in both hazardous materials handling methods and surveying—including GPS, aerial photography, and GIS technology—to produce preliminary digital (CAD) maps in just 30 days." Gone are the "good old days" when two guys stood behind tripods and waved at each other . . . for the most part.

One of the major uses of all those satellites is telecommunications, in a myriad of forms. In *Infomart* magazine, AT&T's Roy Weber, director of new business concepts, asks the question, "What's This World Coming To?" I'd be happy to tell him, but since he's the director for new business concepts, I'm sure he's one of those visionaries who is limited only by his imagination when it comes to what we can do with our technology in the future.

He has promoted a six-theme program which he calls "Plan 2000." These six steps run the gamut from visual communications and telephone automated voice recognition (in other words, it understands your words; you don't have to push a touch-tone button) to "connecting the world" with a multimedia broadband network and numbering *you!* Of course, that's my favorite. It is Weber's Theme Five: ". . . we do everything wrong. We number telephones. You don't want to speak to the telephone. You want to speak to a person . . . we're developing Global Personal Calling Services that will find you [anywhere]."

The editor actually felt obliged—I'm sure because of the content of the article—to insert a somewhat tongue-in-cheek preface between the title and the start of the article. It begins:

> **Editor's note:** In the harsh light of the hospital nursery, the nurses are filling in the blanks on a birth certificate: name, weight, phone number. Phone number? The mere thought of assigning a number to a human being calls forth torrents of ethical and philosophical questions—questions about the relationship between man and machine, about individuality, about privacy. . . .
>
> For Weber, these questions are not simply a matter of intellectual curiosity, they are part of the exercise of inventing the future at AT&T. . . .

And may I remind you that AT&T is right up there with the big banks, MasterCard, and Visa when it comes to development and promotion of smart cards.

Let's see what Schwartau has to say on the subject of satellite telecommunications.

> In under thirty years, satellite communications became an absolute necessity for international transactions. Today, the demand is such that hundreds of new satellite launches are being planned [Author's note: thus my opening comment about the crowded skies]. Motorola's Iridium Project, for example, will ring the planet with sixty-six satellites, permitting portable phone users to talk to

anyone, anywhere, at any time. A true multinational effort is under way, including Japanese money and manufacturing and Russian orbital launch capabilities. Two competing consortiums have also begun staging their own satellite–based competitive global communications efforts.

. . . Charles Reich also noticed that technology and society were at odds. "What we have is technology, organization, and administration out of control, running for their own sake. . . . And we have turned over to this system the control and direction of everything—the natural environment, our minds, our lives."

It's hard to say it much better than that! But as the title of Schwartau's book, *Information Warfare,* implies, he continues to issue warnings about the pitfalls involved.

Not all of the switch connections are made through and across wires of copper and fiber optics. Communications increasingly uses the airwaves, as we can see in the proliferation of cellular phones, Motorola's multibillion dollar Iridium Project, and microwave and satellite transmissions. The electromagnetic ether represents a new battlefield for the Information Warrior.

Cellular phone conversations, for example, are wide open to interception by $179 scanner devices that can be bought from Radio Shack, *Monitoring Times* magazine, or dozens of other sources. Courts have upheld that there is no reasonable expectation of privacy when one is talking on a cellular phone.

Then he proceeds to tell a number of different methods used in *telefraud,* and how much it costs the public. If you are convinced that your secrets (or any other information) are safe—even with encryption devices, because the government has the "back door key"—on the Internet, the information superhighway, satellite telecommunications, your smart card, the Social Security computers . . . you're really just kidding yourself, probably because it's too scary to consider the alternative. Before I conclude this chapter, I will mention just a few more situations involving the GPS.

Here's an interesting use that I have not as yet addressed. An article in *Automatic ID News* entitled "Voice and location tracking systems alert riders of stops" reports that the transit system in Scranton, Pennsylvania, is using a vehicle tracking and fleet management system based on GPS that announces each stop via recorded voice. The in–vehicle tracking unit on thirty–two of their buses provides information such as location, speed, direction, and status. Operators at the Fleetservice Control Center can view the entire fleet at any time. This "talking bus" system has over four hundred announcements, "not just stops, but announcing the beginning and the end of the line, a welcome aboard, one that reminds people there's no smoking, eating, or drinking on the bus. . . ." Theoretically, this is to free the bus drivers from the distraction of having to make any announcements. So the next time you ride a bus, pay attention! It might just tell you where (or when) to get off.

The last article I will share with you on the subject of GPS appeared in *GIS World, Inc.,* June 1994, titled "Satellite Imagery to Track Agricultural Fraud."

> European agriculture will be monitored via satellite imagery. . . . [This] is the largest U.K. satellite monitoring project ever undertaken, *every European Community member state will be monitored. . . .*
>
> The satellite survey involved observing randomly selected farms within undisclosed regions. . . . Digital multispectral images from SPOT and Landsat satellites will be used, as well as the European Space Agency ERS–1 satellite's Synthetic Aperture Radar instrument, which is capable of imaging through clouds and at night.
>
> For each farm, individual field boundaries will be digitized. . . . The resulting information will be compared with farmers' claims, and MAFF will be notified of any irregularities.
>
> "Satellite imagery is a highly cost effective and unobtrusive means to monitor large areas . . . and is a strong deterrent to would–be fraudsters" . . . which proved the success of satellite imagery to help identify ineligible claims of compensatory payments.

Not only is Big Brother watching you, he's watching from the big eye in the sky.

I'm glad that the Word of God says that God's eye is going to and fro across the earth. It's a comfort to know that He is still sovereign and in control of all things. With all that's going on around us in these last days, it's good to remind ourselves of that from time to time. We need to be prudent and be prepared, but we must never operate in fear, as that would give our enemy, Satan, an opening to gain a in foothold in our lives. The New World Order government may be getting all their technology in place to number and track us, but we can be assured that it's all fulfillment of God's prophecies, foretold by His scribes in the Bible. It would be no problem for God to eliminate those satellites if He wanted to, but I suspect even they are part of His plan for the fulfillment of certain biblical prophecies, e.g., the gospel being preached to all nations, and every eye seeing Christ when He returns. Technically speaking, until these latest developments in telecommunications, it wouldn't have been physically possible for *all* the inhabitants of a globe that's round to view His return to one location at the "real time" that it occurred. At best, they could have seen it by tape–delay broadcasting.

Remember, God is the one who creates—technology or anything else. Satan either tries to destroy the creation, steal it for his own purposes, or counterfeit it and *claim* he created it, so he would get the credit.

Now, let's move right along to discuss the cashless society.

CHAPTER SIX

THE CASHLESS SOCIETY

Your buck stops here! Having cash is freedom—and the worst nightmare of dictatorial regimes, since cash provides privacy and anonymity for one's transactions.

If you started at the very beginning of this book and read all the way to this point, you probably already have a pretty good idea of the significance of this subject and how it may work in the near future. However, keeping in mind that many people just check the Table of Contents and read the chapters that particularly interest them, I must be thorough with this subject because of its implications in Scripture, Revelation 13, and its importance in relation to our future lifestyles. So, if you are one of those who faithfully read each page, please forgive any redundancy you find here. There must of necessity be considerable overlap. Yet, I will still strive for brevity, as much of this information will be discussed again in the chapters on identity cards (chapter seven) and biochips (chapter eight).

The New World Order economists are not ignorant of the importance of cash and its ability to inhibit their total control of the world. They are aware that in order to completely control, track, and monitor the global population, *they first must eliminate the use of cash.* With cash, there is no way to know how people are using their finances, whether for or against the government and its agenda. Because control of one's finances typically equates with the control of one's entire life, the advocates of world government for decades have been promoting a move toward totally cashless transactions, via a myriad of banking plans, ATM machines, credit cards, debit cards, point-of-sale machines, and credit data—all funneled through massive computer systems. Eventually, the goal is that all these computers will be controlled by them . . . the *Illuminists* . . . Big Brother . . . the economic leaders of the New World Order system of government.

In the non–banking part of the system, this will be a gradual transformation which will begin in random, innocent activities. Our fascination with the convenience of it all will gradually desensitize us to its pervasiveness . . . until it is too late to reverse the process. I want to quote four paragraphs by Don McAlvany, from the August 1994 edition of his newsletter, *The McAlvany Intelligence Advisor.*

ELECTRONIC FASCISM: TOWARD A CASHLESS SOCIETY

In the high–tech era now emerging, government checks (i.e., Social Security benefits, government pensions, welfare checks, etc.), physical food stamps, and other government benefits are all to be delivered electronically as the Clintonistas implement Electronic Benefit Transfer. Under the system, each recipient's benefits will be credited to an account which can be accessed with special debit cards and eventually via the all–purpose smart (National ID) card.

Food stamp recipients will be able to use the cards to pay for groceries at supermarket check–out terminals, just as many consumers now use credit and debit cards to pay for purchases. Those receiving Social Security, welfare, military pensions, and other public benefits will use the cards to receive cash at automatic teller machines.

The EBT system is already in use in several cities throughout the country and in the entire state of Maryland, and is now being installed in many southern states (i.e., Florida, Alabama, Georgia, North Carolina, South Carolina, Tennessee, Kentucky, Arkansas, and Missouri). The Clintonistas predict that soon $111 billion a year in benefits will be delivered electronically, and plan to spend $83 million over the next three years to implement EBT. Health and Human Services secretary Donna Shalala [Author's note: Shalala is a member of both the CFR and the TLC.] brags that "with EBT, we'll have an electronic audit trail for every transaction, making fraud [Editor's note: or "political incorrectness"] much easier to detect and prosecute."

Similar debit/smart card/cashless systems are being installed throughout Europe and Asia where debit or smart cards are replacing cash (on a mandatory basis) for a host of transactions. *One of the essential elements of the New World Order is a cashless society, where all transactions are forced through the computerized banking and credit card system—eventually via the all-purpose National ID/smart card. One hundred percent monitoring and control of all personal activity is the goal and could become a fait accompli* over the next five to ten years. And if you are "politically incorrect," Big Brother can pull your plug, and you will starve or be frozen out of the system.

In order to justify their meddling and monitoring of our activities, the transactions first must be deemed to be somehow illegal in nature. That lets them be perceived as the "good guys" trying to catch the "bad guys," and in that case, how could we possibly object to whatever means they consider necessary. Unfortunately, in their efforts to track the bad guys, they must have the authority to monitor all of us; therefore, former legal activities have been declared illegal so that banks, businesses, *et al,* can be forced to report your activities. They've even made a law to make it illegal to carefully follow the rules that they have established. They are asking bankers and businesses to judge of your **intent**—it's illegal to follow the "letter of the law" if your intent is wrong. Talk about Big Brother meddling in your life! The penalties for failure to comply consist of large fines and long jail terms, frequently higher than drug dealers. Sound confusing? Below I am reprinting a portion of *The McAlvany Intelligence Advisor* (July 1991), because he has done such an excellent job of taking the confusion out of some of these new laws and their ultimate purpose, which undoubtedly is total control of global economics.

... Linking "smart cards" and the worldwide telecommunications network will open the door to universal electronic transactions in all walks of life. *The era of paper money and coinage is rapidly drawing to a close and the new age of a cashless society is dawning.*

The path to 100% electronic money, and total government financial control of citizens, as Harvey Wachsman explained in the *New York Times* article, is Americard—a "smart card" that does it all. Cash is freedom! A man without money is free to do very little. *If modern electronic credit and debit cards can be substituted for cash, then every financial transaction of your life can be catalogued and stored for future reference and those with the power to cut off your access to electronic money can strangle you in a heartbeat. The potential for totalitarian blackmail and control is incredible,—but most Americans don't even seem to notice.*

1. **CASH REPORT REQUIREMENTS**—Starting about 1987, the U.S. Treasury began enforcing the cash reporting requirements of Title 31 of the Bank Secrecy Act of 1986. These requirements, though not clearly or widely communicated to businesses or the public for over a year or so after the passage of the 1986 Act, called for banks, securities brokerage houses, coin dealers, car dealers, jewelers, and any other financial institution or business to report to the IRS (on Form 8300 for retail businesses and on Form CTR for a financial institution) any customer spending, depositing, or withdrawing cash over $10,000.

Since 1987, by regulatory edict, the IRS has greatly expanded the definition and scope of the cash reporting requirements and the kinds of transactions covered. *Often financial institutions or businesses do not find out the extent of these anti–cash regulations until after they have been victimized by an IRS "sting." Severe jail sentences and fines of up to $50,000 are then meted out to the unwitting businessman, banker, coin dealer, or one of their employees. In this pattern, the government destroys one or two victims from a targeted group or industry, to paralyze the rest of the group with fear.*

Former congressman Ron Paul wrote recently in his newsletter, that with no new authority from Congress, the IRS made the following regulatory changes (recorded *quietly* in the *Federal Register,* May 15, 1991, under "Notice of Proposed Rule Making"):

"Currency Transaction Reports (CTRs) have traditionally been required only for cash, but the new regulations make the CTR rules applicable to *all* monetary instruments, including money orders, cashier's checks, bank drafts, and travelers checks. *By the* *simple method of redefining these instruments as cash, the government now requires that everyone who spends some combination of cash and non–cash monetary instruments in excess of $10,000 in one day (or over a period of twelve months) is required to fill out an 8300 form at retail outlets and a CTR at all financial institutions."*

Cashier's checks, money orders, and the rest are *not* considered monetary instruments if their dollar denominations are in excess of $10,000, however. [Author's note: That's probably because the instrument was already reported to the IRS at the time you purchased it, if it exceeded the $10,000 limit.] What the IRS is trying to prevent is mixed transactions, like half cash and half money order, which are now considered an attempt to evade the law (called "structuring).

a. STRUCTURING—*In 1987, the "crime" of "structuring" was invented, which ruled that suggested or thinking about ordering your transactions to avoid the reporting requirements was also a crime.* This was an historic first for American jurisprudence, to make an attempt to comply with the law, a crime. *If an investor or business "structures" a transaction with multiple payments (i.e., cash, personal check, cashier's or certified funds, or money orders) so that the sum is over $10,000, he is guilty of the money laundering crime of "structuring."*

As former congressman Ron Paul has pointed out: **"The government loves vague laws. They are essential to tyranny and executive discretion."** Examples of such vague laws are the Hooliganism laws in the Soviet Union and the RICO laws in the U.S. If the U.S. government can't find another criminal charge, it can charge you with "racketeering" or "conspiracy." The Bank Secrecy Act prohibits "structuring," which it defines as an attempt to evade the financial reporting requirements. But this law makes obeying the law against the law, a la Orwell's "doublethink."

Big Brother can now fine, convict, or jail *anyone* in the future, for "structuring" violations if he has deposited or withdrawn various amounts of cash (or other monetary instruments) *under* the reporting requirements from his bank *over a twelve–month period. If an investor buys coins, antiques, art goods, or whatever sev-*

eral times in any twelve-month period, paying in amounts of under $10,000 (but adding up to over $10,000 in toto), he can be accused and found guilty of "structuring." The banker, investment broker, or business selling that person the items will also be guilty of "structuring" if he/she/it doesn't report the customer on a CTR, or Form 8300, or if he or she gives the customer any advice or counsel whatsoever as to how to "structure" their transaction(s) to avoid the reporting requirements.

Ron Paul wrote recently the IRS gives a number of examples of structuring: (1) "Under the first, the individual must fill out an 8300: 'D, an individual, purchases gold coins from M, a coin dealer for $13,200. D tenders to M in payment U.S. currency in the amount of $6,200 and a cashier's check in the face amount of $7,000 which D had purchased. Because the sale is a designated reporting transaction, the cashier's check is treated as cash for purposes of section 6050I and this section. Therefore, because M has received more than $10,000 in cash with respect to the transaction, M must make the report required by section 6050I and this section.'

(2) "Under this one, he is not: 'G, an individual, purchases a boat from T, a boat dealer, for $16,500. G pays T with a cashier's check payable to T in the amount of $16,500. The cashier's check is not treated as cash because the face amount of the check is more than $10,000. Thus, no report is required to be made.'

"There are three exceptions. First the customer doesn't have to fill out a form if he can prove the money comes from a bank loan. Or if the money is received in payment on a promissory note or installment sales contract. Or if the money is part of a payment plan that requires one or more down payment.

"This is a highly significant step because it begins to bring non-cash bank instruments under reporting requirements. The next IRS goal is to make personal bank checks qualify as cash under the reporting rules.

"Another major change has to do with the CTRs and 8300s are treated in tax audit. Beginning in a few months, IRS agents will have a complete file of all CTRs and 8300s filled out by the person being audited, and they will be scrutinized heavily."

[Editor's note: One gets the feeling that a businessman, banker, securities, or coin broker will have to be a Ph.D. accountant or Philadelphia lawyer to accurately assess when the form 8300 or CTR must be filed. (Author's note: It's more like they have to be mind readers and fortune tellers, otherwise how are they supposed to know at the time you make your first transaction how many transactions you may make over the next twelve–month period—and that's the time frame the IRS has established for cumulative transactions.) *The IRS has been extremely vague on these rapidly expanding reporting requirements over the past four years, but is still prosecuting and jailing businessmen, bank employees, financial brokers who through confusion or misunderstanding of the regulations have not fully complied.* The reporting requirements and the record keeping they generate are also very expensive for the businessman, banker, or financial broker to maintain.]

b. THE WAR AGAINST COIN DEALERS—The IRS has been indicting coin dealers across the country who either don't understand its confusing cash reporting requirements or who have been entrapped into violating them by very clever "stings." Precious metals are one of the last loopholes of private, trackless investments in America, and the IRS and government bureaucrats would like to wipe out the industry. As the May '91 newsletter for members of the Industry Council for Tangible Assets pointed out: "That we (the precious metals/rare coin/tangibles industry) are a *targeted industry* is not just an IRS policy statement. It's a fact!"

As the *ICTA Washington Wire* described: "Several coin dealers have already been indicted for violations of these regulations. Others are awaiting sentencing or are already imprisoned. The penalties for non–compliance are very severe, ranging from staggering fines and jail time on up to actual forfeiture of your business. *IGNORANCE OF THESE REGULATIONS CAN COST YOU EVERYTHING YOU'VE WORKED FOR!*"

ICTA counsel Victoria Toensing made four points: (1) Cash is a "four letter word"; (2) Illegal cash is *not* just drug money; (3) The penalty for not filing required reports is serious; (4) The penalty for not reporting illegal cash is a mind–blower.

An IRS agent who addressed ICTA's recent dealer convention in Tampa, Florida, said: *"The IRS restrictions were aimed at creating a paper trail."* Another IRS agent said: "The goal of tightening the noose of illegal cash transactions is to make the profits from these illegal enterprises worthless. . . . If one knowingly takes *'cash generated illegally,' the first offense* is punishable by 4.5 to 5.5 years in prison. In conjunction, the new laws regarding forfeiture of assets *are more sweeping than the drug possession forfeiture laws."*

Coin dealers were also encouraged by the two IRS agents to report to them "any suspicious transactions or behavior"—just as bank employees are encouraged to spy on and report depositors who act suspiciously. Doesn't this remind you more of communist Russia or China than the America we have known and loved?

[Editor's note: Think about the above statements. *Not reporting cash transactions is now considered by our government to be a more severe crime, and is more severely punished than drug dealing.* Note the term "cash generated illegally"—that's any cash not "fully taxed." In one IRS sting against a coin dealer, the agent "claimed" to have mentioned "untaxed money"—thereby making the transaction "illegal" because it involved "cash generated illegally."

MIA reader, do you see how serious the government is about pursuing unreported cash, about wiping out ultimately all cash transactions? Cash is truly a four–letter word!]

2. MONEY LAUNDERING ENFORCEMENT—Joseph Battaglia wrote about the evolution of the money laundering juggernaut in the March '91 issue of *The American Advisor.*

"As with so many things the government does, the process of attacking the free economy has been a gradual one. It began with the introduction of so–called anti–money–laundering rule. These rules required banks and businesses to report to the IRS the name, address, and social security number of individuals who engage in cash transactions of $10,000 or more. This rule was established under the guise of attacking drug dealers.

"With the tremendous publicity given to the drug problem and so–called 'money laundering,' the government was able to obtain this repressive, anti–freedom, money–laundering law.

"Subsequently, the government said that drug dealers were evading this money–laundering law and they needed a new tool. *Therefore, they added a provision to make it a crime for individuals to spend more than $10,000 in total cash transactions throughout a year without reporting it.* In today's inflated economy, $10,000 over the course of an entire year is not very much!

"The burden of enforcing this law was placed on private citizens. With this law the government turned businessmen and bankers into policemen. Banking personnel are instructed to report cash transactions of less than $10,000 if they think a customer looks suspicious. *If a bank teller or businessman has reason to be suspicious and does not turn in the individual using cash, he could be guilty of a crime. This is the height of the 'Big Brother' mentality made famous in George Orwell's 1984 and in Hitler's Germany.* [Author's note: The Bible tells of a time in the future when even the children will turn in their parents.]

"To effect compliance with these laws, the government began prosecuting business people across the country. Prosecutions began with the Florida and California drug money–laundering schemes. *In time, they prosecuted real estate brokers, car dealers, coin dealers, and a host of other business people who inadvertently or otherwise accepted cash from an ostensibly legitimate customer. Since this whole affair has been positioned as a part of the war on drugs, the American public has not objected to these repressive measures.* In fact, they have accepted them piecemeal, with hardly a second thought.

"*Now the real significance of these money–laundering rules is about to be felt. All individuals who hold large amounts of cash, but are not drug dealers, will soon find it's impossible to exchange their old currency for the soon–to–be–released new currency.*"

On August 24, 1990, a Money Laundering Enforcement Conference was held in Washington, D.C., sponsored by the American Bankers Assn., the American Bar Assn., and attended by top officials of all federal law enforcement agencies. Together, they comprise the financial enforcement arm of the New World Order. It was agreed that "a new domestic dollar was needed to *hamper private use of cash"* and "a new international dollar to make it more difficult to transfer cash in and out of the country."

The Financial Criminal Enforcement Network (FINCEN) said that *"we currently have nearly all financial information available on every U.S. citizen." In the future, tax violations will be treated as money laundering violations.* (Reread that last sentence!) This and other measures discussed at the meeting will wipe out virtually all vestiges of financial freedom and privacy for the American people.

As Ron Paul recently wrote:

"The IRS has virtually taken over enforcement of money laundering laws. (The 5/8/91 *Federal Register* stated that the Treasury Department was turning over its entire anti–money laundering operation to the IRS—which will have full control of investigations, seizures, and forfeitures of ML cases.) *Virtually all tax cases will be redefined as money laundering (ML) cases thanks to the vague definitions of ML the government uses."*

"About ten years ago, someone at the Treasury had the bright idea that *ML laws provide a better means for enforcement of tax laws than tax laws themselves.* Why? First, Congress is much more willing to pass new ML legislation than tax enforcement legislation, which always leads to complaints from constituents. So far, *no* significant ML bill has been killed in Congress, although a few have been modified to please the banking industry.

"Second, the enforcement of tax laws has a long and detailed court history behind it, and increasingly taxpayers are using that history to their own benefit, witness the number of successful suits against the IRS recently. When convicting on tax laws, the IRS risks getting itself tangled in complex legal webs. ML cases have much lower risks (for the feds).

"*Third, the penalties—both financial and jail—are twice to ten times higher under ML than under the old tax laws.*

"In part, ML is the crime of using the banking system to wash undeclared income, and almost everyone convicted for tax law violations uses banks to some extent. *If a man is paid in cash, for some service, deposits the cash, and doesn't report it, he is a money launderer.*

"Another way to become a money launderer is to "attempt" to "structure" transactions to keep from filling out government forms. No one knows how widely the government plans to interpret the word "attempt." There will be court cases and fights over this during the coming years, but the IRS has *carte blanch* in the meantime.

"*Money laundering will be the term used more and more to identify simple tax violations. I predict that in the years ahead, we will witness an explosion of convictions on ML grounds.* And with the administration's FINCEN apparatus—a detailed financial database utilizing artificial intelligence—the fed will try to turn America into a Ceaucescu's Romania for finance, with the locus of control in the IRS Securitate.

"On 6/11/91 the House passed a severe new piece of money laundering legislation (HR 26) that will expand the powers of the government over everyone's private bank account. The bill:

"1. Enacts severe penalties, like revoking charters and removing deposit insurance, for banks that the feds deem to be participating in money laundering. *This will greatly expand the banks' incentive to act like police instead of financial institutions.*

"2. Gives state financial officials access to the federal government's enormous collection of currency transaction reports.

"3. Grants the Treasury the ability to use state–level financial data on individuals, formerly a violation of the Right to Financial Privacy Act.

"4. Calls on states to license and regulate non–bank financial institutions engaged in check–cashing and money transmittal. [Author's note: That would be like Western Union franchises and others.] They have previously been unregulated, so this eliminates a significant island of privacy.

"5. Makes the operators of money–transmittal businesses subject to five years in prison for participation in money laundering.

"6. Raises the maximum fine (to $50,000) that the Treasury can impose on financial institutions that display a 'pattern of negligence' in policing money laundering.

"7. Requires that banks report the names of customers required to file CTRs on their own behalf, like auto and boat dealers and jewelry stores.

"8. *Prohibits* banks from telling customers when they've had a 'suspicious transaction report' filed on them at the IRS.

"9. Makes the penalty for 'conspiracy' to commit money laundering the same as for actual money laundering. This gives the government a huge advantage in criminal prosecutions.

"10. Gives 'whistleblower' protection to any employee of a bank or other institution with cash dealings who turns in other employees.

"The Senate nearly passed a similar bill last year, so this one's on the fast track. We have seen a dramatic shift toward prosecution of money laundering since the definition is so broad, the powers of the government so strong during investigations, and the penalties so high.

"Broadly defined, money laundering is the crime of using cash—even your own honestly earned and taxed cash—in ways that the government bureaucrats might disapprove of, without telling them first. In a free society, this ought to be no crime."

In addition, the bill would require the administration to expand negotiations with foreign nations on reporting suspected laundering transactions and give it authority to impose sanctions against countries that do not cooperate. The bill's primary author, Rep. Frank Annunzio (D–IL), said in the *New York Times,* 6/12/91, that giving regulators authority to revoke the charter of a federal bank or lift the FDIC insurance of a state bank amounted to a "well–deserved death sentence for the bank—a way to execute a bank." He added: "Those who launder drug money are accomplices to every drug–related murder in the country." [Editor's note: But what if all of us are ultimately labeled as money launderers?]

C. NEW INTERNATIONAL MONEY LAUNDERING INITIATIVES

The administration is making great headway in pushing money laundering enforcement on a global basis. First, there was the United Nation money laundering treaty, which attempts to outlaw bank secrecy. (The U.N. treaty, to which America is a signatory, criminalizes international money laundering, allows seizure of assets, attempts to destroy all bank secrecy laws, and weakens protections involved in the production of evidence, the taking of testimony, and the extradition of offenders.) Then the twelve–nation tax treaty of the Organization for Economic Cooperation and Development was ratified to insure cooperation in harassing taxpayers.

Most recently we have a report from the Research Institute for the Study of Conflict and Terrorism (which works closely with the CIA) which argues that global money laundering is not just the $500 billion it is normally estimated to be, but two to three times that large. The report blames the lack of CTR regulations in most countries besides the U.S., and says that **Swiss, Austrian, Hong Kong, and Caribbean bank secrecy must be destroyed immediately.**

THE NEW WORLD ECONOMIC ORDER

The New World *Economic* Order is one of three aspects of the coming New World Order system of government. The other two are the political order and the religious order (called the New Age movement). All three parts are working together energetically to bring forth the all–enslaving New World Order global government; however, such a system cannot be activated until there is a way to obtain total control over everyone, and that cannot be accomplished without first eliminating the use of cash worldwide. Their goal is to implement a cashless system as quickly as possible.

How will they do it? The laws are in place and the pressure has begun. Don't look for it to let up—from here on, things will heat up more and more and the pressure can't do anything but increase. Let's consider more cogs in the gears leading us to a cashless society.

I believe the primary method probably will be a downhill slide via the convenience factor, i.e., it's safer and easier not to have to deal with cash, then it's easier not to have to bother with the time or expense of writing checks, then it's so simple just to slide our little smart card through the slot to make our purchases, pay our utility bill, or our doctor, or the repairman. But what about having it lost or stolen? Well, since it will be tied to your physical person biometrically (via fingerprints, handprints, facial prints, voice prints, retina scans, or some combination of these), no one can use it but you (allegedly). But we can do better than that . . . just a tiny little RFID transponder (presently no bigger than a grain of rice, and maybe smaller in the future) implanted under the skin is perfect—it can't be lost or stolen, and it can't do all that the smart card can do. Now you have arrived . . . welcome to Revelation 13!

Let me remind you before I go any further that the references to the mark of the Beast in the passage in Revelation have more than just a commercial application. It's true that you will not be able to buy or sell without it, but it is inextricably connected to a spiritual application, as well. No one is going to force you to take this mark—it will be your choice to accept or refuse, because those who accept the mark will also have to *worship* the Beast. Of course, there are severe consequences for refusing, once the Antichrist comes to power. Your refusal will cost you your head, according to another passage in Revelation.

Now, for you diehards who believe it will take more than "convenience" to talk some people out of their cash . . . I agree with you, and there are financial plans already in the works to force the situation. (It is my opinion, though I'd like to believe I'm wrong, that the New World Order economists intend to activate these plans sometime in the near future.)

AN INTERNATIONAL EMERGENCY IS NEEDED

Those in control of the U.S. government, the globalists, the international bankers, the New World Order crowd, and the New World global religious believers (New Agers) all hate cash because it represents privacy, freedom, decentralization, and independence—all the things they are trying to abolish. I am firmly convinced that they are presently advancing their plan to create a series a global economic *emergencies* that will enable them to convince you that cash must be discarded immediately in favor of electronic money. They will insist that such a drastic course of action is necessary in order to eliminate crime and restore order to a world that appears to have crashed—accidentally, of course—into a state of international financial chaos!

THE COMING STOCK MARKET CRASH

Conservative analysts have been predicting a devastating crash for the stock market for quite some time, while at the same time holding their breath and hoping it won't happen. But history and experience, coupled with the facts available, convince them that our economy is artificially propped up, and it's only a matter of time before the establishment can no longer keep it propped up. I agree, but I believe there is something even more sinister going on.

I believe we are headed for a *planned* global stock market crash —and in the near future—unlike anything the world has ever suffered! Such a crash would permit the Illuminists and their cohorts to close thousands of banks in a matter of days, seize most personal assets, confiscate gold and silver, and *eliminate cash*, all under federally sanctioned "declared emergencies," activated by presidential executive order (laws [presidential executive orders formerly placed into law] are already on the books permitting the implementation of such controls, via FEMA and other departments. See the discussions on FEMA in earlier chapters.) After the crash, the worldwide financial system will be restructured into one that provides much more efficient methods of total enslavement—more so than any previous economic system in the history of the world. This will set the stage for the official establishment of the New World Economic Order.

It is expected that the *planned crash* will begin in Japan, then work its way around the globe, toppling the economies of nations like a string of dominoes, virtually simultaneously—*all completely by accident, of course*. Not true! This *accident* is being orchestrated carefully from behind the scenes by the power–hungry globalists.

If this sounds as though I'm on the radical fringe, I challenge you to check the facts for yourself. I'll give you some numbers and locations to help you get started. Go to any major library and ask the librarian to help you locate presidential executive order No. 11490, as listed in the *Federal Register,* Vol. 34, No. 209. This order was signed into law by former president Richard Nixon on October 30, 1969.

In particular, review the third page of this voluminous document (page 17569). Part 3, Department of the Treasury, specifies that in *any* national emergency that might *conceivably* confront the nation, the president is authorized to seize control over and regulate *arbitrarily* virtually all facets of the monetary system. In addition, the same executive order (page 17593) allows him to seize control over and regulate virtually all aspects of the stock market, as well. Are you beginning to get the picture?

Do you think it's possible that all this could be mere coincidence, or do you think, perhaps, there might be an evil master plan behind it? If you concluded the latter, then you have concluded correctly! These soon-coming cataclysmic events have all been strategically planned for the purpose of creating chaos and crisis. And don't rule out the natural disasters occurring around the globe, as we begin to witness more of what was predicted in the Bible for the end of the age, i.e., the unprecedented number of earthquakes and their increased magnitude; the awakening of volcanoes along the Pacific Rim known as the Ring of Fire, as well as in Europe and Asia—volcanoes which for centuries have been considered permanently dormant; the staggering number of devastating killer hurricanes; the floods and the droughts—either too much water to grow food, or not enough. Need I go on? All of these natural disasters take their toll on the global economy, every bit as much as the man-made, manipulated crises and the national and ethnic wars going on somewhere in the world at all times.

ANY CHAOS WILL DO

Once these "problems" have been created, or a sufficiently large natural disaster or war has occurred, a number of prearranged solutions will be brought forth immediately. Such dictatorial "solutions" await only the golden moment of opportunity that will enable their implementation. This will be accomplished under a declared state of emergency during a time of horrible international chaos (of whatever nature) that will permit the New World Order Illuminists to do virtually anything they want, including eliminating all cash globally! But be alert! Watch out for the man who is able to bring order out of all this chaos and crisis. He is described in the prophetic books in the Old Testament, and in the book of Revelation he is called the Antichrist. It says because he is able to restore peace—albeit temporarily—to the world, they will make him the unchallenged leader over all the earth. From this cashless economic system will evolve the New Political Order and the New Spiritual Order—the New Age occult religion of satanism.

How Others Propose to Eliminate Cash

In Don McAlvany's enlightening article printed previously in this chapter, he told us about Harvey Wachsman, *an attorney who advocates the total elimination of cash.* Let's examine some more of Wachman's article, as it "says it all" regarding what's coming in the not-too-distant future. The strange and amazing thing is that—knowing all this—he still advocates it!

First the government would change the color of the currency and require old money to be exchanged at the treasury. Then all the NEW currency would be returned by its owners to the bank of their choice. At that time all banks would be required to open accounts to all depositors free of charge. In place of this paper money, we would receive new plastic cards—called Americards—each *biometrically impregnated with the owner's hand and eye retina prints* to insure virtually **foolproof** identification.

The government would supply all homes and businesses free of charge with scanner machines to read the new Americards, certify the holder's identity, and make instantaneous electronic debits and credits to their accounts. Think of the benefits to the average American. No more check writing would be necessary [Author's note: We're nearly there right now, only they're tapping our accounts automatically for whatever amount is due, based on a one-time authorizations.] because bills would be paid electronically directly from their homes. In addition, individuals and businesses would no longer be able to conceal income. This would be great for the government. **All transactions would be recorded in a computerized bank file that would be easy for the IRS to check.**

Yes, but how "great" would it be for the law-abiding taxpayer? In chapter seven, I deal with the national identity crisis and the uprising demanding a national ID card. But since such a card is the preliminary basis for a cashless society, I will quote some recent articles concerning such a card. Even though the writers are in favor, it is interesting to note that even they recognize the potential for abuse and the probability of the loss of personal privacy.

Lawmakers Clash Over New Call for National ID Cards

... creation of a single, tamper-proof ID card ... any such card would lead to an invasion of privacy ... one can easily manufacture such cards ... there is simply no way to enforce our existing laws without it ... a social security card with a photo, fingerprint, or verifiable bar code ... **a new ID card could lead to a national data bank with information about every American that would pose a threat to individual privacy.**

—*Los Angeles Times,* June 17, 1993

Another article in the *Los Angeles Times,* April 20, 1993, "LA, the Cash Capital," stated the following about the merits of a cashless society: ". . . The idea is to eventually turn greenbacks into electronic blips. . . ." In other words, let's eliminate cash and go into an electronic debit system.

The *San Diego Union-Tribune* (May 16, 1993) ran an article entitled "Automated Teller Machines." The virtues of the cashless society were extolled as follows:

... Americans have heard about the cashless society for the past 20 years, but now the combination of technology and consumer demands for a highly convenient payment system have made the cashless society acceptable and visible on the horizon. . . . Americans in the 1990s presumably are primed and ready for the next financial wonder: the cashless debit card and ATM machines. . . . ATM debit cards subtract the amount of a purchase directly from a bank account. . . . This will enable ATM cards to be used at vending machines, telephones, and parking meters. Such cards would be equipped with tiny computer chips. . . .

Without coming right out and saying so, what they are describing is a smart card, because the other types of credit cards and ATM cards don't have computer chips. And we have been trained (conditioned) to use our ATM cards in this fashion for over ten years. Supermarkets and self-service gas stations for years have had point-of-sale debit machines where you just slide your card through and the purchase is automatically deducted from your checking account. Of course, you may just as easily charge your purchases by sliding your credit card through instead of your debit card.

How convenient(!) it will be when there is only one card to slide through and push a button on a machine to tell it whether to charge your purchase or to deduct it from your checking account. But what if I lose my one and only card? Well . . . you can see where I'm going with this—I've taken you down this road before.

Cashless Society Leads to 666 Biochip Implant

The combined push for a cashless society and a national ID card (a biometrically encoded smart card) will make it very easy for the coming New World Order Big Brother government to enslave us. Of course, the final step in this progression will be implanting your new ID/debit card (in the form of a biochip) just under the skin—it will contain all your data, both personal and financial. See chapter eight for the complete story on biochip technology.

No Cash Equals No Freedom

Earlier in this chapter I pointed out that having a cashless society equates with the total loss of freedom. I want to elaborate on that a bit. A person without cash is free to do very little.

If modern ID cards, credit, debit, smart cards, and ultimately biochip implants can be substituted for cash, then *every financial transaction in your life could be easily stored, catalogued, analyzed, and accessed for future reference* by the New World Order bureaucrats. And if you think they have no interest in the mundane details of your life, think again! They would have at their fingertips the unparalleled, instantaneous power to cut off your electronic buying and selling "privileges" at will. It is a small matter to block access to your funds. It is a simple entry to reprogram a computer to disallow any further transactions to your account. Thereafter, all future purchases would be declined. Such a fate will confront anyone who has somehow failed to "cooperate" with the coming New World Order's 666 system.

It is obvious that such arbitrary power in the hands of big government could easily strangle you in a heartbeat. The potential for comprehensive totalitarian blackmail and control would be incredible! And even though many Americans are beginning to see the "handwriting on the wall" and doing their best to slow the progress of this inevitable system, the majority are still slumbering blissfully where these matters are concerned. As obvious as it is, even when they hear, they refuse to believe. That's too bad.

ACCEPTANCE OF THE NEW 666 SYSTEM

Advocates of world government believe that the only efficient way to handle the complexity of a totally cashless society is to *let the government handle it!* (You expected something else?) However, they assure us that the development of such a system is just around the corner—a system capable of handling electronically the country's $300 billion annual currently–cash transactions. They want everyone to anxiously embrace their wonderful new system, so they must convince you of its flawless ability to handle all your needs, while at the same time being safe from tampering by hackers.

For the majority of people who have been using electronic banking for years—in the form of direct payroll deposits, direct deposit of Social Security checks, use of the ATM (with its myriad of menu selections) to transfer your funds around, withdraw cash, etc., use of credit and debit cards (point–of–purchase machines), use of touch–tone phones to access your account and move funds around, electronic automatic payment of your mortgage payment or utility bills—learning to use the new system will be a snap. You see, the New World Order planners are not stupid. You have been conditioned slowly for years to enjoy all these efficient, streamlined, and convenient forms of enticing electronic enslavement. And the infrastructure now is so firmly and smoothly in place that even those few who may be unfamiliar with electronic banking accounts will find them surprisingly easy to use.

Polls taken around the country overwhelmingly conclude that people approve and appreciate this convenient use of new technology, although many of them were not given a choice. The government instigated EBT payments of welfare benefits and food stamps. It is the only way you can receive benefits—these recipients were almost exclusively cash users who indicated that they preferred the new debit card system. A vast number of Social Security checks are electronically deposited, and the government would like to see it become *all* of them.

Remember, earlier in this chapter, I told you that the pressure was only going to get worse. The April 11, 1995, edition of the *New York Post* carried this article: "Companies Are Hankering for Direct Deposit." Here are some excerpts:

> Corporate America is fuming that Washington is increasingly forcing direct deposit on government workers, while companies can't because of state laws.
>
> The Social Security Administration tomorrow is expected to announce its plans to *require* that all retirees who have a bank account accept getting paid by direct deposit rather than by check.
>
> This year, all 4.3 million federal government employees were strongly encouraged to take their weekly . . . paycheck by direct deposit instead of by check.
>
> The Department of Defense *won't even give an applicant a job unless he or she agrees to being paid by direct deposit.*
>
> The federal government's move to direct deposit, mandated under the 1994 Financial Management Act, is being watched closely by payroll managers and bankers across the country. Many have tried but failed over the past 20 years to get their workers to accept getting paid electronically.
>
> . . . A recent study . . . revealed that while fully 80% of all U.S. companies offer direct deposit to their employees, only 20% of workers actually participate. [Very interesting!]

[In] Japan, direct deposit is used by 99% of all workers, and Europe averages 90%.

Even though Federal Reserve permits companies to mandate direct deposit, . . . 36 states today specifically prohibit employers from making direct deposit mandatory.

On December 20, 1993, an article picked up from AP was printed in the *Los Angeles Times*. It appeared in the "Your Money" section under the headline "Road to Cashlessness Paved with Plastic" and a subtitle, "Technology—a vast information network brings closer the day when money will blip, not jingle." It is a well–written article that tries to take some of the mystery out of what happens after a consumer hands their credit card over to the clerk and they slide it through that little machine hooked up to the telephone lines. I thought the following was very interesting. See if you can figure out what jumped out and caught my attention.

Here's what happens after you hand your card over to the sales clerk:

. . . [The information on your card is read and electronically transmitted over the phone lines.] Once the account information makes it to your bank, the computers ask several questions:

» Is your card stolen?
» Does the purchase exceed your credit limit?
» Is the purchase unusual and way outside your normal buying habits?

The computer answers this question by *instantly examining whether your purchase fits within your established record of buying behavior. Although some consumers might regard that as an invasion of privacy,* it is considered a useful way to help prevent unauthorized use of your card.

I told you they were keeping track of what you were buying! Of course, according to them, that's only for your own protection . . . *so far!* However, I don't truly believe that's all it's being used for, even now. I think it already is being sorted by categories of interest and sold on mailing lists to people who want to fill your box with unsolicited junk mail.

An article written by Phil Patton, entitled "E–Money," appeared in the July 1995 edition of *Popular Science* magazine. It ran with the lead line: "If you thought email changed your life, wait until you get a fistful of this." It reiterates mostly what I've already covered, but it is a comprehensive, well–written report, so I'm including some excerpts below:

> [You use your "stored value card" in telephones, vending machines marking peters, or to board a bus, *et al.*] A text display above the slot where you once dropped quarters tells you how much is being deducted and the remaining value on the card. . . . You add value to the card by inserting it in an Automatic Teller Machine . . . eliminating at last the major encumbrance of home banking: the inability to draw cash. Once e–money is accepted as universally as greenbacks, don't be surprised if a disheveled man on the street steps up to you and says, "Brother, can you spare a little stored value?"
>
> Such is the vision of smart card proponents, who push chip–embedded plastic both as a realistic alternative to cash and a tactile alternative to non–physical money that exists only as numbers on the Internet.
>
> "If we had our way, we'd implant a chip behind everyone's ear in the maternity ward," says Ronald Kane, a vice president of Cubic Corp.'s automatic revenue collection group . . . one of a number of companies and government agencies pushing the frontier of smart cards—the money of the future. . . . The next best thing is giving everyone a card—a high–tech pass with a memory that may, sooner than we imagine, *replace cash in our wallets.*
>
> . . . A true smart card contains a microprocessor. It is in effect a miniature computer, where a recorded balance can be added to or subtracted from. What makes a smart card like cash is that it is a debit card rather than a credit card: It already has value.
>
> . . . Although we may not all end up with a chip implanted under our skin, the even smarter cards of the future may be validated "biometrically" by fingerprints or retinal readers.

Converting to smart cards will require massive, but gradual, refitting or replacement of equipment in stores. . . . *The transition will likely be a quiet, almost unnoticed process,* smart card proponents say. And it's already happening. . . .

Smart cards are moving us toward a cashless society [with] digital global transactions on the Internet. . . .

Smart card systems proven in Europe are likely to be the basis for our future systems. . . . The entire bank payment system in France, involving 22 million people, has been converted to smart card technology. Germany's health care system uses smart cards for patient information and billion.

. . . Fear about security remains the sticking point for the next step beyond the smart card: digital money that does not live in a computerized card but in a system of computers. Beyond smart cards *are no cards at all*—just numbers moving through computers and across phone lines.

. . . These transitional cards will gradually replace the driver's license, medical insurance cards, bank cards, and credit cards. . . .

Space precludes me from including it here, but there is one other article that is very well written and comprehensive. I sincerely urge you to go to your nearest large library and borrow a copy and read it. In fact, it is the cover feature: "The Cashless Society: It's in the cards" (*Information Week,* October 11, 1993).

Plan for an Earth Financial Credit Corporation, an "Earth Dollar," And a New World Economic Order

The World Constitution and Parliament Association, Lakewood, Colorado, an affiliate of the United Nations and other globalist organizations, in 1987 prepared a rough outline for a New World Order financial system. (See "Main Features and Benefits" of the Earth Financial Credit Corp.)

Their thirteen–page booklet, entitled *Plan for an Earth Financial Credit Corporation and a New World Economic Order,* outlines the satanic plan to create a new, global, electronic "earth dollar" unit of exchange. They are planning to install an entirely new economic system, financed by a new global credit concept. It is highly recommended that you obtain your own copies of these documents so that you may personally examine them as to content. Only in this way will you, yourself, fully appreciate the degree to which such plans have advanced. Call the WCPA in Lakewood, Colorado, at (303) 233-3548 for information on acquiring these materials. These are also the people who have available the new *Constitution for the Federation of Earth,* designed to supplant all the constitutions of all sovereign nations on earth.

I think there are many places where Scripture can be applied equally as well to earthly matters as to spiritual concepts, without any irreverence to the Word of God. One such scripture tells us to study to show ourselves approved unto God, workmen who do not need to be ashamed, because we are able to rightly divide (understand/interpret) the Word of truth. I believe that this admonition applies to this subject matter; even though we are dealing with the physical realm, these are circumstances leading to the time of the fulfillment of biblical prophecy. Christians must not turn a deaf ear or put their heads in the proverbial sand, while many of us are crying the warning at the top of our voice. All signs indicate that the hour is late . . . I want you to be aware of just *how* late.

Read on and learn how the noose is growing ever tighter.

CHAPTER SEVEN

AMERICA'S IDENTITY
CRISIS AND THE EMERGING
NATIONAL ID CARD

The 1960s search for *identity* has returned, but this time it is not an idle search for some intangible "self." This time it is for a verifiable *electronic* identity, confirmed by some method of biometrics. Indeed, the word for tomorrow is your *digital identity*. Commercial entities of every variety and government agencies from the IRS to the DMV—and all others in between—are making plans to computerize and identify you electronically.

The term *identity crisis* was coined by German–American psychoanalyst Erik Erikson, a term which he popularized in his theories on identity/identity crisis. Erikson holds that people grow through experiencing a series of crises, from which they must achieve their own identity. In researching *identity crisis,* I ran across an even more interesting concept put forth by one of Erikson's predecessors, psychoanalyst and social philosopher Erich Fromm, who argued that *freedom* was stressful, claiming that in some societies the populace actually followed a dictator in order to be relieved of the stress of having to make decisions for themselves. Frankly, I prefer the stress of making my own decisions to the even greater stress of having someone else make them for me! However, I am addressing another type of crisis in this chapter . . . read on.

America—indeed, the entire world—is experiencing a crisis, but rather than an *identity* crisis, it could be described more accurately as an *identification* crisis. Globalist leaders assert that an *identification crisis* exists worldwide, whereby soon everyone on earth must possess a national ID card of some kind. Why? Because Big Brother and his global government, the New World Order, cannot rise to complete dictatorial power until it can accurately make positive identification of everyone on the face of the earth (beginning with the modern industrialized nations, I'm sure, followed by the third-world countries). In order to enslave you, which is their goal, they first must be able to keep track of you and all your transactions. Positive biometric identification permits surveillance, which leads to control!

Government and/or globalist leaders plan to issue to all of us a unique, biometrically confirmed, digitized ID card that will incorporate a microprocessor, the technologically advanced "smart" card with an integrated circuit chip (IC chip). This smart chip will be capable of storing an immense amount of personal data on everyone. It will result in an unparalleled, illegal invasion of our privacy, and an unprecedented violation of our constitutional rights. This technology will enable the digital profiling and tracking of everyone in a worldwide electronic, all-enslaving cashless society, using a myriad of networked databases sharing information—until they decide to put all the information in *one place.*

Your first reaction may well be, "I'm not important enough for anyone to care—all that spying and surveillance will be reserved for those with access to sensitive data." Don't you believe it—they want to control *you.* It doesn't matter if you work for the CIA, or IRS, or what your job is, or if you are a drug dealer or money launderer. The ultimate goal is to control your *buying and selling,* as described in Revelation 13—and that isn't limited to certain people. It refers to *everyone.*

Information as to what you purchase, and where, and how much, has been collected secretly for some time. And even though no one has publicly confessed that they are accumulating such information on us, they have admitted it in a "backhanded" sort of fashion. In fact, they are so proud of how well it's working, they are now advertising some of the side benefits generated by the collection and sorting of such details. I will give you a couple of examples.

You may have seen a television commercial by a major credit card company, bragging on their terrific efficiency in their efforts to *protect you* and your card from misuse. It was a clever little scenario showing a guy you could loosely call a "slob," who never purchased anything but "slob" stuff. Then one day he went out and bought a tuxedo in which to get married. This terrific, efficient credit card computer determined that this was outside the "norm" for this customer and went "tilt." So someone called to assure that it was really him charging on his card, and not some imposter. Wasn't that a considerate thing to do? As I have pointed out numberous times, it's always for our convenience. But did anyone stop to think about *how they knew it was outside the norm?* Of course, they avoided mention of this in their commercials, but there is only one way . . . the computer has been collecting information about your private transactions long enough to establish a profile on you, and it now knows what is the "norm" for you.

The IRS announced several years ago that it was tying in all kinds of databases so they could tell if your spending was outside the "norm," i.e., the amount of your reported income. They readily admit that this is to eliminate the underground economy, as well as trap illegal banking activities, crime, etc. For example, if you are a waiter who reports income based on miminum wage and meager tips, but the DMV reports you own a Jaguar, Bank of America's computers show you have a big checking and savings account, Visa shows you're a big spender and pay your hefty bills on time, and the state property tax database shows you own a million–dollar home in Malibu . . . stand back and watch the IRS computer go "tilt." All these networked or shared databases will *automatically* sound the alarm when something doesn't fit well within the established profile.

Once the cashless society has been attained, no one will be able to ouy or sell anything without the approval of some computer somewhere. And like overextended credit cards right now, you will hear the term "declined" when someone wants to deny you the privilege of buying or selling. The goal is to control *all* money and *all* information, because those who control the money and information *control the world.* Technically speaking, of course, it won't really be money as we know it (i.e., currency or coins), but probably will be called money, for lack of a better term (although we presently are being conditioned to use the terms *debit* and *credit*). Actually, it will just be a bunch of numbers being pushed around somewhere out there in cyberspace. But that's the goal for the New World Order. Control and surveillance is the name of their game—it's how they will achieve total global electronic enslavement.

Whatever you call it—a national health card, a tamper–proof Social Security card, a state or national driver's license, an electronic benefits transfer cad, or some other universal card—what we are really getting is a *de facto* NATIONAL IDENTITY CARD.

Instead of "your papers" as the Nazis demanded, you will be required to produce your electronically digitized ID card. Upon insertion into the proper automated readers, all there is to now about you may be accessed from the terminal . . . your complete electronic profile from *hundreds* of networked databases.

Just what will these new cards divulge? Virtually everything about you that's stored presently on over 910 databases in America alone—your driving history, digitized photos, arrest and warrant records, bank account balances, Social Security number, marital status, children, health records, home ownership and personal property records, car ownership, various consumer profiles, credit history and profile, employment records, religious affiliation, and even statements from any enemies you may have—all this is now accessible easily on any personal computer via modem connections. All could be instantly displayed on a computer screen at the touch of a button! The more high–tech we become, the more privacy we lose.

What is the excuse being given as the need for a national ID card? There are several, but two of the major concerns are the illegal immigration that has become out of control and the call for health care reform. The New World Order powers in control have deemed the best solution to be the unalterable positive identification of everyone, in order to limit abuse in both areas. A card, linked with some form of biometric confirmation, is likely to be the ID of choice. And since it would only make sense to make the most of the technology at hand, the card of choice would be one which contains the microprocessor chip, allowing the constant updating of information every time a transaction is made or service provided. This kind of technology is referred to as a *smart card.*

It has been in use in Europe for quite some time and is being promoted on this side of the Atlantic by an organization called the Smart Card Forum. *World Card Technology,* February 1995, carried an article written by Catherine Allen, a vice president at Citibank and chair of the Smart Card Forum, titled "Influencing Infrastructure Development in the U.S." Here are some excerpts.

> As evidence of the anticipated growth and interest in smart card technology in the United States, more than 170 companies, as well as the U.S. Treasury, U.S. Department of Health and Human Services, and the U.S. Department of Defense, joined forces in 1993 to create the Smart Card Forum, a consortium charged with developing business specifications and recommending standards for a North American smart card infrastructure.
>
> The Forum's members include American Express, AT&T, Bellcore, IBM, Hewlett Packard, MCI, Microsoft, MasterCard, Visa, International, numerous smart card technology vendors, and several large banks, including Citibank, Chase Manhattan Bank, Chemical Bank, Bank of America, Wells Fargo Bank, NationsBank, Corestates Bank, and National Westminster Bank....
>
> Citibank has taken a leadership position in helping to establish the Smart Card Forum because it is in the Bank's interest....

You will note that the majority of the above–mentioned organizations are either backed by Rothschild or Rockefeller, or members of the CFR or TLC ... or any combination of the above.

According to their literature: "Smart Card Forum, with over 190 corporate and government members, provides an arena for the private and public sectors to foster the development of multiple use/ multiple application smart cards in the North American market. Its objective is to promote communication resulting in market trials of smart card–based payments and information services. . . . Membership is open to organizations with a use or business applications focus. Work groups are active in the areas of electronic purse, health care, government, education, technology, legal and regulatory issues, and telephony."

The Smart Card Forum answers the question "What is a Smart Card? this way:

> Similar to a credit card, a smart card stores information on an integrated microprocessor chip located within it.
>
> There are two basic kinds of smart cards. An "intelligent" smart card contains a central processing unit—a CPU—that actually has the ability to store and secure information, and "make decisions," as required by the card issuer's specific applications needs. Because intelligent cards offer a "read/write" capability, new information can be added and processed. For example, monetary value can be added and decremented as a particular application might require.

A lettter from Catherine Allen accompanied the literature on the Smart Card Forum. It read, in part:

> We invite you to be part of a *cross–industry effort to accelerate the widespread acceptance of smart card technology in the United States....*
>
> The Forum's mission is to accelerate the widespread acceptance of smart card technologies that support multiple applications by bringing together, in an open forum, leading users and technologists from both the public and private sectors. Our goals are to promote interoperability across appropriate business applications of technology, as well as to facilitate market trials.
>
> ... The Forum members think there are some compelling reasons to relook at smart card technology as well as to participate in development of the infrastructure in the United States.
>
> » The convergence of information technologies ...
> » New, non–traditional players are entering the business of financial services, computing, and information services ...

> » The cost of smart card and computer technology continues to decrease rapidly . . .
> » Fraud is rising and firms are searching for more secure technologies . . .
> » Most importantly, consumers are demanding convenience. . . .

Right! But what about the immigration problem and the health care concerns? Do they justify issuing identification cards to everyone? Let's address them one at a time and find out.

IMMIGRATION TIME BOMB: THE CALL FOR A NATIONAL ID CARD

Perhaps nothing poses a greater threat to our civil liberties and personal privacy than the national debate over immigration reform. This topic is *vitally* important, and you must know the implications of new legislation and how it will affect you and your family. A majority of the states are all calling for some form of positive ID for worker verification. Recent proposals all include use of the smart card in combination with some form of biometric data. So how serious is this immigration problem? Not surprisingly, hardest hit are California, Texas, and Florida, as well as New York and Illinois. In six of our largest cities, 20 percent of all arrests are of illegal aliens, while one out of four inmates in federal prisons is an illegal alien.

In Los Angeles, 40 percent of all illegals released from jail are re–arrested for new crimes. Unpaid medical bills cost taxpayers over a billion dollars a year, and each year $24 billion in fraudulent claims are made to collect government benefits. Former presidential candidate Pat Buchanan points out: "It is outrageous that American taxpayers . . . have to provide social welfare benefits for those whose accomplishments are to break the laws to get into the United States and to get on welfare." "Outrageous" seems a conservative term for it! But is the solution to make *everyone* register for a national ID card? The call is no longer just for immigrants, but for everyone to have the card so employers would know who it was safe to hire.

People woke up just in time and raised such a furor about the proposed National Health Card that the idea seems to have been tabled . . . but I'm sure it's only temporary. Watch closely, as I'm sure it will rear its ugly head again, and probably sooner than later . . . perhaps under a new name.

I have now acquired so much documentation on this subject that it is difficult to decide what to omit and what to include. I still have to cover some of the more important functions of smart card technology (in addition to its commercial uses, such as banking and purchases), for example, EBT cards, health cards, motor–voter cards, new–style pilot's license, and perhaps the most important of all— the MARC card.

As more and more people gain access to more and more information about you, your privacy diminishes in direct proportion. I am sure these ID cards are nothing more than a predecessor to the implantable biochip (described in the next chapter); in any event, they are establishing the beachhead for the positive identification of every person. In the July 15, 1994, edition of *USA Today,* the following article ran under the heading "Today's debate: PROVING CITIZENSHIP." The article was titled "National ID cards let Uncle Sam spy on you," and was followed with, "OUR VIEW: The idea is hot in Washington and carries a heavy price both financially and in loss of privacy." The writers are extremely astute. Here are some eye–opening excerpts:

Think the federal government already knows too much about your private life? Hang on. The granddaddy of all privacy invasions—a national ID card—is marching onto Capitol Hill.

Startling numbers of Democrats and Republicans, liberals and conservatives, are embracing variations of the identity card—all in the name of immigration reform. They contend the cards could keep illegal immigrants out of American jobs by requiring potential bosses to use the cards and accompanying national database to verify citizenship.

Sound like a cheap and harmless fix? Wrong. The cards present gargantuan potential for abuse with enormous costs.

. . . Fear of constant harassment is wrong. Having to carry a card to guarantee your freedom is not what the Founding Fathers had in mind.

Then there's the price tag. Most plans on Capitol Hill—and there are dozens in various bills—require all U.S. citizens, not just recent immigrants, to get cards.

. . . Proponents believe the means justify the end—closing the jobs door to illegals. They believe "tamper–proof" IDs, verifiable through the national database, will stop the use of fraudulent documents. . . .

National ID cards are an old idea and a bad idea. The last thing the federal government needs is another peephole on personal privacy that ends up costing U.S. taxpayers more money that it saves.

In the October 17, 1994, issue of *Forbes 400*, editor–in–chief and former presidential candidate Malcolm S. Forbes, Jr., included the following on his editorial page:

1984 Updated?

A cry for a national identification card is rising again. The catalyst is the desire to get a tool that will cut illegal immigration. We should resist the temptation. Such a card will rapidly be used for far more than employment. The loss of privacy outweighs any gains.

It is disconcerting enough to know that computer snoops can dig up a lot of supposedly confidential information about our lives. The IRS recently admitted that thousands of its employees routinely, without authority, examine tax returns of friends, enemies, and the famous.

Assurances that laws would protect our privacy rightly ring hollow. With a national ID card your whole life could end up on a government central computer file. All tax returns, all banking transactions including cash taken from ATMs, all medical records including individual prescriptions, every hotel stay, every store purchase, every moving and parking violation, etc., would be centrally accessible.

Do we as a nation of individualists really want that? Do not be fooled by the idea that a Social Security or national ID card can be made counterfeit-proof by having our photos and fingerprints on it. Warped technological wizards will find a way to beat any government-designed system.

It's hard to say it any better or more precisely than that! Unfortunately, many people can't see the handwriting on the wall . . . or they are part of the Big Brother New World Order crowd who will gain more control over us . . . or they are just naïve and capitulating for a modicum of convenience.

Mike Hale, executive administrator for Florida's Information Resource Commission, said: "One of the biggest forthcoming issues in government is going to be on the development of a universal card for citizen identification." He believes states need to take a close look at issuing everybody one card for identification and the delivery of services, from health care and human services to libraries and special events. "The card can become a way to standardize service to the citizens," says Hale.

To expedite the "telling of this story," and to condense much of the documentation, I am going to put many newspaper and magazine articles in chronological sequence and just take excerpts from them below. Source, date, and title of article will be given on each for verification purposes.

As early as April 12, 1992, an article appeared in both the *Los Angeles Times* and the *Las Vegas Review-Journal* announcing the unveiling of credit cards with the cardholder's photo right on the card. This is where the infrastructure began to be laid for the full-blown smart card technology to follow. In trying to combat fraudulent use, these new cards were issued by Citibank, who reportedly sustained a $1 billion loss from credit card fraud in 1991.

By the next month, the term "smart cards" was being used widely. The following, written by Jeffrey Blair of the Associated Press, appeared in the May 31, 1992, edition of the *Law Vegas Review-Journal*, in an article titled "Smart cards: Convenience and market data rolled into one":

> It looks and acts like your average bank card, but it knows a lot
> more about you than you may think.

The smart card—a piece of plastic with a computer chip on its face—is slipping into the United States with uses from defense and health care to retailing and transportation.

The cards have replaced food stamps for some Ohio shoppers and meal tickets for students in college. Marines and peanut farmers are whipping them out for boot polish and crop reports.

Someday they may also pay highway tolls, or unscramble satellite TV signals, as they're used in Europe today. . . .

"The average American who has a dozen pieces of plastic in their pocket probably doesn't even know what a smart card is. . . ."

So first, an introduction to these data dynamos:

» Unlike today's financial cards, the smart card doesn't need a magnetic strip on the back.

» Instead, it's equipped with a wiry silicon chip, often displayed at left center but sometimes hidden in the plastic. (Smart cards may also have embossed account numbers, holograms, graphics, and photos on the front or back.)

» Like a bank card, the smart card is slipped into a computer. Then the owner enters a four- or five–digit ID number and uses the card to make purchases, convey information, or both.

» The card can hold three pages worth of typewritten data, compared to one line of type for a magnetic–strip card. That means several accounts could be loaded onto one smart card. . . .

» Smart cards cost from about $1 each for a disposable card to $4 for the most common cards to about 10 times that for security cards that hold complex information such as voice patterns or retina scans [linked to biometric identification].

Since newspaper articles are generally written for the laymen rather than the scientist or technician, this is very clear and concise. But as with all computer technology, several years can make a great deal of difference in capabilities. For example, as I covered in detail earlier in this book, EBT is no longer available only in Ohio; it is being used in many states and the federal government is presently laying the infrastructure to use it in all federal benefits programs, from welfare, to Social Security, to health care. The highway tolls are already being collected in several places by smart card technology. Probably the greatest improvement in the technology is that "three pages" of data is now obsolete; in certain types of cards well over a thousand pages of data can be stored on your smart card (some can store nearly two thousand pages).

In a June 17, 1993, article in the *Los Angeles Times* titled "Lawmakers Clash Over New Call for National ID Card," we read:

> Creation of a single, tamper–resistant identification card to verify employment eligibility—a controversial proposal designed to reduce illegal immigration—received a largely sympathetic hearing Wednesday from members of a House subcommittee.
>
> . . . Rep. Anthony C. Beilenson (D–Woodland Hills) has introduced a bill to establish a national identification card for all eligible workers. "There is simply no way to enforce our existing law without it."
>
> Civil liberties groups contend that a new identification card could lead to a national data bank with information about every American that would pose a threat to individual privacy.

The following are excerpts from an article that appeared in the July 1993 edition of *Monetary & Economic Review.*

Smart Cards: They Make Our Enslavement So Convenient

Last month in *MER* we briefly touched the subject of the "smart card" and its important role in the New World Order. It is these little pieces of plastic and metal that will control the everyday happenings of the individual. Your purchases can be tracked, your bank account observed, and your entire history can be stored on these cards. They are capable of containing information from blood type to background, all in a package no bigger than a regular credit card. But just how close are these new threats to personal freedom? Right around the corner, and closer than anyone ever thought. [Author's note: Keep in mind, this was written in 1993.]

You may be familiar with the latest commercials from AT&T. Views of a world of ease based upon new technological break-throughs. The first picture is the portable fax machine, followed by the video phone, and finally we observe a card capable of containing your personal history and medical records. It would seem that AT&T has taken the lead in the smart card industry and is now implementing the cards into daily life. According to AT&T, the smart cards are small, 8-bit microcomputers with their own operating systems, capable of storing 3 kilobytes of information. The cards are contactless, meaning that the microchips are fully enclosed, reducing wear while making it possible to scan the cards like a normal credit card. [Author's note: The ones linked with biometric data are designed to scan from a distance, without even putting it into a reader/machine.] The information on the card can be read through either a special card reader or through a regular hook-up to a personal computer.

We can already see the beginnings of the smart card in our everyday life. Many banks offer debit cards that replace checkbooks for their customers. Virtually every phone company has a card with your account number on it for access to long distance calling without the hassle of finding change. Your credit card is an instrument of trade that has in many cases become easier for people to use than cash. These are but a small taste compared to the newest advances of smart card technology.

In Italy, the Olivetti company, along with AT&T, installed a new pension management system using smart cards to keep information on pensioners and their accounts within their pension fund. The pensioners must have their card in order to withdraw any of their money and the card keeps a record of all transactions.

Also in Italy, the government has installed systems on toll roads that require smart cards to pay the toll....

In many corporations around the world the cards have been implemented for building security.... The company can literally track the location of individuals at any time....

It all sounds so nice and easy, but consider the ramifications. Your assets can be frozen in the blink of an eye; anyone with the authority could bring up all of your history and background. Every single one of your records could be accessed by the Internal Revenue Service, the FBI, or any other government agency in an effort to control the actions of the people. It all reminds me of those futuristic movies where the people become a number rather than individuals, whose efforts are put toward the goals of the state. All privacy, whether it be personal history or financial, would be gone forever.

If this sounds far off, consider this: the cards are being set up for use in the United States as they are in the rest of the world. In southern California the smart card is being used on new toll roads. . . . AT&T Smart Cards has openly stated, "equipped with smart cards, commercial vehicles could be located, classified, weighed, and identified for taxation and other purposes while in motion." [Author's note: Again, this is another technology that has been implemented in several states since this article was written.]

If it is possible to be used in commercial trucks, could it not be used in an individual's car? National Cash Register has teamed up with AT&T to produce a dual smart card and voice print identification system, for use on automated teller machines. The voice print on the card must match your voice while making the transaction in order to be validated. Even the United States government uses smart cards in the form of employee identification. . . .

It is easy to see the advantages and sheer ease this allows the New World Order crew in the supplying of information on governments, corporations, and individuals. Though the beginnings of the smart card in society are scattered, it is very simple to take all information from several smart cards and move all files to a single card. It is just a matter of time before the people of this nation and others allow the full use of smart cards in their businesses and private lives. **Remember, the goal of the New World Order crowd is to control the economic and social behavior of everyone. Many people will succumb to this financial slavery out of mere convenience.**

After those last two articles, almost anything else I add will be redundant, but I will make brief reference to the other articles just so you can see the sheer *weight* of the evidence.

» *Los Angeles Times*, September 10, 1993, "Wilson Expands on Plan for ID Card"

> **Immigration:** Governor wants the state to be a testing ground for the tamper-proof documents. But he admits that it would probably be impossible to come up with a foolproof system. . . . There have been periodic proposals for a national ID card, but they have always run up against strong opposition on civil liberties grounds. . . .Wilson said any identification card is the key to the enforcement of any of the sanctions written into federal law. . . .

» *Los Angeles Times*, December 24, 1993, "Orange County to Test Medi-Cal 'Credit Cards'"

> **Welfare:** Program is designed to speed reimbursement and to cut down on fraud. . . .
>
> The new California Benefits Identification Cards will be mailed to most of the 230,000 people in Orange County who are eligible for Medi-Cal health insurance and the almost 42,000 elderly, blind, or disabled residents who receive benefits under the federal Supplemental Security Income program. Four other counties also will participate in the pilot program; all of the state's 5 million Medi-Cal recipients are expected to have the new cards by June.
>
> A magnetic strip on the back of the card—similar to automated teller machine cards—will be run through a machine to link doctors with computer information in Sacramento. The computer also will show if the card has been lost or stolen. . . . In addition to controlling fraud and abuse, the computerized system will give the state access to new information such as "improper or potentially deadly prescription usage."
>
> "This puts the technology foot in the door for future benefit issuances, such as food stamps, and [welfare] payments." . . .

» *Legislature Reporter,* Manitoba, Canada, January 25, 1994, "New card to track drug use" by Paul Saymn

> A new Pharmacare tracking system to start April 1. . . . The arrival of the computerized Pharmacare system—which will use the new purple Manitoba Health Services Commission card—is likely the first step toward the so-called "smart health cards" that would allow health professionals to tap into a person's entire medical history. "It will be like a little travelling medical file. . . . It will go further than protecting our system (from abuse), it will also protect our health." . . . With a push of a button, druggists will know what medication a customer is on—and if he or she is abusing the system. . . . The new system would immediately alert a druggist if a prescription for any drug had been recently filled elsewhere.

» *American Banker,* March 25, 1994, "AT&T's Smart Card Chief Plans Two-Front Push"

> The president of a new AT&T business unit sees 1994 as a crucial year in the development of a U.S. market for smart card services. . . .
> **Smarter Smart Cards.** The chips in AT&T smart cards currently [1994] have about 3 kilobytes of memory. By the end of the year . . . the standard AT&T card will boast 8K, and plans call for 100K card in the next few years.
> With the larger memory, cards could carry personal information such as medical records, in addition to the financial and identification data that banks would likely put on the cards.
> Experts say that expanding the smart card's utility beyond financial transactions will hasten consumer acceptance. . . .

» *Security Management,* April 1994, "TVs to Toll Booths: Smart Card Capabilities"

> Organizers of the 1992 World Expo in Seville, Spain, needed a way to allow holders of season passes to enter the expo area quickly while preventing them from granting others access on the same

ticket. They solved the problem with smart cards and biometrics. A fingerprint biometric terminal controlling each season ticket holder turnstile was installed. More than 100 turnstiles were implemented—52 for the 110,000 season pass holders, and an additional 48 for the 30,000 expo workers. The season passes and the workers' passes were personalized at more than 60 fingerprint digitizing and recording stations. The system was capable of passing one person through a turnstile every 8 seconds, with complete confidence in the validity of the pass and of the holder.

» *USA Today,* July 13, 1994, "National citizen ID is proposed"

All U.S. citizens and legal immigrants would get the equivalent of a national ID card under an expected proposal to Congress by the Commission on Immigration Reform. Similar proposals have been embraced by Congress but vehemently opposed by some immigrant and privacy advocates as costly and prone to abuse. The new Social Security–type cards, including photo and finterprints, would allow employers to verify work eligibility *through a national database.*

» *Orange County Register,* July 13, 1994, "U.S. may issue ID cards to citizens"

IMMIGRATION: Gov. Pete Wilson wants California to be the test state for "Employee Verification Registration," a TV report says.

The federal government, in a response to its inability to control illegal immigration, may soon ask every American to carry a national identity card. . . .

"Rather than wait for the development of a nationwide system, I strongly recommend you designate California as the first state in which a working system can be implemented on a fast track," said Wilson.

[A national identity card] "will create a neo–Nazi state in the United States where we will be required to tell on each other. . . . Next thing you know, we'll have tattoos on our bodies," [said Enriqueta Ramos, vice president of Rancho Santiago Community College's board of trustees].

. . . Other lawmakers expressed concern that the program would be ineffective, costly, and an incursion into personal privacy.

"Will government really be able to do the job it is claiming? And if not, we've just spent billions of dollars and just given up some major, some severe privacy rights for nothing," Rep. Xavier Becerra, D–Los Angeles, told CBS.

There is another piece of technology which would appear to be the ultimate in identity cards . . . at least for today. The **Lasercard** is an optical memory card produced by the Drexler Technology Corp. It is an updatable, credit card–sized, multi–megabyte data storage card which can accommodate up to 1,600 pages (i.e., 4.11 megabytes) of information on the carrier. It is based upon optical recording technology—the process of writing and reading with light.

The Lasercard has ample memory to store personal identification numbers (PINs), digital photos, signatures, voice prints, fingerprints, hand geometry, retina scans, and virtually any form of personal biometrics or biographical data on the cardholder, i.e., text, graphics, voice, pictures, software—virtually any form of information that can be digitized. In its literature, Drexler says that it can produce up to 40 million Lasercards a year.

» *Orange County Register,* August 18, 1994, "O.C. Mexicans have no voice in vote . . . CARDS: Underdog supporters protest plan"

> The voices of about 600,000 Mexicans living in Orange County and an additional 4–5 million living in California will not be heard at the Mexican polls Sunday.
>
> The reason: A tamper–proof voter–identification card, which was issued only to residents of Mexico, and has shut out millions of Mexican citizens living abroad. . . .
>
> The government says the cards, with a photograph, fingerprint, hologram, invisible ultraviolet coating, barcode, and plastic laminate, are tamper–proof and will guarantee the most honest elections in Mexico's history.

But not everyone agrees. . . . "People will always find a way to cheat, even with the cards. . . . The reason these cards were approved was to eliminate people from the process."

» *Government Technology,* September 1994, "MasterCard Moving to Chip Technology"

That magnetic stripe on the back of your credit cards is about to go the way of the Dodo. MasterCard International, the credit association owned by member banks, has begun a program to move toward chip–based 'smart cards.' The group's goal is to have all its payment systems including chip technology by the year 2000.

» *Houston Post,* December 15, 1994, "High–Tech ID: New Driver's License Debuts Jan. 2"

Magnetic and photogenic are the key words for Texas' new high–tech drivers' license, which the Texas Department of Public Safety will begin issuing on Jan. 2. The new licenses will have a magnetic strip on the back containing basic information printed on the license. DPS squad cars will carry devices like credit card machines which can scan and verify data on the back. The system also may be used by retailers scanning for hot–check artists.

» *World Card Technology,* February/March 1995, "Multi–Functioning Cards"

The buzz word in the smartcard market today is "multifunction cards." The concept behind these is to reduce the number of cards in the consumers' wallets by integrating many applications like banking, health, GSM SIM, etc., all on one card. . . .

. . . In this age of multifunction cards, the semiconductor manufacturer must find a way of cramming a great number of memory cells into a smaller space. This is done by introducing smaller geometrys. Today the standard transistor cell size is 1.2 um (a human hair is an average 40 um thick). Motorola is actively developing new, dense EEPROM cells to support multi application cards, which are significantly less than 1 um in length. *This will make smartcard devices with more than twice the EEPROM capacity a reality by the end of the century.*

» *Wall Street Journal,* March 21, 1995, "Three Banks, Visa Hope to Catapult 'Smart Card' Use at Summer Olympics"

Three largest Southeast banks in cooperation with Visa plan the most ambitious launch yet of a "smart card" in the U.S. in time for the Summer 1996 Olympics in Atlanta.

While the new cards look like credit cards, they're different in concept. A credit card represents a loan. A smart card, which is already popular in Europe, is an electronic purse that holds electronic cash. Each time it's used, the amount of the purchase price is automatically deducted by an electronic reader. When the "electronic purse" is empty, the card can't be used anymore.

Visa said the new cards, powered by a microchip, will come in two versions: a disposable one that will be discarded after the value has been spent; and a reusable or rechargeable card, that can have new buying power added by loading it into an automatic teller machine. The second type would be incorporated into a multiuse bank card that also functions as a debit card and bank–machine card.

"This will be the first rollout of the technology in the U.S.," said a Visa spokesman. . . .

Visa said the 1996 Atlanta Olympics makes for the perfect locale to trot out the smart card because of the large international audience it will bring, including many Europeans who are already comfortable with the technology.

» *Automatic ID News,* April 1995, "Technology adds functionality to ID cards"

Get ready to replace that bulging purse or wallet–full of cards with a single, multifunction card. Now that's smart! . . .

The smart card population is going to increase its rate of growth. The increasing volumes of production and chip evolution prompted *Business Week* to forecast 1 billion smart cards to be produced in 1996. The United States market will mainly consist of pilots for prepaid cards, financial transactions, security access control, and portable databases. *The road–toll solutions are well established and growing rapidly. The military logistics and related applications are now proven....*

» *Charlotte Observer,* April 10, 1995, "Social Security streamlining in the works/Changes in store for retirees"

The White House plans to streamline the Social Security Administration by changing the way future retirees receive their checks and apply for benefits....

Officials also said they would seek to move all retirees with bank accounts into a direct deposit program, and may allow banks to issue a single debit card that would add Social Security benefits to other federal payments, such as welfare or food stamps, that are now paid via "smart cards."

» *Denver Post,* April 21, 1995, "Bombing may spark national identity cards," by Richard Reeves

[The Oklahoma bombing] will change many things in the United States....

Many of the changes in America were already well under way. To cash a check in trusting California now, you have to show a photo–ID California driver license. If you do not drive, the Department of Motor Vehicles issues plastic identification cards so you can do the business of the day. So, in effect, California already has the kind of identity card—"Your papers, please?"—that Americans have always resisted as the internal passport of police states.

The California licenses have the usual magnetic strip across the back, and although officials swear that only relevant height and weight information is encoded in the strip, we all know that the things are capable of retaining every fact of a life, plus the Encyclopedia Brittanica.

And soon they will, I am almost certain. One of the results of this crime against the American soul will be some form of national identity card.... I know there will be government and police abuses of such cards but ... the information on each of us is already out there somewhere....

And now—whoever did this—.... the worst part of it will be restrictions we must put on our own freedoms.

» *Government Technology,* May 1995, "Students Like Cards & Kiosks"

... Currently 40,000 students, faculty, and staff use the FSUCard, which serves as an ID, security card, library card, food and vending card, ATM and telephone calling card. John Carnaghi, Florida State vice president for finance and administration, calls the FSUCard "the most creative administrative tool I've ever encountered."

FSU and MCI also introduced FSU Connection Interactive Kiosk Network, which allows students to use their FSUCards to update local or permanent addresses, print transcripts and class schedules and apply for graduation. Eventually the kiosks will allow students to pay tuition and register for courses.

» *Automatic ID News,* June 1995, "ID cards cut postage and fraud in food stamp programs" This article covers the use of ID cards in Los Angeles county and other California counties that are about to duplicate LA's successful efforts in the automation of their food stamp programs. Elimination of fraud, as well as savings due to the automation, are cited as the primary reasons for use of this new technology.

» *Los Angeles Times,* June 12, 1995, "Big Brother, Make Room for Big Sister." The following article by Ron K. Unz is one of the most astute and honest commentaries, as well as comprehensive analysis, that I have seen on the subject of identity cards and their potential for disaster in many different areas of our lives.

Immigration: Sen. Feinstein wants everyone to carry an encrypted, database–linked national identity card.

Timothy McVeigh, alleged perpetrator of the Oklahoma City bombing, is said to have believed that, while he was in the Army, the government implanted a microchip tracking device in his buttocks. Most of us would dismiss this as the ravings of an obvious madman. But to Sen. Dianne Feinstein, McVeigh is just a bit ahead of his time; she is a believer is "biometric" tracking of all of us. She proposes, as part of legislation for tougher control of illegal immigration, a national identity card for every man, woman, and child in America.

Captivated by advanced technology, Feinstein says that such a card could include a magnetic strip or microchip containing a digitized form of each citizen's vital statistics, photograph, fingerprint, voiceprint, and retina scan. The card would be linked to massive new federal computer databases, and would be presented whenever an American applied for employment or government benefits. The card would have to be renewed annually, presumably requiring refingerprinting to verify identity.

Now, subjecting every American to the humiliation of annual citizenship checks could hardly win popular support if presented purely as an employment program for tens of thousands of new federal document inspectors and file managers; an overriding justification must be found. In the past decades, the magic words *national security* might have persuaded Americans to meekly sacrifice their traditional liberties. The Cold War is no more, but Feinstein has found an equivalent: the current "war" against illegal immigration. Once the 260 million legal inhabitants of America have been scanned, everyone caught with their fingerprints not on file might be presumed illegal and deported or imprisoned, solving the problem once and for all.

Whether Dianne Feinstein actually cares so deeply about the scourge of illegal immigration remains open to considerable doubt. Aside from happily placing her own home in the care of an illegal alien some years back, she strongly supported throughout the 1980s various San Francisco ordinances that declared the city a "safe haven" for all illegal immigrants and prohibited any local cooperation with immigration authorities. But politicians follow the polls, and if catching those illegal nannies and gardners now requires every American citizen to carry a microchip, so be it. Gov. Pete Wilson endorsed much the same approach just before the 1994 election when he said that actually Proposition 187 would probably require establishment of a national ID card.

Compared to Feinstein's proposal, Pat Buchanan's foolish idea of building a massive wall across the thousands of miles of our southern border is far less harmful to American freedom.

A national ID database represents the slipperiest of all civil liberty slopes. A system employing tens of thousands of government clerks and administrators and costing tens of billions of dollars to build and operate would surely not remain limited to catching illegal nannies. Why not use it, at virtually no additional cost, to track convicted child molesters, as well? Who would dare object? Why not then also track the movements of convicted murderers. And rapists. And drug dealers and felons in general. And fathers behind on child support. And tax-evaders. And "political extremists." Members of "religious cults." Drug addicts. AIDS carriers. Gun owners. With each turn of the political cycle, left and right would add their favorite batch of social enemies to the surveillance list.

Or consider employment issues. Since every private employer would have to obtain federal authorization before offering any individual a job, a database record of race, ethnicity, and gender could be used as an extraordinarily direct means of enforcing future affirmative action regulations. Imagine business owners receiving computerized responses such as "employment permission denied; you already employ too many white males."

Perhaps considerations such as these have persuaded the Clinton Administration, Sen. Edward M. Kennedy, and other leading liberal members of Congress to put aside any civil liberty concerns they might have and fully endorse legislation along the lines of Feinstein's "Big Sister" proposal. Some moderate Republicans such as Sen. Alan Simpson of Wyoming and Rep. Lamar Smith of Texas are also on board. However, leading conservative Republicans and libertarians—House Majority Leader Dick Armey of Texas, strategist Bill Kristol, the Cato Institute, the National Federation of Independent Businesses—are absolutely opposed, as are civil liberties groups such as the ACLU.

Requiring the law–abiding 98 percent of America's population to carry a national ID card or undergo retinal scanning is un–American in the strongest sense of the word, and the only long–term beneficiaries of such federal policies would be the recruiting sergeants of the Michigan Militia. Our fractured society already contains large numbers of violent and paranoid individuals terrified of imaginary government plots against their freedom. [Author's note: I believe there is enough documented evidence in this book to convince anyone that these "plots" are no longer "imaginary."] Politicians who would give true substance to such fears by affixing microchips to every American's identity must be held accountable for the likely consequences. One Oklahoma City bombing is enough.

» *Honolulu Star–Bulletin,* June 24, 1995, "Liberals, conservatives on immigration." This is another superb article by an excellent writer, Thomas Sowell, a senior fellow at the Hoover Institution.

Few things illustrate the difference between liberals and conservatives as clearly as the different approaches to the immigration issue by liberal Democratic Sen. Dianne Feinstein and conservative Republican presidential candidate Pat Buchanan.

Pat Buchanan would act directly against immigrants by a moratorium on even legal immigration and by fortifying the borders. Whatever the merits or demerits of this approach, it focuses directly on immigrants.

Dianne Feinstein advocates a national identity card that all Americans would be required to have and that all employers would be required to see to prevent hiring illegal aliens.

It is the classic liberal response of using a particular program created by particular people to expand the government's power over other people. The same pattern is seen in liberal responses to crimes committed by people with firearms by cracking down on the far larger number of people with firearms who are committing no crimes.

Nothing polarizes the political left and right like the idea of a national identity card. Yet it is obvious why, in principle, this should be a liberal–versus–conservative issue.

Everyone should be against people escaping personal responsibility for their actions by pretending to be somebody else or by relocating to places where their sordid past is not known, thereby permitting them to victimize more innocent people.

Some hard–nosed conservatives have urged that sex offenders in particular be identified and not allowed to escape their past and continue to prey on unsuspecting neighbors, or those neighbors' children, in the future.

Would not a national identity card also prevent other kinds of criminals, deadbeat dads, and other parasites from escaping their past and jeopardizing other people's futures?

Despite the many potential benefits of a national identity card, the painful fact is that battle lines are drawn over this issue for one reason: We cannot trust the government in general, and liberals in particular, to stop at a national identity card to be used to enforce immigration laws or to deter crime.

Control is the name of the game for liberals, even when they call it "compassion." A national identity card would not [be limited to merely] greater government snooping into people's private lives. The information gathered would lead to more laws forcing more people to do more things the way the politicians want them done. *It is a down payment on totalitarianism.*

Lack of trust is not some purely psychological reaction or paranoia bred by militias or talk show hosts. History is full of reasons to distrust governments in general and the political left in particular.

Most Americans probably have no more objection in principle to a national identity card than to some form of gun control. It is only in practice that we know that it will never stop there.

Put differently, many of the benefits that we could get from many policies must be forfeited because of the greater dangers created by the untrustworthiness of those who believe in big government as a means of imposing their own superior wisdom and virtues on others.

At the very moment when the liberal media are blaming "anti-government" feeling for such things as the Oklahoma City bombing and blaming conservative talk show hosts for promoting such feelings, the Supreme Court of the United States has given a free home demonstration of betrayal of trust by striking down term–limits legislation passed by overwhelming majorities of voters.

Nothing in the Constitution forbids the states to pass such legislation. Moreover, the 10th Amendment clearly sets forth the principle that the federal government *can do only* what it is specifically authorized to do, while the states and the people can do whatever they are *not* forbidden to do. [Author's note: It seems as if they are overlooking that executive order process which permits "end runs" around the framers' intent for the Constitution.] But the learned justices decided to turn this principle upside down and claim that the states need specific authorization to act.

All this dishonesty served only to impose their preferences and prejudices on the rest of us. Instead of saying where in the Constitution such laws as term limits are forbidden, the Supreme Court majority quoted previous decisions by their predecessors, who also made it up as they went along.

In addition to the immigration problems, terrorist threats have been used as one of the primary reasons for implementing stronger security measures, including positive identity methods and expanded surveillance of groups with an agenda not considered "politically correct." The threat can be genuine or imagined . . . and achieve the same result. It can be domestic or foreign in origin; the work of a group or a disturbed individual.

The following article deals with the seventeen–year ongoing mail bombings by the single person dubbed the "Unabomber," who has created massive confusion in airports on the west coast by announcing he had planted a bomb on an aircraft. Extra security measures were implemented immediately and caused not only added time and inconvenience to passengers, but created delays in mail delivery because all large letters and packages were being subjected to extra scrutiny at every airport.

» *San Francisco Chronicle,* June 29, 1995, "Unabomb Security Clampdown/All airline passengers must show ID"

> Responding to the Unabomber's threat to blow up a jetliner, authorities yesterday took unprecedented security precautions at airports around the state and temporarily shut down California's air mail system.
>
> "Further examination has confirmed that this letter originates from the Unabomber subject. It is a credible threat."
>
> . . . Yesterday, in what aviation experts said is the strictest case of domestic airport security in U.S. history, airport officials required all passengers to show photo identification that matched the name on the passenger's ticket. Luggage belonging to people who failed that test was opened and searched for bombs.

» *USA Today,* July 13, 1995, "Cracking Down on Fake IDs." This was the front–page feature, continuing on the whole of page two. Even though it focuses on fake IDs, the estimated cost of all that fraud, the ease with which they can be obtained, and the changes being made to the drivers' licenses in an effort to eliminate the fakes, one portion deals with the high–tech aspects of future ID methods by various concerns—both businesses and agencies.

> The growing crisis costs the living billions of dollars—and the dead their identities. Photo caption: Wanda Jones died at age five in 1944. Her identity has been assumed by the unknown woman in the ID card above.
>
> Experts say fraudulent identities are epidemic, and its victims are the living as well as the dead.
>
> Voiceprints, hand geometry, bar cards, magnetic stripes, and fingerprints—they're all soldiers in the war on fake IDs.

"Big Brother is here," says Jim Gaughrin, a fraud investigator for the U.S. Secret Service. "If somebody gets your name and Social Security number and applies for credit, you're screwed. Wouldn't it be better if nobody could get credit unless they matched your fingerprint?" [Author's note: Is that supposed to be a rhetorical question?!?]

That attitude is behind the push by government agencies, the credit and banking industry, and security businesses for counterfeit-proof IDs.

» At Kennedy, Newark, and Toronto airports some international travelers put their hands on a *Star Trek*-like computer that scans various shapes and distances—their hand's geometry—as part of an Immigration and Naturalization Service test program.

» The INS also is testing voiceprints for legal immigrant work cards. If the process works, a worker could call a computer and say a phrase into the phone, and the computer would verify that person's identity. Now, a person who is not eligible to work can counterfeit a work card and get a job illegally.

» Even fingerprinting's going high-tech. Banks are using barely visible inkless methods to fingerprint non-customers who cash checks.

» Drivers' licenses now come with a credit-card look and holographic images to make tampering difficult.

Vital statistics—name, height, weight, hair color—are printed over ghost images of photos or state seals, making it tough to replace accurate information with false. License bureaus are using digital photography so a picture can be filed in a computer and called up on a screen with the touch of a button. Some states require a thumbprint.

Increased security doesn't stop with driver's licenses.

Credit card companies—which, depending on who is counting, lose between millions and billions of dollars annually because of fake IDs—are stepping up their efforts, too.

Visa has slowed fraud through a computer system that watches for the same address or phone number used on multiple credit applications, often a sign of fraud.

"Let's face it—if 350 applications are coming from a P.O. box in the Bronx, we've got a problem," says Allan Trosclair, vice president of fraud control for Visa USA. Trosclair credits the new computer system with helping Visa push its rate of fraudulent credit cards from 6 percent to 3 percent since 1993.

Even the Social Security Administration, *in the past extremely secretive with its information, is verifying records for driver's license bureaus.*

But crackdowns come at a price, privacy advocates say.

» Two articles appeared side by side in *Government Technology*, August 1995

Privacy Group Warns Congress

Congress should keep a cool head in the wake of the Oklahoma City tragedy, the Electronic Privacy Information Center (EPIC) wrote in a letter to Sen. Orrin Hatch (R–Utah), chairman of the Senate Judiciary Committee. The Clinton administration has been using the bombing to renew its request for encryption controls and other ways to prevent what it says is terrorist activity using the Internet for communications.

EPIC, a Washington group pushing computer privacy, urged Congress to take "careful and deliberate consideration of any proposal that would alter current guidelines for government investigation and monitoring of domestic political activity or the collection and use of personal information."

UK Opens National ID Card Debate

After months of rumors and press reports, the British Government announced plans for the introduction of a national ID card system. According to Prime Minister John Major, however, the plans are far from rigid, and the idea is still very much at a discussion state.

The UK has not had a national ID card system since 1952, when the wartime ID card system was scrapped. In a recent report, the government steered clear of a firm decision in favor of any one ID card proposal and, if anything, only serves to cloud the issue in the UK still further.

British opinion polls show that most people—up to 75 percent in one survey—now back the idea of national ID cards.

It never ceases to amaze me how people can become so deluded about something when all the current evidence is so readily available, in addition to the historical evidence in the case of the British.

» *U.S. News & World Report,* October 2, 1995, "The Road Worriers: Can Electronic Tolls Be a Tool for Big Brother?"

Imagine driving from Maine to Maryland virtually nonstop, breezing through hundreds of miles of turnpikes and bridges, never stopping at a tollbooth. This traveler's dream is actually a step closer to reality. The governors of Connecticut, Delaware, Maine, Maryland, Massachusetts, New Hampshire, New Jersey, New York, Pennsylvania, Rhode Island, and Vermont agreed this month to work toward setting up a multistate system of using ETC—electronic toll collection.

. . . The crucial issue, says Phil Agre, communications professor at the University of California at San Diego, "is whether the systems capture individually identifiable information"—that is, information that might identify drivers. Besides raking in tolls, transportation departments also can suck up tons of personal information about a traveler, including driver's license data, license plate number, destination, highway speed, vehicle identification, and time of day of travel.

Anonymous? Who controls this information? Will it be sold or merged into other databases available to insurance companies, credit bureaus, marketers, and law–enforcement agencies? [Author's note: There's another one of those rhetorical questions.] The opportunities for mischief are enormous. . . .

» November 2, 1995, *Kansas City Star,* "FBI seeks extensive wiretap plans: Submitted proposal calls for upgraded monitoring system" (this article originated in the *New York Times*). *Look out . . . Big Brother is getting bigger!*

The FBI has proposed a wiretapping system that would give law enforcement officials the capacity to monitor simultaneously as many as one out of every 100 phone lines in some high crime areas of the country.

Such a surveillance ability would *vastly exceed the needs* of law enforcement officials around the country, who in recent years have conducted an annual average of fewer than 850 *court-authorized* wiretaps—or fewer than one in every 174,000 phone lines. [Author's note: "Court-authorized" is the key phrase here . . . there is no way of knowing how many *unauthorized* taps are conducted by the ATF, IRS, FBI, CIA, Secret Service, *et al ad nauseam*.]

The plan, which needs congressional approval for financing, would still require a court warrant to conduct wiretaps.

Generally, FBI officials contend that an advanced, high-capacity monitoring system will be necessary as more of modern life—and crime—takes place as voice or computer conversations over digital phone lines.

On digital lines, communications are transmitted in electronic pulses represented by the 1s and 0s of computer code. Such communications are harder to monitor than with the old-fashioned analog lines in which conversations are transmitted as electronic signals corresponding to audible sound waves.

An FBI spokesman declined to elaborate on the need for such an expansion of its wiretapping abilities.

"The full implementation is absolutely essential for law enforcement and public safety," said Mike Kortan, an FBI spokesman in Washington. "We are in ongoing discussions with the communications industry. Therefore, it would be inappropriate to comment further at this point."

The plan was published in the *Federal Register* on Oct. 16, but has not drawn much attention yet outside law enforcement and industry circles. It is the first comprehensive outline by the FBI of the surveillance capabilities it will require under the Digital Telephony Act that President Clinton signed in 1994.

Do you recall our discussion earlier in this book about Big Brother wanting a key to the "back door" so they could override any encryption you might use on your communications and Internet use to ensure privacy as you conduct your business transactions? Remember the Clipper chip . . . and the big bill they tried to stick on the telephone companies (which ultimately got stuck on the taxpayers) to develop a way they could quickly and with great ease eavesdrop on conversations on the new fiber optic systems? Well, there has been no announcement as yet, but I give you my guarantee . . . *this is all wrapped up together somehow!*

And an article has appeared entitled "Automated FAA Certifications?"

> The Federal Aviation Administration is exploring the possibility of using an automated system to collect and validate the information needed before issuing pilot certificates and ratings. The new Airman Certification and Rating Application (ACRA) system would use a DataCard with an *embedded computer chip* [smart card] to record the applicant's information . . . and transmit it, along with the applicant's digital signature, to the Oklahoma City Airman Certification Branch for processing. The DataCards, more impressive than the current flimsy paper certificates, resemble thick credit cards and feature a color photograph and bit–mapped signature of the applicant. According to FAA officials demonstrating the application process at the EAA Fly–In at Oshkosh, the data chip on the card has the capacity to store a variety of additional information about the cardholder.

Americans and Europeans are not alone . . . the whole world is going cashless (just like Revelation 13 says it will).

This documentation could go on indefinitely, but I will end it here and make brief mention at this point of each of the special subjects to which I referred earlier in this chapter.

EBT (ELECTRONIC BENEFITS TRANSFER)

As the title implies, these are some form of government benefits which are now, or soon will be, dispensed by electronically transferring the funds, food stamps, Social Security checks, welfare assistance, etc., directly into an account in your name, which you may access by way of a smart card to be issued to you. At the moment, individual programs are handled separately, but studies are well underway to determine how they may be combined onto only one card. Many states and a number of federal programs currently use this system, and many more will soon follow. Here are excerpts from just a couple of the articles.

» May 1994, *Personal Identification News,* "Vice President Announces National EBT Strategy"

> **Eight–Point Plan and Nine–State Prototype Outlined in Official Ceremony**
>
> Vice President Gore officially embraced a national strategy for the widespread adoption of Electronic Benefits Transfer . . . saying, "I am firmly committed to making this happen."
>
> EBT, the card–based delivery of a wide range of benefits in social service programs, may eventually encompass over 31 million cardholders and $120 billion of payments. The program has become one of the hottest initiatives in the Federal government's efforts to reinvent itself. . . .

» April 1995, *Automatic ID News,* "NJ grocer installs online debit card reader for food stamp transactions": "Twin County grocers became the first grocery store chain to install integrated card readers that can process food stamps, credit, and debit card transactions for the Families First electronic benefits transfer (EBT) system.

MOTOR–VOTER–WORKER

Not to be outdone by the Postal Service, which claims it can issue 100,000 ID cards on very short notice, the directors of the state departments of motor vehicles are meeting with each other and representatives of the federal agencies to discuss the feasibility of tying your driving, voting, and working privileges all together on one identification card—your driver's license (managed by the state DMVs), since the driver's license currently is recognized as the ID of choice in all states. In fact, if you don't drive, the DMV will issue you an official "ID card" so you can cash checks, check into hotels, rent things, etc. This proposed system is referred to as "Motor–Voter–Worker," which is really just another way of saying "National ID Card."

You may be familiar with the term "Motor–Voter." It is a phrase that was coined to describe the process of registering a person to vote at the same time they are issued a driver's license. Now it is proposed to link the system with the Social Security Administration (SSA), as well, using the SSA as a clearinghouse for the comprehensive driver's license, to verify that all the information is correct. Like I said, no matter who ends up issuing it, it is still nothing more than a national ID card.

As early as 1991 the state of California DMV issued information to its offices statewide about the new style of license that would be issued in the future. It would be plasticized and "similar to a credit card in size, thickness, and consistency." The important thing to note from this memo is that the "new process involves capturing and storing the applicant's photo, fingerprint, and signature in digitized form, along with the application data, on a cassette." The cassette will then be used to produce the card/license and to create a centralized database containing all this information for future retrieval, display, or exchange.

The importance of this information lies in the fact that everything is digitized, which is a prerequisite for later moving us into syringe–implantable biochip technology. Eventually, this information will be linked together in one giant database; at present, twelve states already are in it.

INSPASS

INSPASS ostensibly was developed for the convenience and expediency of the frequent international traveler. It is a combination of a

smart card and biometrics (hand geometry). *Business Week* (May 1, 1994) describes it this way:

A Better Passport: The Human Hand

Fed up with waiting in long passport lines when you get back from an overseas flight? If you're one of the nearly 10 million passengers who returned home last year through John F. Kennedy or Newark International Airports, the U.S. Immigration and Naturalization Service is offering a way to zip you through. You won't even have to show your passport.

The INS Passenger Accelerated Service System (INSPASS) allows you to use an electronic hand reader to verify that you are who you say you are. The key to the quick ID review is the human hand. Like fingerprints, every hand pattern is unique. The INS digitally captures the design of a participant's hand and embeds it on a wallet–size white plastic card, which the traveler carries. Readers located in INSPASS kiosks at arrival terminals then can identify the person by matching the print on the card against his or her hand laced palm down on the machine. [Author's note: This is the *right* hand you must insert into the reader.]

The program is open to all U.S. citizens and most Canadians, Japanese, and Western Europeans. Expansion to more international airports is anticipated.

PRESSING TOWARD THE "MARC"

The prototype for the national ID card is already being used by the U.S. military. The MARC card (**M**ulti–technology **A**utomated **R**eader **C**ard) is a smart card now being issued by the Department of Defense (DoD) to military personnel. This is not just one of those "rumors"; it has been occurring for quite some time and is fully documented in this chapter (see sample on previous page).

This smart card uses several information–storage media: a standard 3-of-9 barcode, magnetic stripe, embossed data, printed information (including a digital photograph), and an Integrated Circuit (IC) computer chip.

The combination of several media on one device gives the MARC its unique versatility—it can interface with a variety of technologies and systems. The DoD initiated the MARC project several years ago to provide itself with the ability to instantly track and control all U.S. military personnel worldwide. It is a prototype for the national ID card which probably will be issued to every U.S. citizen as we slide ever closer toward biochip implantation.

The MARC card's IC will be used by the DoD to store and manage all your personal data, both prior to and during your military service. It will be used to manage all medical information on all military personnel worldwide, first individual records on an individual's own card, then downloaded into the mainframe computer's enormous database. It will store (and update as needed) all personal data about the cardholder, i.e., legal information, family information, educational background, police record, religious background—everything you would expect to find on a highly detailed job resumé, *and then some!*

Think of the MARC as your ever–so–enhanced dog tags. The DoD considers one of its most important functions to be the ability to continually identify and track the location of the holder—worldwide—at all times. On certain bases, the MARC has already replaced the meal card. It is keeping track of meals eaten, and without it you don't eat on base! . . . or buy food or other goods at the base exchange. Without the card, you are denied access to treatment in military medical facilities.

The DoD and civilian project coordinators presently are evaluating the MARC card for use in paying personnel (just like the EBT cards). The MARC will be linked to the electronic banking system and the military person can kiss his cash goodbye—all financial transactions will go through a computerized banking system. Using their "captive audience" as guinea pigs, the government will work out the bugs, then move to issuing the MARC to **all** military personnel. From there, it is just a short hop to issuing them for all U.S. civilians.

An Information Paper has been prepared by Lt. Cmdr. Michael D. Sashin at the Pentagon, reporting the results and personnel responses concerning the use of the MARC. Hawaii's Channel 4 TV News (January 5, 1995) did an interview with military personnel espousing the great convenience of the MARC, the reduction in paperwork, etc.

The *1995 Advanced Card and Identification Technology Sourcebook* had this to say about the MARC: "The first 20,000 of over 300,000 MARC cards were issued to soldiers and their dependents in Hawaii in late 1994. . . . The cards are truly multipurpose cards used in force readiness, cafeteria, logistics, and personnel applications. . . . The cards are truly multifunction cards used for health insurance, medical records, small purchases from PXs and cafeterias, skills inventories, equipment sign–out, and an increasing number of related uses."

April 11, 1995, Gemplus issued a press release:

Gemplus Receives a 60,000–Microprocessor Card Order

Gemplus Card International Corp. announced today the receipt of a 60,000–microprocessor card order to supply cards to the Department of Defense. The Gemplus MCOS16K EEPROM cards are being supplied as a part of the Department of Defense's AIT contract. . . . MARC . . . cards will be issued to military personnel in Oahu, Hawaii, to test the concept of multiple applications and technologies on a single card.

"We are optimistic that the MARC card concept will be rolled out DoD–wide. . . . Gemplus is also providing the Gemplus Pocket Reader to the MARC program." The goal of the test is to develop a joint military services multimedia tool . . . and to demonstrate the feasibility of *complete DoD implementation.*

They also were issued to the troops dispatched to Haiti, with similar success.

In the January 25, 1994, edition of *Current News* (published from the Pentagon) there appeared an article titled "National Health Plan Is Tracked," in support of smart cards worldwide, the MARC in particular: "The use of MARC as the DoD's "smart card" for patient care and tracking follows closely with National efforts to define universal health benefits and access to health care using smart card technologies. The National Smart Card Forum [Author's note: described fully early in this chapter] . . . was attended by several DoD representatives. A significant interaction . . . created an extremely worthwhile alliance between commercial an government interests."

Whether or not that could be considered a truly "worthwhile alliance" probably would upon just whom you asked! I don't much believe in coincidences, so I surely find it amazing that when the implantable biochip technology replaces the DoD's present MARC/smart card technology, the name of the device still will be the **MARC.** Could the military's new MARC be used as the final sales gimmick to condition society into readily accepting the evil "MARC of the beast" when it finally arrives?

In the book *Revolution* (Harcourt Brace Jovanovich, 1988) by Martin Anderson, whose newspaper articles we have referenced much throughout this book, he relates an experience that occurred during the Reagan administration. It was another immigration problem, and the proposed solution was the same—a national ID card. Here is how Anderson describes the incident.

. . . One day in 1981, the attorney general came to present his border–control plan—for reasons he thought were good—to the president and his cabinet. Attorney General Smith was a patrician lawyer from Los Angeles who was smart and able, and he had done his homework very well with other members of the cabinet. Smith was Reagan's former personal lawyer and held his trust and confidence. He was seated, in accordance with long tradition, almost directly across the table from President Reagan, speaking directly to him.

I was seated a couple of feet behind the attorney general, in one of the soft leather seats along the back wall that were reserved for senior White House staff, again in accordance with long tradition. I could see the back of Smith's head, nodding slowly up and down, as his agile brain directed the flow of the flawless, brilliant presentation. It was working. As he moved on from point to point, the members of the cabinet were becoming persuaded. The national identification system was described simply as upgrading the social security cards to make them counterfeit–proof. Not a single objection. It all went down smoothly. A few minutes later Smith was through. He stopped an I knew he was smiling. The president looked up and around the room to see if anyone had any comments. I knew there weren't going to be any. The subject was complex. Nobody else in the cabinet had spent much time on it. And Smith's presentation was very, very good.

So I raised my hand.

I knew I was breaking an unwritten rule, the rule that says senior staff members may sit in on cabinet meetings but they are not to speak unless spoken to. But in the second or two I had to think about it I reasoned that I did not want to be part of the administration that foisted a national identity card on Americans, especially when most of the cabinet seemed to be quite unaware of what they were doing. The worst that could happen to me was to be fired, and if I were fired I would have to go back to sunny California, which didn't seem like a bad prospect at the time.

After a few seconds went by there were no comments coming from the cabinet and the president noticed me. I guess it was pretty obvious, my hand was raised directly over the back of the attorney general's head. He simply said, "Yes, Marty."

And I began to speak. One reason I loved Reagan was his casual neglect of unnecessary protocol and formality. He liked to do things that worked. I assume he figured I had something worthwhile to say or I wouldn't have raised my hand. Anyway, the room grew quiet and a lot of eyes, some topped by slightly raised eyebrows, focused on me. I knew this wasn't the time for a longwinded, theoretical critique of national identity cards, so I decided to try humor, leavened with a little shock.

"Mr. President," I said, "one of my concerns about the national identity card is that the Office of Management and Budget has estimated that it could cost several billions of dollars to produce a counterfeit–proof social security card for everyone." The statement didn't seem to make much of an impact. By that time a billion dollars or two didn't bother anyone in the cabinet.

"I would like to suggest another way that I think is a lot better. It's a lot cheaper. It can't be counterfeited. It's very lightweight, and impossible to lose. It's even waterproof."

"All we have to do is tattoo an identification number on the inside of everybody's arm."

There were several gasps around the table. A couple of the cabinet members looked as if they had been slapped. No one said anything for a long time.

The first to speak was James Watts, secretary of the interior.

His thick eyeglasses sparkled as his booming voice rolled across the table, "Why, it sounds to me that you are talking about the mark of the Beast. That's terrible."

Most of the people seated around the cabinet table looked puzzled. Except for the president, few of them knew that the mark of the Beast was a biblical reference to Revelation 13:16–18. But now they wee alert. Watt was an astute politician, especially knowledgeable about the political thicket populated by right–wing Republicans. You could see the questioning looks come over their faces, each one crinkling and moving in his or her own special way. Nobody seemed to know quite what to say. First the image of Nazi concentration camps and now the mark of the Beast. What next?

The attorney general started to shift back and forth in his chair, getting ready to quell the incipient mutiny. But President Reagan cut him off. The president spread his hands forward across the polished surface of the table, leaned back and looked directly at the attorney general. Smiling broadly, he joked, "Maybe we should just brand all the babies."

For about ten seconds everybody laughed and smiled, and that was the end of the national identification card for 1981.

Somehow, I don't think we will continue to be so lucky. Remember, it has been suggested by some that a chip be put behind the ear in the maternity ward . . . and, trust me, they weren't making a joke!

There's another "coincidence" of which I'm not too fond— Chapter 666 of Public Law, dated August 10, 1939 (it's a matter of public record—just look it up), was called the "Social Security Act Amendments of 1939." Since all this national identity business was spawned and implemented by the Social Security Act, somehow I seriously doubt the "coincidence" theory.

And when it comes to conditioning us (or as I prefer, desensitizing us), the government doesn't have a corner on the market. The New World Order crowd has permeated every avenue of our daily lives, not the least of which is the media and entertainment business. I have quoted enough newspaper and magazine articles throughout this book that the liberal bias of the media has been more than proven to my satisfaction. But the entertainment industry is at the same time covert and blatantly overt in their messages. Whenever they present a Christian or other devout religious person, they are always represented as anything from just a weird kook and "nerdy," all the way to downright evil; and their evil acts are done, of course, because God wants them to be a serial killer, or He told them to commit some awful act. Usually the most heinous individuals are portrayed as "Christians" or "born again." This type of conditioning affects people . . . it's sort of like advertising: they say it has no real effect on people, but if they really believe that, why are they wasting all those millions of dollars every day to convince us to buy their pet product or service?

It used to be that the message was very subtle, but no longer. Science fiction used to be "good, clean fun" and a way to just let your imagination run toward how technology might be in the future. If you live just a few years longer, you usually find out that what was science fiction technology in the past is sitting on your kitchen counter today, for example, microwave ovens. Hollywood has put out movies like *The Fortress* and *Demolition Man*. And there is a television program called "Babylon 5," on which they all have their communicators implanted in their right hands. This is the same communicator they use when they want to access some of their "credits" (cyberspace money), identify themselves, make phone calls to earth (or Mars colony or wherever), be tracked/located by "the bridge," and a myriad of other functions. And I wonder how they came up with the name of "Babylon" for their new station in space. I'm sure that most of you are familiar with the connotation of that name. Co-incidence? I doubt it, but maybe I'm just suspicious.

Whether or not they conspired in the physical realm to desensi-tize the public in this way, that is what they are accomplishing. And if it is not an intentional conspiracy, I see only one other alternative . . . it must be a spiritual conspiracy. Now, doesn't that sound just like the devil . . . by the time the technology (which is already here) is developed to the stage of becoming the mark of the beast, the teen-agers who have grown up on this stuff will be adults, and they won't even blink, much less resist, when they are offered this "wonderful, new technology."

The only answer for a spiritual problem is a spiritual solution. We must be diligent now, even as we watch programs of this nature with our youngsters, to be careful to point out these things and ac-quaint them with biblical prophecy, especially Revelation 13. We must introduce them to Jesus Christ . . . being a born-again believer in Jesus is the only escape from what is to come.

But we still have a little legislative ground to cover before we can move on to the chapter on syringe-implantable biochips.

STATEMENT OF
U.S. REPRESENTATIVE STEPHEN HORN

Stephen Horn (R–CA) testified before the Subcommittee on Immi-gration, Senate Committee on the Judiciary, on May 10, 1995. Since this is a matter of public record, and you may obtain copies if you desire, I will be selecting only a few excerpts for this chapter (as I will with the Marshall Rickert testimony, reported further below).

> . . . America is the only industrialized country without a national identification system. It is time we looked seriously at the "func-tional equivalent" of such a system. [Author's note: I wonder if he ever considered the possibility that this is why America is number

one in the world, that the majority of the other nations are referred to as "third world countries," and that so many people want to immigrate here, even if they have to do it illegally.] . . . Bold measures had to be taken. . . . The House Subcommittee on Government Management focused its March hearing on the Jordan Commission's most debated recommendation—setting up a nationwide employment verification registry. . . . The Commission's national computer registry makes sense. . . . We already have, in state motor vehicle databases, substantial information which could be linked together . . . shared with Federal agencies . . . linking together the various databases. . . . I would propose standards for counterfeit- and tamper-resistant cards and for a positive link between documents and their bearers [biometrics] . . . for positive personal identification.

On the same date, verbal and written testimony was presented by Marshall Rickert, Motor Vehicle Administrator, State of Maryland, on behalf of the American Association of Motor Vehicle Administrators (AAMVA).

The AAMVA represents state and provincial officials in the United States and Canada. . . . The Association's programs encourage uniformity and reciprocity among the states and provinces, and liaison with other levels of government and the private sector. [Author's note: "Liaison with the private sector" means they sell for commercial purposes anything in their files on you or anyone else that anybody wants to buy!]

There has been much talk of a national identification card. The Oklahoma disaster supports such a concept and I would submit that such a system is already in place . . . the driver's license.

. . . The final program draft should be adopted by . . . August. Once approved, the working group will begin developing training materials and procedures to assist members in implementing the model program.

A key element of the program is the development of a unique identifier which *will allow a person to be tracked throughout North America* [biometrics]. AAMVA is recommending that the social security numnber serve as the unique identifier and that the number be verified through the Social Security Administration prior to issuance.

The Social Security Administration published a notice in the March 29, 1995, *Federal Register,* of their *intent to allow the motor vehicle administrators (MVAs) access to their computer system (SSAs) for the purpose of verifying the identity of drivers license/ID card applicants.*

The Association is also taking steps to obtain electronic access to the Immigration and Naturalization Services computer system. . . . INS has been mandated by Congress to share information . . . in its computer files with criminal justice agencies for enforcement of criminal laws. *Such access should be extended to MVAs*

. . . The Association developed a Drivers License Reciprocity (DLR) program . . . to electronically transfer information regarding automobile, motorcycle, and light–weight truck operators. . . . The Association is developing standards for the transmission of digitized images and use of bar codes and magnetic stripes.

. . . [Presently] nothing requires a person to provide his/her social security number. . . . To ensure state compliance with many of these issues, federal requirements/sanctions must be effected. . . . Sanctions should be severe enough to discourage fraud. . . .

L.U.C.I.D.™ 2000

As I have pointed out previously, prior to this time in history a system of computerized global control was not technically possible. *All that has changed!* Such a system is presently being installed right before our eyes, as it were, though few are aware of it. Its secular designers have named it "L.U.C.I.D.™ 2000." In my opinion, L.U.C.I.D.™ 2000, in concert with the Internet, will be the means by which we ultimately will lose control over both our privacy and our finances, completing the final link in our electronic enslavement.

Although you may not have heard of it, L.U.C.I.D.™ Net (as it is frequently called) is an extremely complex and sophisticated international system of networked, computerized identification databases that will transfer information on us digitally and instantaneously anywhere in the world. The worldwide Internet will serve as the electronic medium through which future local, national, and international cyber–bartering must pass. This global cashless society is being encouraged by business, government, and the media. You will be spending "e–money," that is, if you have the proper "mark" to do any buying or selling.

WORLD CITIZENSHIP?

To conclude this chapter on our identity crisis, I want to include some evidence that it doesn't stop at our own borders . . . they want us to be good citizens of the world. And if you think that's just a figure of speech, think again. There is an organization called the World Service Authority, based in Washington, D.C., who is ready to "sign you up" right now . . . in writing . . . on paper! And they've been around for awhile—they were founded in 1954. When I made inquiry about their organization, they promptly mailed me an application form "for registration as a citizen of the World Government of World Citizens."

Apparently, joining entitles you to all kinds of documents. "All World Service Authority documents—including the WSA passport, *World Identity Card,* World Citizen Card, and World Birth Certificate are in seven languages: Arabic, Chinese, English, Esperanto, French, Russian, and Spanish." They also issue "International Exit Visas and International Residence Permits." In the case of the latter, "only registered World Citizens may apply."

Here is some of what they have to say:

> You are already a World Citizen by birth and in fact. By registering as a citizen of the World Government of World Citizens—which does not require renouncing any lesser allegiances [Author's note: Referring to my patriotism for America as "lesser allegiances" makes me very hot under the collar, as by now you may have concluded about me on your own.]—you are joining a fast–growing, sovereign constituency which has committed itself to establishing social, economic, political, and ecological justice throughout the world in accordance with the fundamental moral codes of all major religions [Author's note: Can you say *New Age?*], with basic

human rights and with scientific techniques of organization.

As a registered World Citizen, you have the opportunity to help evolve just and democratic World Laws through the World Syntegrity Project, launched July 1993, a unique, ongoing strategy to evolve a democratic world constitutional process valid for the next millennium. [Author's note: I don't know about you, but I plan to spend my next millennium under the thousand–year reign of peace of Jesus Christ! And as rapidly as things are progressing, I don't think it will be too many more years.]

The World Government of World Citizens in fact is already functioning in representing you and your needs on a global level. It issues World Passports, World Citizen Cards, World Identity Cards, World Birth Certificates, World Marriage Certificates (all in seven languages), and World Postal Stamps. These represent you human rights and are mandated by the Universal Declaration of Human Rights, proclaimed by the General Assembly of the United Nations 10 December 1948.

I should have seen it coming . . . there's the tie to the U.N. Sometimes it pays to just skip to the bottom line—but don't do that yet. All the groundwork has been laid, and it's time to move on to the most important chapter in the book, biochip technology and where it's leading us. So, save "The Bottom Line—A World in Disorder" (my summary) until you have learned all about biochip implantation—present and future.

CHAPTER EIGHT

BIOCHIP IMPLANTS & RFID TECHNOLOGY: THE MARK OF THE NEW WORLD ORDER?

We are not part of a military program to implant tags in humans. In fact, we are not part of *any* plan to implant tags in humans, but a glass encapsulated animal tag only begs the question of the definition of what type of animal, and if that definition is "a mammal," certainly it would include man. Are humans running around somewhere on the globe with tags—RFID tags—implanted in them? Yes! Absolutely, conclusively so.

—Donald G. Small, Hughes Identification Devices
Excerpted from the video *Mark of the New World Order*

Let me begin this chapter with a categorical disclaimer and a warning to those action-oriented individuals who might choose to react radically toward any of the companies mentioned in this book, and in this chapter on biochips and other RFID technology in particular.

I wish to make it *very clear* at this point that *nowhere in this book* am I accusing any manufacturer of radio frequency identification devices (RFID) of working directly for the devil in helping him bring about biochip ID implants! Such accusations are absurd!

Most officers and employers of biochip transponder–producing companies are very fine people who simply believe that they are helping to advance identification technology that one day will benefit society. Most are completely unaware of the New World Order crowd's ulterior plan eventually to use this technology for identifying, numbering, and controlling people.

Therefore, I wish to state clearly that this book was written to expose *Satan's SPIRITUAL PLAN* to fulfill the Bible's "last days" or "end times" prophecies, rather than to accuse any particular RFID manufacturing company, officer, or employee of being involved in a diabolical plan to harm or enslave anyone. I hope I have made myself clear in this regard. Now, let's get on with some very important information.

THE MARK OF THE NEW WORLD ORDER: MARK OF THE BEAST—666

For centuries Christians have speculated about the concept of the mark of the beast as described in Revelation 13:16–18. A few liberal theologians have suggested that the mark of the beast in the hand or forehead is not a literal concept at all. They have said—and some still say—that the mark is an allegorical, or perhaps even mythological concept. Other Christians have said the mark is nothing more than a spiritual concept revolving around Catholicism and the pope. More recently, Christian fundamentalists have pondered over whether or not barcode technology eventually would be used as the *literal* mark of the beast in the right hand or forehead, since interpreting scripture literally is always the best first approach. This subject seems to confuse many people when it really should not. It is quite easy to understand, given modern technology and proper interpretation of the original language of the text.

Allow me to put to rest all further speculation by making the following statement: It is my well–researched opinion that the mark of the beast, as related in Scripture, is *absolutely literal*. Soon, all people on earth will be coerced into accepting a mark in their right hand or forehead. I am convinced that it will be an injectable passive RFID transponder with a computer chip—a *literal* injection with a *literal* electronic biochip "mark." Exactly as Scripture says, without the mark, people will not be able to buy or sell anything anywhere in the world. I believe that such an implanted identification mark *literally* will become Satan's mark of the beast, as we will discuss further in this chapter.

However, before proceeding further into microchip implant technology, we first need to spend a few moments analyzing the scriptural basis for my position.

"And he [the Antichrist beast] causeth all, both small and great, rich and poor, free and bond, to receive *a mark in their right hand,* or in their forehead: And that no man might buy or sell, save he that had *the mark,* . . . count the number of the beast: for it is the number of *a man* [the Antichrist]; and his number is *Six hundred threescore and six* [**666**]" (Rev. 13:16–18).

THE KING JAMES VERSION

Pay particular attention to the above scripture that says the mark will go *in*—not on—the right hand. This is the key to correct understanding of the technology that must be used to carry out its implementation. Nearly two thousand years ago, John the Revelator received a vision from God that no one on earth would be able to buy or sell in the "last days" without the devil's mark *in* his hand. To help you grasp an accurate understanding of this concept, let's examine the definition of the words that appeared in the *original Greek manuscripts* of the Bible in additional to secular dictionary sources.

The English word *mark* (*Strong's Exhaustive Concordance of the Bible,* No. 5480) is from the Greek word *charagma* (pronounced khar´-ag-mah). *Charagma* is connected by the *Expanded Vine's Expository Dictionary of New Testament Words* to *stigma, Strong's* No. 4742, in which *Strong's* references *stigma* back to the Greek word *stizo,* then defines *stizo* as follows: ". . . **to prick, stick, incise, or punch for recognition of ownership.** . . . Scar of service: **a mark.**"

This is perhaps the best definition of HOW the mark of the beast will be given to everyone. I think it is a clear picture of the identifier being placed into and under the skin . . . and for now, the technology that fills the bill is the biochip RFID transponder.

The secular *American College Dictionary* defines *mark* as: ". . . an impression upon anything, such as a line, cut, dent, stain, bruise, brand . . . an affixed or impressed device . . . a sign or token . . . a distinguishing feature . . . to put *a mark on for identification. . . .*"

It also defines *stigma* as: "A mark of disgrace or infamy; a stain or mark of reproach; a mark or sign of defect or degeneration; a mark on the skin; *a mark made* by a branding iron *on the skin of a criminal or slave.*"

Another secular reference, *Rodale's Synonym Finder,* lists the following synonyms for *mark*: ". . . cut, gash, scratch, slash, scar, pock, notch, chip, nick, pit, dent, impressions, bruise, sign, symbol, indication, *brand, identification; marking,* token. . . ."

By this time it ought to be obvious to anyone with an open, unbiased mind that the mark of the beast of the Antichrist will be used to *identify* those who are owned by him during the seven–year period known as the Great Tribulation. Without his mark of ownership in the skin of the right hand or forehead, no one on earth will be permitted to buy or sell anything. Remember, the Greek word *stizo* indicates that the mark will be *"pricked, stuck, incised, or punched"* into the skin "as recognition of ownership." Doesn't this sound incredibly close to having an ID microchip/biochip transponder the size of a grain of rice injected with a twelve–gauge hypodermic needle through and under the skin? Could this be merely a scientific coincidence . . . or could it be an exact fulfillment of "end times" scriptures, such as Revelation 13:16–18?

Think about it for a moment! Does this leave any room for other methods, such as barcodes or tattoos? You know what I think, but is there any evidence from secular sources within the media or identification industry that supports my convictions? The answer is a resounding, "Yes!" (probably the most profound of which is the quotation with which I began this chapter). In fact, there is such a deluge of evidence in the media and in industry brochures and news releases that I have had to omit the preponderance of the documentation because of space constraints.

Technological advances are pushing us rapidly toward this method of global identification, and it is my goal through the rest of this chapter to present you with overwhelming evidence from all possible sources that this event is not only on the horizon, but probably will occur during our lifetime.

COMPUTER CHIPS IN PEOPLE

Computer chips/biochips are already in use widely in animals and inanimate tracking protocols, but the question on everyone's mind is, "Can they do it in humans . . . or more important, *will they?*"

Popular Science (October 1994), in its "Computers & Software" column, printed an article titled "Future Watch: The Body Binary."

> Within the next ten years, we'll have miniature computers inside us to monitor and perhaps even control our blood pressure, heart rate, and cholesterol. Within 20 years, such computers will correct visual and hearing signals, making glasses and hearing aids obsolete.
>
> At least that's how Bertrand Cambou sees it. As director of technology for Motorola's Semiconductor Products in Phoenix, Cambou has been a part of the miniaturization of microprocessors and the development of wireless communication technologies. Both would have central roles in putting computers inside the human body.
>
> It's now possible, notes Cambou, to put the sensors, processors, and wireless radio frequency (RF) devices for an internal computer onto a single, tiny chip. The RF signaling would permit accurate readouts of vital statistics without attaching anything to—or drawing anything from—the body. Even more amazing, internal computers might enable the deaf to hear and the blind to see. A chip implanted on the optic nerve, for example, could correct defective images or simply transmit entire images to the nerve.
>
> The notion of putting computers inside the body may be more realistic than it sounds. "We are not aware of any current obstacles to the encapsulation and implanting of electronic devices within the body, and the transmission characteristics [of radio frequencies] through the body are well known," says Cambou.

Now if that doesn't qualify for an Oscar in the category of "We're only doing it for your own good," nothing will! And there is no question that technology will bring with it many benefits—we have never denied that point. Our concern is over the excess baggage the benefits bring with them, not the least of which is the loss of privacy, as all these new medical marvels will be tracked and monitored. And failure to do so brings hefty penalties and fines (read about the Safe Medical Devices Act described a few pages later).

Helping you see and hear better is only the beginning. The February 1, 1994, edition of the *Wall Street Journal* carried a frightening article headlined, "Nervy Scientists Move Toward Union of Living Brain Cells with Microchips." Below are excerpts.

> Researchers said they took a key first step toward creating electronic microchips that use living brain cells.
>
> The researchers they had learned how to place embryonic brain cells in desired spots on silicon or glass chips and then induce the brain cells to grow along desired paths. The scientists hope to be able within the next six to twelve months to get the brain cells, or neurons, to grow connections to each other that will crudely mimic the circuitry that neurons form in the brain.
>
> "I want to emphasize this is fundamental research," said biophysicist David L. Stenger of the Naval Research Laboratory in Washington, worried that the research might be misinterpreted as a fledgling effort to make an artificial brain.

And with good reason, I suspect. Their alleged purpose is for the development of better computer networks of artificial neurons. "It also may be possible to eventually make 'biochips' that drug makers could use to see if new compounds might interfere with, or perhaps enhance, functions like memory or learning." Your name doesn't have to be Frankenstein to see where that research is headed!

By March, the research was reported in a comprehensive article in *Defense News*. The headline read, "Naval Research Lab Attempts to Meld Neurons and Chips: Studies May Produce Army of 'Zombies.'" Before you read on, I think it would be appropriate to ask you to keep in mind, this *isn't* one of those "the aliens have landed" articles in the *National Inquirer.* Here are some excerpts:

> Battles of the future could be waged with genetically engineered organisms, such as rodents, whose minds are controlled by com-

puter chips engineered with living brain cells. . . .

Such a scenario could become reality within the next 15 years if research conducted at the Washington–based Naval Research Laboratory pays off, they said.

The research . . . grows living neurons on computer chips. . . .

"This technology that altars neurons could potentially be used on people to create zombie armies," Lawrence Korb, a senior fellow at the Brookings Institution, said March 16. [Author's note: In my opinion, Brookings is a New World Order think tank; therefore, this is quite an admission by Korb.]

"It sounds like science fiction, but science fiction is only 10 to 15 years ahead of [these kinds of] novel technologies," said Kyle Olson, vice president of the Chemical and Biological Arms Control Institute. . . .

The research has captured the attention of the U.S. intelligence community. [Author's note: No surprise there! Can you just imagine what the CIA, Armed Forces, FBI, NSA, etc., could do with perfected research of this nature?]

"Once this technology is proved, you could control a living species. . . . For all the desirable applications, it may have horrific application." . . .

In the near future, Navy scientists hope to create living neural computer networks that can learn. . . .

"This opens up whole new applications in bioelectronics, where you could use the memory on a [biological] chip, pop it into your head, and learn French." . . .

"This is a class case of military [research and development]. The door swings in two directions. You've got this Frankenstein-type weapon on one hand, and it can deal with problems of the human condition on the other," Olson added.

However, experts say it is unlikely that Pentagon officials would ever unleash genetically engineered soldiers on adversaries.

Now, doesn't that give you a sense of safety and assurance? When has the Pentagon ever given us cause for concern? Well, just ask the people who lived near the nuclear power plants who were intentionally subjected to released hazardous waste without their knowledge (because the researchers wanted to know what effect it would have on people) . . . and of whom more than half have died of cancer or other related diseases. Or ask the farmers near Rocky Mountain Arsenal in Colorado, after they finally found out why all their sheep were dropping dead. After all these years, the government has admitted being guilty of a limited number of such incidents, and has even made financial restitution in some cases. I am confident, however, that this is only the tip of the iceberg, and that we don't even have a clue as to the extent to which innocent Americans have been used as guinea pigs in some government experiment . . . not to mention military personnel who are guinea pigs in just about everything the government wants to try out before it foists it off on the masses.

In Winn Schwartau's book *Information Warfare*, he addresses this subject (p. 360).

> Futurists in the bioelectronic industry are looking at ways of merging conventional electronics with *living systems* to increase speed and density, and reduce power and heat in a new generation of information systems. Widespread commercial applications are not likely to come about for twenty years, but we inch towards such goals with pacemakers and remote triggered electrical stimulation for behavior control. [Author's note: Read further in this chapter, as well as the article "Walking Prisons," by Max Winkler (*The Futurist,* July–August 1993), about proposed methods for monitoring released sex offenders and child molesters.] This is about as personal as an information system can get. As information systems are embedded within the human body, the ethical and legal perplexities are only compounded. Will they make us think better and remember more? Or perhaps they will help postpone the aging process by optimizing the body's functions. . . . Or can they be used to manipulate and control the unwilling? Both.
>
> While biochips are on the horizon, direct man–computer communications is here now. The military calls them SQUIDs, or Super Quantum Interference Devices. SQUIDs are placed on or

near a subject's head to detect brainwave pattern activity. The SQUID and the subject learn from each other, so that when, say the pilot of a jet fighter thinks about arming and firing an air-to-air missile, it arms and fires. In the coming years SQUIDs will evolve and will be able to electronically read minds as Hollywood imagined in the Natalie Wood movie *Brainstorm*. When SQUIDs become reversible and can communicate thoughts and information right into the brain, that's when we really have to watch out.

In the future, the ultimate form of Information Warfare may prove to be the direct insertion of information into an adversary's brain from afar.... Can minds be forced to act in one manner or another or even to shut down by remote devices targeted at specific individuals? We're already examining the possibilities in research on nonlethal weaponry.

So, you see, RFID biochips to track vehicle and people movement seem to be "small potatoes" when compared with some of the other research and development on the drawing boards of some of our nation's leading labs and engineering departments (primarily military or government funded).

In the July 24, 1994, issue of *The New American*, William F. Jasper tells us about the kind of advice the Clinton administration received from the people with whom they chose to surround themselves. The article is titled "High-Tech Nightmare." Below are some excerpts:

The "smart card" is also a central feature of the Clinton "health care reform" program. However, some "Friends of Hillary" have even grander visions. Mary Jane England, MD, a member of the executive committee of the White House Project and president of the Washington Business Group on Health, a national outfit comprised of some of the nation's leading corporate welfare statists, is especially excited about the potential for implanting smart chips in your body. Addressing the 1994 IBM Health Care Executive Conference last March in Palm Springs, California, Dr. England said: "The Smart Card is a wonderful idea, but even better would be the capacity not to have a card, and I call it 'a chip in your ear,' that would actually access your medical records, so that no matter where you were . . . we would have some capacity to access that medical record. We need to go beyond the narrow conceptualization of the Smart Card and really use some of the technology that's out there. The worst thing we could do is put in place a technology that's already outdated, because all of you are in the process of building these systems. Now is the time to really think ahead. . . . I don't think that computerized, integrated medical records with a capacity to access through a chip in your ear is so far off and I think we need to think of these things."

Martin Anderson wrote a priceless article that appeared in the *Washington Times,* October 11, 1993, under the headline "High-tech national tattoo." Of course, he immediately recognized the proposed health security card as the *national identity card it truly is,* and after telling of the dangers inherent in such a system of tracking individuals and their daily activities, he gets right to the bottom line: What if you should lose it?

> . . . Can anyone who finds the card or who steals it get access to the information?
>
> There is another solution, although I hesitate to mention the idea because one of Mr. Clinton's White House aides may take it seriously.
>
> You see, there is an identification system made by the Hughes Aircraft Company that you can't lose. It's the syringe implantable transponder. According to promotional literature it is an "ingenious, safe, inexpensive, foolproof and permanent method of . . . identification using radio waves. A tiny microchip, the size of a grain of rice, is simply placed under the skin. It is so designed as to be injected simultaneously with a vaccination or alone."
>
> How does it work? Well, the "chip contains a 10-character alphanumeric identification code that is never duplicated. When a scanner is passed over the chip, the scanner emits a 'beep' and your . . . number flashes in the scanner's digital display."
>
> Sort of like a technological tattoo. . . . Of course, most Ameri-

cans will find a surgically implanted government microchip repugnant. At least for the foreseeable future, the use of this ingenious device will be confined to its current use: the tracking of dogs, cats, horses, and cattle.

But there is no difference in principle between being forced to carry a microchip in a plastic card in your wallet or in a little pellet in your arm. The principle that Big Brother has the right to track you is inherent in both. The only thing that differentiates the two techniques is a layer of skin.

Once you denigrate the idea of privacy, all kinds of innovative government controls are possible, things that didn't even occur to Aldous Huxley when he wrote his chilling novel, *Brave New World.*

The Bible tells us that in the *last days knowledge will increase, meaning that it will increase exponentially.* Anderson's article was written in 1993, and at this writing I can list a number of ways in which biochips are now used in humans, some in bracelets and anklets (early parole prisoners, Alzheimer's patients, 50,000–plus refugees housed at Guantanamo Bay Naval Station, and others) and some inside the body (mandatory in body parts implants effective August 29, 1993), and allegedly in some military personnel used as guinea pigs in testing the technology. We've come a long way, baby!

Although the Bible states the implant will be in the right hand or forehead, and even though most of the biometric technology is using "right hand" verification, a number of people still seem to like the spot behind the ear. The July 1995 edition of *Popular Science* carried an article called "E–Money." Although it was primarily about smart cards, digital cash, and the electronic cashless society, Ronald Kane, vice president of Cubic Corp., stated: "If we had our way, we'd implant a chip behind everyone's ear in the maternity ward." In lieu of being able to do that, "the next best thing is giving everyone a card."

As early as April 2, 1989, the *Marin Independent Journal* (Marin County, California) carried an in–depth article titled "Future shocker: 'Biochip—Science fiction technology here.'" Writer Teresa Allen carefully outlined the whole plan, including scanning your hand (with the biochip) after you scan your purchases, and the strong aversion people have to being implanted. And even though written five years prior to the revelation of the experiments on living brain tissue, it alludes to such technology by stating: "Within 15 to 20 years, the regular microchip will be outclassed by a biochip made out of living protein."

THE SAFE MEDICAL DEVICES ACT

Legislation has been enacted, effective August 29, 1993, known as the Safe Medical Devices Act, for the express purpose of tracking and identifying medical implant devices. Failure to comply can bring severe civil penalties and heavy fines on manufacturers ($15,000 to $1 million). The Safe Medical Devices Acts (Public Law 101–629) was signed into law by President Bush on November 18, 1990. It was published in the *Federal Register* dated Monday, August 16, 1993, Part IV Department of Health and Human Services, 21 CFR Part 821.

Manufacturers must adopt a method of tracking devices that are permanently implanted in a human, and they are required to conduct post–market surveillance for certain devices, including permanent implants. The tracking device of choice seems to be the Hughes RFID biochip, which will contain information about the implanted device, its manufacturer, date, model, name of patient, patient's doctor doing the procedure, etc.

Below are excerpts from a Medical Device Bulletin that was published October 1993.

FDA Issues Final Rule on Manufacturer Tracking of Certain Medical Devices

The Food and Drug Administration has issued a final rule designed to protect patients with critical medical implants and life–supporting devices if malfunctions arise.

The rule . . . requires manufacturers of 17 implants and 5 other medical devices to keep track of patients who receive the devices so they can be contacted if problems develop that would threaten patients.

Manufacturers will be required to have systems to track certain products from the manufacturer through the distribution chain to the patient. . . .

. . . Manufacturers will be required to update the information in the tracking system and to audit the system twice a year for the first three years and once a year thereafter.

No specific method of tracking is required. . . .

Medical devices to be tracked are:

» Vascular graft implants
» Ventricular bypass devices
» Implantable pacemaker pulse generators
» Cardiovascular permanent pacemaker electrodes
» Annulopasty rings
» Replacement heart valves
» Automatic implantable cardioverter/defibrillators
» Tracheal implants
» Implanted cerebellar stimulators
» Implanted diaphragmatic/phrenic nerve stimulators
» Implantable infusion pumps
» Breathing frequency monitors
» Continuous ventilators
» DC-defibrillators and paddles
» Silicone inflatable breast implants
» Silicone gel–filled breast implants
» Silicone gel–filled testicular implants
» Silicone gel–filled chin implants
» Silicone gel–filled angel chik reflux valves
» Electromechanical infusion pumps
» Jaw implants
» Inflatable penile implants

Other devices will be subject to tracking in the future, as necessary to protect the public health.

It is my understanding that future devices may be added to this list simply by publishing that intent in the *Federal Register.*

Here are some other pertinent questions.

Who has primary responsibility for the tracking of a medical device? The manufacturer. Does the regulation require a specific method of tracking? No. Is a manufacturer's tracking method subject to FDA inspection and audit? Yes. Routine inspections will include a review and audit of tracking systems. FDA will inspect tracking systems at any other time that it feels necessary. Does a patient have the right to refuse to participate in tracking? Yes. A patient may refuse to have their device(s) tracked. Such refusals should be documented and be provided to the manufacturer by the product, model, and serial number. The manufacturer must maintain these records for the useful life of the products. Must a final distributor *obtain a written consent from the patient in order for the patient's tracking information to be released* to the manufacturer? **No.** The regulation does not require that a patient give written consent to have a device tracked or to release their identity to the manufacturer.

In the August 17, 1994, edition of the *Los Angeles Times,* an article by Kathleen Wiegner appeared under the headline "Giving Surgical Implants IDs." Here is what it had to say:

At least 6 million medical devices a year worldwide are surgically implanted in people—everything from breast implants to chin implants, vascular grafts and penile implants. Years later, if a patient visits a doctor because of problems, medical information such as the manufacturer of the implant or the name of the surgeon may not be available.

No problem, if the patient's implant carries an implant of its own—a microchip on which all relevant information has been encoded. Called SmartDevice, the chip, which is about the size of a grain of rice, is manufactured by Hughes Identification Devices, a subsidiary of Hughes Aircraft Co. In the event of complications with an implant, a doctor could retrieve the information from the chip using a "gun" that emits a radio beam. The gun operates in much the same way that decoders in supermarkets decipher bar coding. The information on the chip would also be recorded on a computer–linked global registry.

LipoMatrix Inc., 33% owned by the biotechnology company

Collagen Corp. of Palo Alto, has been issued a patent for the use of SmartDevice in medical devices and has begun putting them into its soybean oil breast implants. SmartDevices are already in . . . LipoMatrix breast implants tested since October on women in Britain, Italy, and Germany.

Stanford University Medical Center will conduct a study on the breast implant chips starting in September.

There you have it! Biochips implanted in the medical implants headed for human bodies for the express purpose of tracking you. And they will be aided by a "global registry" (just another tentacle of the octopus network of databases linked together so the New World Order crowd can keep tabs on everyone). These body parts, containing the same biochip currently being implanted in pets and livestock, will be tracked globally, as the FDA mandates that the manufacturer must be able to reach the implant carrier in ten days or less, or pay the consequences of violation of the Safe Medical Devices Act.

Even Oprah Winfrey has considered the ramifications of biochip implants on her popular talk show. In a program on February 25, 1994, in a show titled "Your Life in the Year 2000," Winfrey and her guests had been discussing futuristic technology, including virtual reality games, smart cards, and the cashless society, never being lost anymore because of the automatic highways, and other subjects, when one guest announced, "We're going to have little chips implanted. You'll be able to track a child that disappears and get them back globally . . . because we'll all have our little memory chip." To which the other guest promptly responded, "I hope not. . . . I don't want a chip in me."

To that I say a big "Amen!"

MINIATURIZATION OF COMPUTER CHIP TECHNOLOGY

Smaller and mightier is the goal of the producers of computer chips and other electronics. Make it hold more, make it do more, and make it fit on the head of a pin? Not as farfetched as you might think. In July 1993, *Popular Science* carried an article titled "Integrated Circuits:

Chips Reach the Atomic Level." We tend to think that something has gotten as small as it possibly can get . . . then someone announces that they have shrunk it again. I'm not sure when we will be "maxed out" when it comes to downsizing the hardware. I suppose it will be when it gets so small they can no longer create tools small enough to manufacture it, but then they will just change directions and figure out how to make the present size hold more capability and operate more efficiently (see above reference to merging living brain cells with manmade chips).

Sematech Corp. announced in 1993 that they had developed a device 1/200th the size of a hair (0.35 micron), and they are working on smaller chips—only 0.10 micron in size. Sematech is a consortium of prominent developers and producers of computer chips and other electronics. Fourteen large electronics corporations have joined forces—their research and development teams are working together to further advance and miniaturize computer chip technology. One of their goals was to bring dominance in the industry back to the United States, which they believe they have now accomplished.

Although Sematech does not make biochip implants, one of their partners, Texas Instruments, does. Obviously, this advanced technology will spill over into transponder implant biochips, allowing them to eventually get smaller, as well.

No one can tell their own story better than Sematech, so below is a reprint of a Sematech press release dated January 21, 1993.

0.35 Micron: Gateway to Talking Computers, Home Medicine & More

Sematech's ability to make semiconductors containing devices as small as 0.35 micron on all–American equipment helps pave the way for U.S. production of 64–megabit and 256–megabit computer chips.

According to industry observers, these high–density chips— in the form of microprocessors and dynamic random access memories—will usher in a high-tech future of talking computers, lifetime telephone numbers, and sophisticated in–home medical tests.

"As transistors get smaller . . . they allow more things to be done inside a single electronic package," author David Gabel writes in a recent technology forecast in *Electronic Buyers' News.* "Thus, higher device density doesn't just get more bits per square micron, but it also allows designers to put processors, memory, and I/O (input/output) control on the same chip."

This capability, writes Gabel, could translate into real–world improvements like:

» A personal communicator—smaller than a cellular phone and more powerful—that fits in your pocket. Keyed to your personal phone number and linked to a global network, it lets you take calls virtually anywhere in the world. [Author's note: Think iPhone, Blackberry, etc.]

» A "medical module" linked to your home computer that lets you do your own blood test and then alerts you and your doctor to any real or potential health problems.

» Office and home computers which carry on intelligent conversations with you and can also recognize and respond to the voices of your spouse, children, and co–workers.

Similarly, a 1989 speculative piece in *Electronic Business* envisions mind–stretching potentials from chips with internal devices of 0.35 micron and below. These include:

» Workstations as powerful as today's supercomputers and supercomputers able to process billions of instructions per second.

» Intelligent automobiles equipped with chips that monitor and control everything from fuel mixture to the suspension system.

» Medical imaging equipment with higher resolution and improved high–definition television.

More forward leaps from semiconductor technology are predicted by *Business Week* in a Sept. 7 cover story. The article, "Your Digital Future," does not specifically discuss semiconductor technology, but it does forecast digital applications that can be achieved only through denser chips. Some of these applications include:

» Interactive TV that lets you watch a lion hunting game

from the lion's point of view.

» Flat–panel wall displays that show you a Van Gogh painting one day, a soothing nature video the next.

» Stereos with "surround sound" that mimic the acoustics of your favorite concert hall.

» Videophones that give clear images, take messages, and handle faxes.

Whether all these technically feasible advances actually happen depends on outside factors such as investment, marketing, and public acceptance. But there's little doubt in the semiconductor world that "denser," "more powerful," and "more advanced" will be the passwords to the next century of electronics.

And the Sematech consortium plans to be leading the way! As Walt Disney envisioned—ahead of his time—"It's a small world after all." The time of clichés, such as "the bigger, the better," seem to have outlived their usefulness, in favor of other clichés, such as "good things come in small packages."

The History and Advance of Implantable Biochip Technology and Manufacture

Let's get a brief explanation of RFID and how it works. RFID is an acronym for a **R**adio **F**requency **I**dentification **D**evice, which uses radio signals to "read" identification codes and other data stored in an RFID transponder and is a reliable way to electronically detect, control, and track a variety of items, information, animals, and people.

The core of the technology is a small, low frequency transponder attached to an object. A reader sends a radio signal to the passive, or battery–free, transponder. The signal charges the transponder, allowing it to return a signal carrying a unique ID code. Lasting less than one–tenth of a second, the process can take place within a "read range" of up to fifteen feet. The data collected from the transponder either can be sent directly to a host computer through standard interfaces or stored in a portable reader and later uploaded to the computer for data processing. RFID transponders are designed for long life—up to 175 to 250 years according to Donald Small, Hughes Identification Devices.

It all began so innocently. During the late 1980s, pet owners and animal shelters around the country became increasingly aware of the need to identify or track animals in order to return lost pets to their owners and decrease the growing number of animals euthanized. This seemingly harmless and beneficial idea gave rise to an entire industry now devoted to this very purpose; however, this technology has ominous overtones for anyone concerned about the potential for human application. Although I cannot yet document its occurrence, this is precisely what some futurists and intellectuals are both predicting and suggesting, and it *is* thoroughly documented that the RFID technology is being used on humans today; we just can't prove injection of an implantable biochip at this time.

Mike Beigel first introduced the basic prototype for the microchip used in the biochip transponder in 1979. AVID, Inc. (American Veterinary Identification Devices) was incorporated in Norco, California, in 1985, and spent the next six years in research and development. Implantable microchips were first tested in 1987 when International InfoPet Systems, based in Agoura Hills, California, started marketing a microchip made by Destron IDI. By 1991 the market began to heat up and Destron IDI sold its identification card technology to Hughes Aircraft, converted its Boulder, Colorado, location to a research facility, and merged with a Minnesota–based firm.

Destron–Fearing Corporation now offers a wide selection of implantable biochips. Also in 1991, InfoPet changed hands and became InfoPet Identification Systems, which markets a microchip developed by Trovan. Trovan is a German–based subsidiary of AEG/Telefunken, which is the major supplier of this technology in Europe. Countries using this technology include Austria, France, Germany, Holland, Ireland, Spain, Italy, Switzerland, and the Scandinavian countries, as well as Australia, the United Kingdom, and the United States. At this same time, AVID, Inc. introduced a third type of microchip, and Texas Instruments had gotten into this growing market. By 1993, one industry observer described the implantable ID market as a "mosaic of technology."

Various animal shelters, clinics, and human societies began calling for a unified ID system. "Last spring, the National Animal Control

THE MARK OF THE NEW WORLD ORDER

Association, members of which include animal shelters and humane societies, suggested a boycott of microchips until the companies agree to share enough information so any chip could be read by any scanner" (*Orange County Register,* March 7, 1993). AVID and Destron agreed on the need to develop a standard system.

In 1992, Destron entered negotiations with Texas Instruments to develop jointly a worldwide operating standard for animal ID. Daryl Yurek, chairman of Destron, says, "Developing and implementing a worldwide standard paves the way for governments and government agencies to adopt electronic identification without worrying about being locked into a single proprietary technology."

Doesn't a worldwide operating standard for electronic identification sound like a great idea? Just think of all the happy pets and pet owners who will benefit from this wonderful technology! Try to imagine a future world dictator getting hold of this technology and you will have some idea what the New World Order is all about. Better yet, try to imagine this kind of power for surveillance and control falling into the hands of a dictator, and him *not* using it to his own advantage. I believe the latter is the bigger challenge!

Regardless of manufacturers' claims, even the best of existing low-frequency passive transponder technology is limited in its read-range capability. Existing technology is generally limited in its transmission range to within less than two feet from the animals into which transponders have been injected; the majority are limited to a two to twelve inch read-range. However, fish in Europe have been tracked with some type of long-range radio frequency transponder technology which are inserted into the stomachs of these fish. They are apparently tracked by long-range satellites or GPS.

The technical description is given above, but here is a good layman's version of how implantable biochip technology actually works. The basic system consists of an implantable biochip transponder and an external scanning device. The transponders come in various sizes, the smallest of which (at this time—but remember, everything is getting smaller) is about the size of an uncooked grain of rice (11 mm). The transponder is a glass tube made of soda lime glass, which is known for biocompatibility. During manufacture, this glass tube is hermetically sealed so it is not possible for any body fluids to reach the internal electronics (or vice versa). There are only three components inside (see illustration). The first is a computer microchip (a custom integrated circuit), which contains the unique ID number which has been etched onto the surface of the microchip. Once the microchip has been encoded by the manufacturer, it is impossible to alter. The second component is a coil of copper wire wound around a ferrite (iron) core. This coil functions as a tiny radio antenna to pick up the radio signal from the external scanner and to send back the encoded ID number. The third component is a capacitor, which tunes or facilitates the signal to and from the microchip.

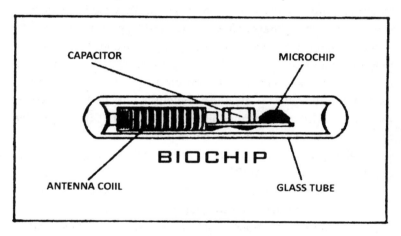

This type of transponder is a passive device, meaning it has no batteries and can never wear out. It is energized by a low–frequency radio wave from the scanner. Most scanners use a 125 kHz, the signal used by AM medium–wave broadcasting. These low–frequency radio waves can penetrate all solid objects except those made of metal. Electronic ID based on these radio signals is referred to as RFID. Once the scanner is activated, it digitally displays the decoded ID number on a liquid crystal screen. Destron can encode up to ten digits on their smallest biochip. Texas Instruments has a brand new chip which will allow the encoding of up to nineteen digits. By combining the digits in a variety of combinations, the smallest biochips can be programmed with up to 34 billion code numbers. A spokesman from Trovan says that with the latest technology, "the number of possible code combinations is close to one trillion." That's a lot of identification capability!

One of the more interesting features of implant technology is the injection system. The trademark name for Destron's injection system is called "LifeChip." It would be hard to imagine a more deceptive title than this, especially as this technology moves closer and closer to human applications. "There is a way which seemeth right unto a man, but the end thereof are the ways of death" (Prov. 14:12).

Each transponder comes pre–packed inside a sterilized needle, which is discarded after use. Because of the sharpness of the needle, "there is minimum discomfort." Special injectors are necessary because most transponders come with an "anti–migration tip." In order to prevent the biochip from moving around, one end is sheathed in a polypropylene shell. This coating offers a surface with which fibrous connective tissue begins to bond within twenty–four hours after injection. In other words, once the biochip is implanted, it becomes part of you with an "unlimited lifespan" (Trovan). "Once implanted, the identity tag (RFID) is virtually impossible to retrieve. Surgical removal, using the most advanced radiograph techniques available is extremely difficult" (AVID).

The final stage in the biochip technology is the ability of the scanner to transfer ID codes to a variety of external computers and printers. InfoPet has a "Recovery Network" with a 24–hour hotline. Government animal regulation and control agencies, shelters, and clinics participate in this network. InfoPet can identify any of its registrants through the microchip number . . . pet's name, owner's name, Social Security number, zip code, or telephone number. AVID is participating with the PETtrac, which is a national computer network. The average cost for pet identification is $40.

The Canadian Kennel Club, as well as nearly five hundred humane societies, has endorsed the Destron chip. Destron president Jim Seiler is enjoying his firm's success, but he also is aware of concerns which trouble the public and assures us that Destron "is not considering human application." Mr. Seiler may not be considering human application, but others certainly are—in fact, in their considered opinions, the sooner the better.

Though other applications are covered in detail elsewhere, it still should be noted here that this technology is definitely not limited to pets, livestock, fish, or wildlife. The developers at Trovan envision a day when transponders will replace the barcode system. Possible applications include coded automobile chassis numbers, automatic tolls, parking, copyright protection for video and computer software, passports, ID cards, credit cards, badges, warehouse/stock handling, valuable items registration, insurance, shipping containers, luggage tags, ammunition, arms, aviation parts, body parts, customs, seals, and laboratory applications. It is not surprising to see European firms way ahead of everyone else when it comes to advanced identification technologies. Scripture clearly indicates that the Antichrist will rise out of the European theater and use the technology which is already available (Dan. 2:2–45; 7:19–27; 9:27; Revelation 17:8–18).

One such individual is Tim Willard, executive officer of the World Future Society. In a disturbing article appearing in the *Marin Independent Journal* (April 2, 1989), Willard openly suggested using biochip technology on humans. "The technology behind such a microchip is fairly uncomplicated and with a little refinement could be used in a variety of human applications. Conceivably, a number could be assigned at birth and go with a person throughout life." Most likely the biochip would be implanted on the back of the right hand so that it would be easy to scan. Willard says it would be like a universal ID card, replacing all other forms of ID. "At the checkout stand at the supermarket, you would simply pass your hand over a scanner and your bank account would automatically be debited." Sounds so convenient, doesn't it?

Remarkably, Willard goes on to suggest that a human microchip identification system "would work best with a highly centralized computer system." Willard comments, "While people over the years may have grown accustomed to artificial body parts, there is definitely a strong aversion to things being implanted. It's the 'Big Brother is watching' concept. People would be afraid that all of their thoughts and movements were being monitored." (And rightfully so, I might add!) Willard adds, "People tend to be romantic about their independence and privacy." Mr. Willard, and others like him in the New World Order crowd, always display their arrogance when it comes to sentimental notions like freedom, independence, national sovereignty, and privacy. After all, this is a new age, isn't it? And we have to think globally, don't we? Wake up, folks! If we let our freedoms be taken from us, we will not be able to resurrect them just by wishing it was so.

I think by now you have more than sufficient information on how the biochip system works and why we are escalating so rapidly to its extensive use on a global scale. Now let's see the extent to which it already has been implemented, and future uses currently on the drawing boards.

THE TREND TOWARD ELECTRONIC TRACKING OF EVERYTHING . . .

The trend toward tracking everything from packages to garbage to freight to animals to people is expanding at a staggering rate. This is truly a burgeoning business and, furthermore, it is a global business.

Even though freight lines (truck, train, and ship), parcel handlers (UPS, FedEx, etc.), and retailers (merchandise identification) are still using barcodes, the trend is moving away from barcodes to RFID transponders, some of which are "read–only" and others "read/write," which allows all shipping details to be placed on the microchip and updated at each stage of the shipment. And the barcodes that remain are becoming much more sophisticated. In chapter four of this book, I described 2–D barcodes and other more advanced models coming into use. Yet, even with these advances, it seems that RFID is becoming the preferred technology of the future.

. . . FROM PETS TO HUMANS

Biochips in pets and livestock is old news, and their use now is being extended into tracking of fish and wildlife to determine their numbers and ability to survive when their species becomes endangered.

» *San Diego Union–Tribune*, December 3, 1992

Vets chip in for pets: Tiny implants can provide foolproof ID
Your precious pet iguana has turned up missing, and the guy down

the street is suddenly showing off a new reptile that looks suspiciously familiar.

Now, how would you be able to positively ID an iguana?

With a microchip, of course.

Dr. Bob Stonebreaker, a Del Mar veterinarian, reports that the microchipping of all ostriches and emus in San Diego County is virtually complete.

"It was a big job; must have been a couple thousand or more to do," said Stonebreaker, who breeds the giant birds as a sideline.

The veterinarian said "a lot of ostrich rustling occurs in this county. These birds are worth a lot of money, and this is a surefire way people can ensure their birds are permanently ID'd." ...

"Besides, tattoos can be altered. The microchip solves the problem."

» *Orange County Register*, March 7, 1993. The following letter to the editor by Linda Stearns of Tustin, California, appeared under the heading, "The ramifications of microchip pet implants," and begins to recognize some of the implications of this technology when projected further into the future.

Often things begun with the best intentions are easily transformed into procedures that are less than desirable.

Implanting microchips in our animals sounds reasonable enough. We own our pets. If they are lost, we have a better chance of finding them if they are picked up by animal shelters that are equipped by scanners.

However, it seems to me that we are in the beginning stages of a larger experiment. Suppose these chips could be enhanced to emit radio waves that are readable at greater distances? We would then have a tracking device. Suppose we implanted microchips in our littlest children in case they are lost or stolen. We already have programs to fingerprint them, why not implant them? But in the process of protecting them, aren't we, in effect, declaring ownership of them? At what age would we declare that person sovereign? Perhaps it would be decided to leave the chips in place to aid in census taking or some other benign purpose. [Author's note: She apparently was not aware that the chips are virtually impossible to remove—even by high-tech surgery.]

We could conceivably have the beginnings of a whole society of people registered by some agency and traceable anywhere in the world. Perhaps we could find dead-beat fathers; perhaps we could all be monitored for our movements and associations.

Suppose those chips were further enhanced to receive? What kind of messages might be programmed into an individual? And from whom? [Author's note: Sounds like she's been reading Schwartau's book . . . except he didn't write until 1994!]

This may sound like paranoia or science fiction, but the technology isn't that far away. Implanting sounds like a good idea when we're talking about dogs. What will we say when it's suggested for humans?

Congratulations! That's very astute of you, Ms. Stearns!

Usage by county and city animal control departments and local humane societies, in addition to use on a personal level by local vets and pet owners, has become commonplace. In a matter of just a couple of years, usage has escalated from some strange experimental process to worldwide and nationwide acceptance by the mainstream in animal control. In fact, in certain places animal implants are already *mandated* by local authorities, and there is no doubt that the number will grow rapidly with the reports of success of such programs.

Amelia F. Donald founded the International Equine Recovery Net in 1990 after researching the problems and solutions of horse theft as it touched her life. She sees electronic identification technology (RFID) as the "battle in defense of honesty." The June 15, 1993, edition of the *San Francisco Chronicle* ran an article by Dan Turner headlined "High-Tech Horse Branding: Microchip implant may replace traditional way to track livestock."

Stealing horses might seem like a rather old-fashioned way to make a living, but a rash of California horse thefts in recent years has led to a very modern solution.

Veterinarians are beginning to implant microchips beneath the skin of horses, which provides a way to identify the animals if they are stolen. The method, which has been used to identify pets since the late 1980s, is just starting to replace the brand as the best way to track livestock.

Horse theft is a lucrative business that seems to be just taking off in California. Although horse meat is not sold in the United States, it is popular in parts of Europe and Japan and prices have risen markedly in the past two years.

There are 13 slaughterhouses for horses in the U.S., four of them in Texas. They will pay up to $1 a pound for grade A horse, said . . . Great Western Meat Co. in Morton, Texas, the biggest horse slaughterhouse in the country.

With a well–fed animal, that could mean as much as $1,000 for the horse thief.

Theft is not the only reason horses are being "chipped." Quarantine and preventing the spread of disease is high on the list of priorities for positive identification of animals. The Louisiana Department of Agriculture and Forestry is dealing with an outbreak of Equine Infectious Anemia (EIA) which is spread by the horse fly and is usually fatal. Sellers must produce a clean bill of health for animals before they can sell them. "Beginning February 1, 1993, horses tested for EIA must be individually and permanently identified. The department is recommending the new microchip implants for identification."

And TIRIS is getting into livestock identification abroad, as well as its involvement in inanimate object RFID. In Australia, unbreakable, reusable RFID pellets are being injected into the rumen of cattle for purposes of identification and tracking the history of the animal. The pellet settles in the rumen, stays with the animal for life, is removed at the time of the slaughter, and is available for use again—the perfect definition of recycling.

Earlier in this chapter we mentioned the fish that caught the fisherman (sort of a takeoff on that old cliché that "dog bites man' is not news, but "man bites dog" is news). Here's the article: "RF–

tagged salmon catches poacher." It appeared in the August 1994 edition of the *Automatic ID News*.

> A poacher was tracked to his home after netting RF–tagged salmon from the river Hirnant, near Bala, Gwynedd, U.K.
>
> The tags transmitted radio signals to bailiffs at the National Rivers Authority as the poacher walked home with his illicit catch. Able to pinpoint exactly where he lived, bailiffs arrived at the poacher's home to find four prime salmon lying on his kitchen table.
>
> Tagged salmon transmit data over great distances to ichthyologists tracking migratory habits, allowing them to estimate numbers entering the river each season.
>
> "This case should act as a warning to other poachers," the National Rivers Authority said. "Although the microchip usually tracks migrating habits, it can also track poachers."

As I said before, I am investigating this because—at the moment—I am not aware of any technology this advanced. I assume that it is based upon some type of GPS technology. If this is a *passive* RFID system, the readers are more powerful than anything I have yet encountered. However, the way technology is advancing exponentially, it would take more than this to surprise me.

This next article in the *Orange County Register* advances the tracking systems from animals to humans:

> **Keeping track: Electronic device can monitor people and pets**
> Whether you need to track an endangered species or an errant grandparent, Spence Porter can help.
>
> Porter, president of Communications Specialists, Inc. in Orange, is one of a handful of manufacturers in the nation who design devices to monitor the movement of birds and other animals.
>
> He has developed transmitters worn by the crème de la crème of endangered species: bald eagles; California condors [*et al*]. . . .
>
> . . . People will see stories about transmitters on condors and bald eagles "and call the zoo and ask if they could put one on grand-

pa or their dog." He is experimenting with the new system and has donated several devices to people with Alzheimer's disease.

The June 6, 1995, edition of *USA Today* carried an excellent article entitled, "Embedded electronics, a chip off sci–fi," written by Mike Snider. It carefully points out how biochip technology—the implanted computer chip—is not–so–gradually becoming embedded in our popular culture.

> » In the new movie *Johnny Mnemonic,* Keanu Reeves plays a 21st–century courier with an overloaded data chip embedded in his head.
>
> » Robert Ludlum tosses a chip into his latest mega–selling espionage novel The *Apocalypse Watch.* Nazis brainwash a secret agent and implant a mind–control chip.
>
> » In the news, Timothy McVeigh, charged in conjunction with the Oklahoma City bombing, told acquaintances that the U.S. Army implanted a computer chip in his buttocks to monitor his whereabouts.
>
> » And, in an outside–of–court conference earlier this year, Colin Ferguson, the man found guilty of the Long Island railroad murders in 1993, accused the CIA of implanting a computer chip in his brain.
>
> Other recent chip–ins include the 1994 MTV series "Dead at 21," in which the main character carried a chip implanted at birth, set to self–destruct at age 21. And in ABC's 1993 miniseries *Wild Palms,* a cult leader tried fusing a chip into his brain to gain immortality.
>
> Believe it or not, science isn't so far behind science fiction.

Then he tells about pet implants. Next, he proceeds to the medical uses, starting with pacemakers, implants, and prostheses. He then moves ahead to future medical uses for the technology, speculating about helping the deaf to hear, the blind to see, and the paralyzed to stand. To me, this sounds more like miracle (or maybe sci–fi) than technology. But then he settles down to some future uses that are actually in the realm of possibility in the foreseeable future, such as implants that contain personal information about you, including your medical records, X–rays, MRI images (not to mention your positive identification, with biometrics, and your financial info, etc.). Then they extrapolate this data out to some *really* wild projections. I strongly recommend that you read the whole article.

Now for some of the uses presently in practice in the tracking of humans: these use RFID technology—they just aren't *implanted* as yet (that we know of). Instead, they are attached to the body in some way—actually, in a variety of different ways.

Athletics are turning to RFID technology because of the accuracy of both identification and timing. In Europe entrants in a triathlon are issued an RFID wristband (which, by the way, must be worn on the *right arm*). Here is how it works:

> The beauty of the IPTA system is its simplicity. Each athlete wears an IPTA wristband which has a built–in [TRIS] transponder. . . . Special antenna are installed in the timing boxes for reading these. . . . Boxes are located at the beginning and end of each transition zone and at the finish line. The athletes slap the box [with their *right* hand] as they pass each zone and their exact time is record-ed. As the times are recorded, they are sent via cable to individual computers at each zone and then via radio frequency to the host computer. In order to be sure that absolutely no data has been lost during the radio transmission, the data from the individual com-puters at each zone is loaded into the host at the end of the event for figuring the final results.

This same technology usage was discussed in the July 1995 edition of *Automatic ID News* in an article titled, "Chip chipping in to run honest race." This article by James E. Guyette discussed a number of different kinds of races and RFID technology being used to make them more accurate, and to keep them honest. Runners and swim-mers have the transponders in a Velcro bracelet. Bike racers have them mounted on bikes. "The new system prevents participants from taking shortcuts in an effort to win. Checkpoints play a crucial role in these types of events." This is especially true in marathons, where one person got caught trying to better his running time by taking a three–mile shortcut.

A number of articles have appeared about prisoners being fitted with home–monitoring devices and confined to their homes to alleviate the overcrowding of jails and prisons. February 17, 1992, *The Orange County Register* carried an article, "More prisoners serving their time out of jail," with a photo of the monitoring device. On July 31, 1994, the *North Jersey Herald News* carried another such article, "Anklet is put back on parole."

Without a doubt the most extensive use of RFID bracelets has been by the United States Department of Defense (DoD) for the processing and tracking of over 50,000 Cuban and Haitian refugees interned at Guantanamo Bay Naval Base in Cuba.

Automatic ID News ran a front–page article in its December 1994 issue, complete with photos, under the headline "New DoD system tracks refugees: Navy deploys RFID–based human tracking system to cope with the Haitian/Cuban exodus." Then they told the story of how our government was not only endorsing but implementing a program for identifying and tracking human beings by permanently riveting a bracelet transponder on their right wrist. Some of the refugees later devised ingenious methods to remove them, with great difficulty, I might add, but when this was discovered, the government took steps to stop it by embedding strips of metal in the bands to reinforce them and prevent their removal. Even the children got banded. However, even the smallest adjustment on the bracelet kept slipping off their tiny wrists, so the navy just turned them into "ankle bracelets." Here are some excerpts from that comprehensive article:

> Banks of sophisticated computer workstations are connected . . . to CCD photo cameras, fingerprint scanning terminals and . . . RFID transponder readers. . . . The entire 2,000–square–foot interior of this former base restaurant has been converted into a state–of–the–art computer processing center to identify and track the more than 50,000 Cuban and Haitian refugees who flooded into this 45–square–mile base between June and September of this year [1994].
>
> Last June, the United States Atlantic Command (USACOM) . . . implemented the Deployable Mass Population Identification and

Tracking System (DMPITS) . . . Now, having performed beyond its designers' greatest expectations, the DMPITS system has also been purchased by the U.S. Department of Immigration and Naturalization Service (INS) and installed October 1, 1994, in border patrol stations in the San Diego area. A new era of tracking illegal aliens and immigrants with automatic identification technology has begun.

At its peak, the 81–person DMPITS unit was processing 400 to 500 people an hour, 24 hours a day. A total of 22,000 Creole-speaking Haitians and 32,000 Spanish–speaking Cubans passed through the system. . . . Approximately 8,000 Cubans volunteered to be moved to more comfortable refugee camps in Panama. (Another complete DMPITS system was ordered for the Panama operation.) The transfer of so much humanity taxed the capabilities of the DMPITS unit to the max. [FingerPrint USA] received emergency orders for three more complete systems for the Navy and two complete systems for INS within three months. . . .

How it works

. . . Military personnel place a black plastic wristband on the person's *right* wrist. The wristband contains a read–only AVID RF transporter containing a nine–digit identification number. It is secured using an aluminum metal pop riveter. Small children have the wristband attached to an ankle. Infants are identified with a wristband placed on their mother's left arm.

Since the pop riveter resembles a large metal drill, Paschall was concerned that it would frighten some refugees, especially children. After some dress rehearsals with marines, it was decided that the crew would wear civilian clothing, and the job of fastening on the wristbands would go to women soldiers. However, it soon became clear that the problem was not as big as expected. Said Paschall, "Once the first individual did not scream in agony, it tended to be much easier after that."

The enrollee places the right index finger on the glowing red surface of the Touchprint scanner. A reproduction of the fingerprint appears in the window on the DMPITS enrollment screen.

The system searches the entire database to see if that fingerprint has already been recorded. If not, the left index finger is scanned. The individual's picture is recorded by the Panasonic CCD camera and also appears on the screen. The name is key entered into the proper field. Finally, the processor interrogates the individual's wristband with the RFID reader, recording the unique identification number. With the aid of interpreters, some demographic information is obtained; name, sex, date of birth, age, place of birth, nationality, names of family relations, point of origin, whether the individual is the head of a family, any perceivable handicaps, and whether the individual is an unaccompanied minor. Finally, the individual's camp number, tent number, and cot number are recorded. . . .

When refugees are transferred between camps, or transferred off the base, their ID bracelets are read. The system updates the camp's population census and creates a manifest for departing ships and flights. Couriers accompanying Cubans who have chosen to move to the Panama camp carry DAT tapes with the DMPITS records of the people on each flight. Upon arrival, those records are downloaded into the Panama camp's database and verified.

In this same issue, Mark David, editor–in–chief of *Automatic ID News,* wrote on the DMPITS operation: "It is an incredible application—one of the first to cross a controversial line and tag humans with RFID transponders." They failed to mention, however, why people were trying to rid themselves of the offensive bracelets by trying to chew them off, or cut them off with crude knives. In a previous chapter I gave you the full story, but let me remind you that one of the refugees was unhappy with the technology because it reminded him of the *mark* that people would be forced to receive in the book of Revelation . . . that was a pretty sharp refugee!

Just how big a leap can it be to progress from *wearing* your RFID transponder on your right wrist to *implanting* your RFID transponder in your right hand? Not nearly as big as I would like. In fact, as far back as July 20, 1989, the *Arizona Republic* carried an article suggesting a program of implantable biochips to find lost or kidnapped children and runaway teens. Jack Dunlap envisioned a program called KIDSCAN, where parents would have their children "chipped" and assigned an identification number. A veteran of the missing–persons division of the Phoenix Police Department admitted that some parents would be nervous of the "Big Brother" aspects of KIDSCAN, but still thought the concept attractive. "Any technology that can be used to detect missing children and children that are in danger would be welcomed." At that time Dunlap was not aware that passive biochips have to be scanned at short range . . . in fact, since he expected "signals" to be picked up on satellites to provide the location of the subject, it sounds like he had a battery–powered unit in mind. But 1989 was still very early in this technology, and things are progressing!

In his editorial in the August 1994 *Automatic ID News*, Mark David raised the question, "If 'chips' are for pets, why not for kids?" Their cover story that month discussed the advantages of "chipping" animals, then continues:

> A recent newsletter from tag maker Destron/IDI picks up a report from the *Sydney Morning Herald* about a 2½–year–old boy who was found wandering in Blacktown, Australia, with his dog, neither of them with any idea of where they lived. The dog, however, wore a tag indicating it had been chipped. Officials took the dog to a nearby vet clinic, where it was scanned. A quick call to the national chip registry identified the dog's owners—the boy's worried parents. . . .
>
> This happy tale got me thinking about the possible advantages of "chipping" children. After all, not all 2½–year–olds found wandering the streets are lucky enough to be with their dogs, whether tagged electronically or not.
>
> [Author's note: Mr. David seems suddenly to find himself in a dilemma when he considers the possible impact of what he is proposing. Read on.] Now, the idea of electronically tagging humans is not one that I could easily embrace. Numbering humans is tainted with the air of jails, concentration camps, and people–as–numerals totalitarianism. For as long as I've been sitting in this editor's chair, I've been railing against the oft–repeated notion that humans will

soon be branded with barcodes. . . .

I'm also aware of the Big Brotherly potential for database abuse and invasion of privacy that grows with every scan of every item in our grocery carts.

[Now, here's that dilemma I mentioned.] But as the father of three small children, I can't help but feel there could be some legitimate arguments made for the voluntary "chipping" of kids. [Author's note: Voluntary for whom? The parents or the child? And when the child grows up, he is still going to be carrying around the chip . . . as an adult who *did not* volunteer to get the implant. At what point does a child become a sovereign individual, and after he does, what—if anything—can you do about the existing implant?] After all, just yesterday, my senseless 18–month–old, Joe, made his way out the front door (which we thought was locked), down the steps, and out onto the sidewalk before we realized he was missing from the house. And any parent who has ever had the experience of losing a child in a crowded store or theme park would quickly wish that every mall and park had a lost–child patrol equipped with RF scanners.

Mr. David goes on to extrapolate this concept to include more sinister disappearances, health benefits, and even making a "net" by installing RFID "portals" at the entrance of such "kid magnets" as zoos, theme parks, and McDonald's to catch children listed as missing. The biochip would give their true identity, no matter what name was given by the adult with them. He supposes that the ultimate finder system would combine elements of infrared personnel tracking systems with the wide–area anti–theft systems which allow police to locate and track stolen cars via RF tags. However, after carefully weighing all the factors, Mr. David gives a hearty "thumbs down" to this use of the new technology: "Despite these potential advantages, I can't sign off as an advocate of such a concept: The idea of chipping children just doesn't fit comfortably under my skin. And if chips are for kids, why not adults too? No thanks. The potential for abuse seems too great and the sacrifice of personal freedom too high."

Unfortunately, a lot of people disagree with him. In the November 1994 edition of *Automatic ID News,* the following letter to the editor was submitted by a reader from Mountain View, California:

> I was compelled to write to you after reading your editorial in the August issue of *Automatic ID News.* The title of the editorial was, "If 'chips' are for pets, why not for kids?" While I can understand your reservations over using RFID technology for tracking people, I am troubled by your firm lack of support of this application.
>
> While our forefathers wrote the Declaration of Independence and formulated a guideline for civil rights, I don't think they had in mind that there would be a time when repeat criminals are allowed to roam free. Conversely, if they did envision this time, they certainly never offered a plan that would enable families to recover their children safely after an abduction, from the home no less.
>
> Privacy issues appear to be a matter of subjected interpretation of the law that makes no distinction between when or whose privacy should be protected. Therefore, we must ask ourselves whose privacy should be protected in a variety of circumstances. In cases where a child has been abducted, I would think the privacy issue would be clearly defined. Certainly, the child would want to have his or her privacy unprotected if it meant a speedy rescue from the prospect of being brutally raped and/or murdered. Maybe the criminal would want his or her privacy protected in the midst of a crime, but does society as a whole?
>
> Instead of worrying about the abuses of this application, we should explore the benefits. I believe that if we look closer at the number of child abductions, we may find an age group that may benefit from using this technology. I also believe that "chipping" inmates would be a good idea if it meant that the inmate could be quickly located after an escape. Furthermore, chipping repeat offenders that are out on parole could also prove beneficial in cases where the parolee chooses to "skip town."
>
> In a final note, I want to say that I applaud the RFID industry and the technological advancements industry participants have made. I will continue to applaud and support this industry and I look forward to the day when a child is safely recovered just min-

utes after an abduction. I ask you to reconsider your opinion of this application and put it into the perspective of how you might feel just minutes after you realize one of your own children was abducted.

This person probably will be at the head of the line when the national identity cards are passed out and later on when the mark of the beast is implanted.

There are many other newspapers and magazines I could quote, including a very thorough article by Lisa Crosby in the June 15, 1994, edition of the *Tucson Weekly* titled "Electronic Leash: The Implantable Biochip Is Already Here. Is Big Brother Just Around the Corner?" And one by Wayne Laugesen in the October 19, 1995, edition of the *Boulder Weekly* titled "Under Your Skin: Biochip implants could find missing children or end personal freedom." The latter is a well-written article which contains much of my personal research. I believe there is a mountain of evidence to support my conclusion that some form of the syringe implantable biochip based on RFID technology will become the mark of the beast described in Revelation 13.

RFID is becoming increasingly prevalent as the price of the technology decreases. In January 2003, Gillette announced that it had ordered 500 million tags from Alien Technology. Gillette VP Dick Cantwell said the company paid "well under ten cents" for each tag.

In 2006, RFID tags were included in new U.S. passports. The U.S. produced 10 million passports in 2005, and it was estimated that 13 million would be produced in 2006. The chips store the same information that is printed within the passport and include a digital picture of the owner. The U.S. State Department initially stated the chips could only be read from a distance of 10 centimeters (4 inches), but after widespread criticism and a clear demonstration that special equipment can read the test passports from 10 meters (33 feet) away, the passports were designed to incorporate a thin metal lining to make it more difficult for unauthorized readers to "skim" information when the passport is closed. The department also implemented Basic Access Control (BAC), which functions as a Personal Identification Number (PIN) in the form of characters printed on the passport data page. Before a passport's tag can be read, this PIN must be entered into an RFID reader. The BAC also enables the encryption of any communication between the chip and interrogator.

The new Passport Card also incorporates RFID technology. The Center for Democracy and Technology has issued warnings that significant security weaknesses in the Passport Card could be used to track U.S. travelers are apparent in the specifications of the card design as outlined by the U.S. Department of State. The Passport Card now ships with an Identity Stronghold Secure Sleeve which shields the card and blocks anyone from reading its contents while the card is inside the sleeve.

Note at left, the photo of a man's LEFT hand and the proposed location of his soon-to-be injected RFID chip implant.

The second photo below was taken just moments after the operation to insert the RFID tag in his LEFT hand had been completed.

Implantable RFID chips that were originally designed for animal "tagging" are now legally being used in humans!

An early experiment with RFID implants was conducted by British professor of cybernetics **Kevin Warwick**, who **implanted a chip in his arm in 1998**. In 2004 Conrad Chase offered implanted chips in his night clubs in Barcelona, Spain, and in Rotterdam, The Netherlands, to identify their VIP customers, who in turn use it to pay for drinks.

In 2004, the Mexican attorney general's office implanted about one hundred and eighty of its staff members with the Verichip to control access to a secure data room.

Security experts have warned against using RFID for authenticating people due to the risk of identity theft. For instance a man-in-the-middle attack would make it possible for an attacker to steal the identity of a person in real time. Due to the resource constraints of

RFIDs, it is virtually impossible to protect against such attack models as this would require complex distance–binding protocols.

Most fundamentalist Christians have now come out against the device due to biblical prophecy where all persons must receive the mark of the beast "in their right hand or on their foreheads" as described in Revelation 13:16–18, **in order to participate in any economic activity under the government of the Antichrist**.

This concern is compounded by the fact that, according to a recent ABC News article, **there have been reports of other chips being implanted in patients' right hands**. However, the chip has also been seen being implanted in the left arm or hand as well as other areas. It is often surmised that the sixteen digits in the chip stand for the last digits of **666**, the original mark of the beast. The Greek word *charagma* (which stands for 666) **describes the piercing bite of a snake (SATAN?)**, which is akin to using a needle to place the device under your skin.

Unusual Usage of RFID Systems

People with very creative minds are developing some very innovative ways to use RFID technology in commercial situations. Some of these ideas are quite unique.

One clever use of RFID is the merging of the human with the inanimate in order to enable function. An example is the "smart gun," which would employ user–recognizing devices to eliminate the possibility of firing (accidental or otherwise) by an unauthorized user of the firearm. The safety can be released only when it "recognizes" the proper biochip implanted in the gun hand of the holder of the weapon. An article called "Future Firearms" in *Omni '95* explained all this and more. A similar article called "Gun Control Is Bad Medicine" appeared in the February 1994 edition of *American Rifleman*. They included a futuristic projection of what it might be like to purchase a firearm in the year 1999. It was humorous, but too close to the truth to really be very funny.

Similar technology is now proposed so that in the future your vehicle ignition won't engage unless the biochip in your hand is compatible with it. This system is already in use at present, only it must match the RFID in your key instead of the biochip in your *right* hand (ignitions in vehicles are always on the right side, of course). And since the majority or people are right–handed, most of the implants to operate a firearm, naturally, will be in the right hand, as well.

As the Scripture admonishes, don't let those days take you unaware.

VERICHIP'S SO-CALLED "DIGITAL ANGEL" RFID CHIP: THE "DIGITAL DEVIL" FROM HELL!

VeriChip is the first Food and Drug Administration (FDA)–approved human–implantable radio–frequency identification (RFID) microchip. It is marketed by VeriChip Corporation, a subsidiary of Applied Digital Solutions, and it received United States FDA approval in 2004. About twice the length of a grain of rice, the device is typically implanted above the triceps area of an individual's right arm. Once scanned at the proper frequency, the VeriChip responds with a unique sixteen–digit number which could then be linked with information about the user held on a database for identity verification, medical records access, and other uses. The insertion procedure is performed under local anesthetic in a physician's office and once inserted, is invisible to the naked eye. As an implanted device used for identification by a third party, it has generated controversy and debate.

Destron Fearing, a subsidiary of Applied Digital Solutions, initially developed the technology for the VeriChip. Digital Angel, Inc. (NASDAQ: DIGA) develops global positioning satellite (GPS) and radio–frequency identification (RFID) technology products for consumer, commercial, and government sectors worldwide. Headquartered in Delray Beach, Florida, their products offer security for people, animals, the food supply, government/military arena, and commercial assets. Included in this product line are RFID applications, end–to–end food safety systems, GPS/satellite communications, and telecommunication, security infrastructure, and the controversial Verichip human implant, a product which has caused concern among advocates of civil liberties as well.

Applications for this technology include pets, wildlife and livestock identification using implantable RFID microchips, scanners and antennas.

Digital Angel has also researched and developed GPS search-and-rescue beacons that integrate geosynchronous communications for use by the military and the private sector to track aircraft, ships, and other high value assets. Digital Angel GPS and RFID products enable the rapid and accurate identification, location tracking, and condition monitoring of people. Applications of their products include identification and monitoring of pets and fish with implantable RFID microchips, identification of livestock with ear tags, GPS-based search-and-rescue beacons for aircraft, ships, boats, and individuals.

Digital Angel's website (www.digitalangel.com) says this about its product line:

> Digital Angel GPS and **RFID products are utilized around the world to SAVE lives**, ensure the safety of our food supply, reunite loved ones, and improve the quality of life. We are a leading developer of technologies that enable the rapid and accurate identification, location tracking, and condition monitoring of what is important to people. Applications of our products include identification and monitoring of pets and fish with our **implantable RFID microchips**, identification of livestock with our ear tags, GPS based search-and-rescue beacons for aircraft, ships, boats, **and individuals.**
>
> **Implantable microchip technology goes well beyond identification devices.** Currently, an area of immense potential is the use of implantable microchips as diagnostic devices to sense an animal's physical condition.

In the beginning of 2007, the Verichip Corporation created Xmark, its corporate identity for healthcare products. Xmark incorporates the Hugs and the Halo system of infant protection; the RoamAlert system of wandering protection; the MyCall emergency response system; and the Assetrac asset tracking system.

Privacy advocates Katherine Albrecht and Liz McIntyre are

among a few of the most prominent opponents of implanted micro-chips. They are coauthors of a position paper on the use of spychips, "RFID: The Big Brother Code," the books *Spychips: How Major Corporations and Government Plan to Track Your Every Move with RFID* (2006) and *The Spychips Threat: Why Christians Should Resist RFID and Electronic Surveillance*, and the antichips.org website.

Their work broadly overlaps that of CASPIAN, a grassroots privacy group founded by Albrecht in 1999 to oppose the use of "loyalty cards" to track consumer purchases in supermarkets. Associated sites include spychips.org, a site opposing RFID chips hidden in consumer goods, and nocards.org, with more general discussion of privacy issues.

Indeed, will RFID chip implants be utilized as the 666 mark of the beast and will the Antichrist's brand of choice be the VeriChip Digital Angel injectable transponder? Frankly, I'm personally convinced of it, but only God Himself knows with absolute certainty what the 666 mark will be. However, if Digital Angel is it, then such a product seems to fit in perfectly with where Satan's technology is taking us globally. Having a Digital Angel chip in one's body allows one to be easily tracked wherever he goes. And who will track us? I'm convinced it will be America's National Security Agency, better known as the NSA. The NSA is capable of tracking everyone globally!

WILL THE NSA's "BLACK WIDOW" COMPUTER TRACK AND CONTROL THE VERICHIP "DIGITAL ANGEL"?

During 2008 the NSA's newest computer system became operational and went online. Indeed, the NSA's colossal Cray supercomputer, code-named the "Black Widow," now scans millions of domestic and international phone calls and emails every hour. The NSA's new Black Widow performs hundreds of trillions of calculations per second as it searches through and reassembles key words and patterns, across many languages internationally.

Therefore, Barack Hussein Obama is now in command of the biggest, most capable, most sophisticated domestic and international spying operation in world history. As stated, its prime engine is the National Security Agency (NSA), located at its huge, guarded, Fort

Meade, Maryland, facility (about ten miles northeast of Washington, D.C.). A brief glimpse of its ever-expanding capacity was provided on October 26, 2008, by the *Baltimore Sun's* national security correspondent, David Wood.

In July 2008, George W. Bush signed into law the FISA Amendments Act of 2008, which gives the NSA even more power to look for patterns that suggest terrorism links in Americans' telephone and Internet communications.

Amazingly, the socialist ACLU immediately filed a lawsuit on free speech and privacy grounds. The new Bush law provides farcical judicial supervision over the NSA and other government trackers and databasers. While a senator, Obama voted for this new system; now he is in charge of it. The ACLU stated this about the new system's capabilities: "The government is now permitted to conduct intrusive surveillance without ever telling a court who it intends to spy on, what phone lines and email addresses it intends to monitor, where its surveillance targets are located, why it's conducting the surveillance, or whether it suspects any party to the communication of wrongdoing."

This truly scary Big Brother technology would have shocked even George Orwell, who wrote the now classic novel, *1984*. This new supercomputer technology gives the word "dragnet" an especially chilling new meaning.

The ACLU's Jameel Jaffer, director of its National Security Project, adds that the new statute warming the cold hearts of the NSA "implicates all kinds of communications that have nothing to do with terrorism or criminal activity of any kind."

What particularly outraged civil libertarians across the political divide was that the FISA Amendments Act gave immunity to the telecommunications corporations—which for seven years have been a vital part of the Bush administration's secret wiretapping program—thereby dismissing the many court cases brought by citizens suing those companies for violating their individual constitutional liberties. This gives AT&T, Verizon, and the rest a hearty signal to go on pimping for the government. But that's apparently just fine with Obama.

Under the new FISA Amendments Act, there are no limits on where this stream of data can be disseminated. As in the past, but now with "legal" protection under the 2008 statute, your suspicious "patterns" can go to the FBI, Homeland Security, the CIA, and state and local police that are also involved in "fusion centers" with the FBI. Consider the enormous and bottomless databases with which the government—and its powerful NSA—can have a ball!

In James Bamford's book, *The Shadow Factory* (Doubleday)—a new book that leads you as far as anyone has gone into the bowels of the NSA—he notes: "For decades, AT&T and much of the rest of the telecommunications industry have had a very secret, very cozy relationship with the NSA." In AT&T's case, he points out, "Its international voice service carried more than 18 billion minutes per year, reaching 240 countries, linking 400 carriers, and offering remote access via 19,500 points of presence in 149 countries around the globe."

There's a lot more to come that we don't know about yet. In *The Shadow Factory*, James Bamford quotes Mike McConnell, Bush's director of national intelligence, as saying that this wiretapping program was and is "only one program of many highly secret programs approved by Bush following the attacks on 9/11." McConnell also said of the NSA's nonstop wiretapping: "This is the only aspect of those various activities whose existence has officially been acknowledged."

Regardless, AT&T, Verizon, *et al.*, don't have to worry any longer, thanks to the new law.

Hey, why the name, "Black Widow," anyway? Honestly, what corporation in its right marketing mind would name its newest computer after a mate–devouring spider? Well, one can only speculate about such a DARK name as follows: black widow spiders construct a cobweb, i.e., an irregular tangle of sticky silken fibers and frequently hang upside–down near the center of their webs, waiting for insects to blunder in and get stuck. Then, before these insects can extricate themselves, the spiders rush over to bite them and swathe them in a silken shroud for later consumption. Moreover, black widow spiders received their name because the females frequently consume their males after mating, leaving them widowed. Well, that about covers it doesn't it?!

James Bamford agrees by writing that "the insatiable NSA is developing an artificial intelligence system designed to know what people are thinking." Hello—here come the thought police! Wake up America!

SECULAR "BIG BROTHER" OR BIBLICAL ANTICHRIST? WILL THE REAL SON OF SATAN PLEASE STAND UP?!

Author George Orwell popularized the expression "Big Brother" in his 1948 novel *1984*. This famous novel is set in an allegedly imaginary future where freedom of both thought and action have utterly disappeared. In Orwell's scenario, humans are under the constant scrutiny of an all-powerful, all-enslaving global government symbolized by *Big Brother,* a male dictator whom the world must worship and follow. Posters everywhere warn citizens, "Big Brother is watching." Children are taken from their parents and love relationships are strictly forbidden. The secret police control and monitor all individual thought and movement by continuous surveillance. Personal privacy is both nonexistent and illegal.

The term *newspeak* is a concept popularized by this novel. In *1984,* the world is enslaved by totalitarianism, wherein the thoughts and actions of each individual are controlled and manipulated by carefully designed "brainwashing" propaganda. All truth is replaced with redefined language called *reverse-speak, doublethink, double-speak,* or *newspeak.* An attribute of newspeak is the ability to hold two *contradictory* opinions simultaneously, whenever the government so dictates. The purpose of newspeak is to condition the mind to the ideology of the Big-Brother police state and to make it impossible to find words to express any other "heretical" thought—which, of course, was any thought contrary to Big Brother's. In newspeak, words like *justice* and *democracy* no longer exist, and the word *free* can never be used to convey the thought of *political* freedom. Such circumstances seem to resemble more closely the present-day New World Order than some fictional tale from the 1940s, do they not?

The cover of *1984* contains the following quotation from Mr. Orwell: "I do not believe that the kind of society I describe necessarily WILL arrive, but I believe . . . that something resembling it COULD arrive. I believe also that totalitarian ideas have taken roots in the minds of intellectuals everywhere."

Grolier's 1994 Multimedia Encyclopedia has some very interesting things to say about Orwell's *1984*: ". . . Although *1984* is sometimes thought of as *science fiction,* it is actually a notable work of *Utopian literature* that emphasizes what Orwell believed were the *dangers inherent in modern, bureaucratic society."* What does this encyclopedic "doublespeak" really mean? It means that *1984* isn't really a *novel* at all; rather, it is a *forecast of things to come* in our modern world!

Grolier's also has some very interesting things to say about Orwell, himself. It indicates clearly that "Orwell was a socialist." Then it defines socialism as: "A comprehensive set of beliefs or ideas about the nature of human society and its *future desirable state."* It continues the link, by way of Marx and Engels, to the Communist Manifesto, the only logical conclusion of which is that socialism is the initial stage of communism. When the New World Order achieves ultimate power and authority, what we will have, in reality, is global communism. Can you see this progression in world affairs today?

The only important thing missing from Orwell's *1984* vision of global control by Big Brother was the biochip implanted under the skin of everyone's right hand—and if the technology had been available at the time, I'm sure Orwell would not have overlooked such an efficient device of tracking and spying on everyone. It probably would have been called the "Mark of Big Brother," but the result would have been the same, without a doubt.

THE NEW WORLD ORDER, NATIONAL ID CARDS, AND SYRINGE-IMPLANTABLE BIOCHIPS

If space permitted, I would go into a lengthy dissertation on socialism and communism, because the history of these two philosophies is important to understanding the basis of the New World Order philosophy. Of course, we are being told otherwise by our socialist, leftist, liberal media, as well as by our socialist, leftist, liberal government leaders. That's right! We are being told lies on a daily basis by our media and politicians. Even the ones claiming to be conservative constitutionalists are coming into question now. Many are turning out to be wolves in sheep's clothing—don't accept any at face value; verify everything! That's why I have used so many pages of this book documenting my statements and allegations.

They are plying us with Orwellian newspeak (read that "double-crossing double-talk") to mentally prepare us for the final transition from capitalism to communism. The New World Order means exactly that!

Accordingly, the government concept of hard-core communism is now being *repackaged and remarketed as global democracy.* You may ask, "How does all this tie into the subject of this chapter on biochips?" Well, I'm about ready to tie it all together for you . . . read on.

"Global democracy," and other such deceptive terms, is just a *newspeak* lie. This "new thinking" is being sold to us by means of the most sophisticated, satanically-inspired, effective propaganda campaign the world has ever witnessed. As a result, most of us are so brain-dead and asleep from years of having been exposed to such mind-control conditioning that we're not even aware of how close we actually are to being conquered and enslaved.

Here's that connection I promised you . . . before we can be enslaved and controlled completely, we must first be **positively identified.** *Without a sophisticated, computerized system of positive biometrically verifiable electronic identification, we cannot be surveilled. Here is where the New World Order ID cards and biochip implants emerge.*

In 1933, Americans were assigned their first national ID cards in the form of a newly inaugurated Social Security system. That same year, all Russian citizens received their mandatory national ID cards, as well. The Russian cards allowed communist leaders to totally enslave, control, and surveil their population. Americans didn't suffer the same consequences concurrent with the issuance of their Social Security cards, but now everything is nearly in place to allow this to happen.

In 1986, author James W. Eaton published a very informative book on national ID cards entitled *Card–Carrying Americans: Privacy, Security, and the National ID Card Debate.* On page 102 of his book he makes some very interesting observations about the Russian national ID card system, as it pertains to control and surveillance of the populace: "The Soviet control system relies heavily upon personal identification documents. Each resident is issued an ID document at age sixteen. The document includes the bearer's picture, name, and date of birth. The document provides officials with basic personal data which can be used to enforce existing travel restrictions. In Russia, no one can visit anywhere for more than seventy–two hours without police permission. The secret police (the KGB) can insert restrictions in the ID document, effectively preventing a holder from traveling, and risking arrest if he does so."

On page 100, Eaton says this about Americans' opposition to a national ID card system: "Opponents of an American national identity program fear that it could lead to *a universal card and totalitarianism.* No one can dismiss such a concern lightly."

On pages 1–3 Eaton writes:

Computers have woven a net of information about nearly every adult American. A growing number of personal information files, under public as well as business management, utilize the Social Security number to facilitate the process of matching and comparing information about any given individual in different files. However, it is difficult for the average person to access his own records and monitor what they contain and make corrections to erroneous data. . . .

A thoughtful minority of Americans are concerned about America's transformation into an "instant information" society. They fear that traditions of individual freedom and privacy are in grave danger. They often refer to George Orwell's classic novel, *1984.* Years ago, Orwell envisioned people being manipulated to serve the whims of a computerized "Big Brother." At the time *1984* was written, the technology of such computerized surveillance was not yet developed, but it now approaches perfection.

I believe that Joseph Eaton's observations above express all I need to say about this.

It should be obvious to all by now what is happening in this regard. First, Americans will be forced into a new computerized, international identification system (infrastructure) with instantly accessible digitized personal data. New sophisticated ID cards will be issued to everyone in order to make the system work. Shortly thereafter, all existing ID cards, debit cards, drivers' licenses, and credit cards will be consolidated into a single, technologically advanced *multiple-use smart card* with an embedded integrated circuit chip capable of storing both electronic money and personal identity information.

Almost simultaneous with this, the world will have been taken cashless, and all currency and coin will have been illegalized so that we must all buy and sell via computerized exchange . . . just a bunch of numbers floating around in cyberspace. Then, we'll be informed that our new cards can be easily lost or stolen, and if they are, we'll not be able to function in the New World Order. In the final step, Big Brother will tell us he has a solution to these problems. He will cause us all to receive an injectable ID biochip transponder under the skin of our hands that will replace our ID cards. Upon taking the chip implant, we will all have been properly identified or MARKED in the new system of global communism called the New World Order. No one will be permitted to buy or sell anything without it. It will be the *mark of the New World Order!* And it will enslave us for eternity.

> And he causeth all, both small and great, rich and poor, free and bond, to receive a mark in their right hand, or in their foreheads: And that no man might buy or sell, save he that had the mark, or the name of the beast, or the number of his name. Here is wisdom. Let him that hath understanding count the number of the beast: for it is the number of a man; and his number *is* Six hundred threescore *and* six.
>
> —Revelation 13:16–18

Shakespeare said, "a rose by any other name would smell as sweet."

Whether the coming global dictator is called Big Brother or Antichrist, or the New World Order is called global democracy, socialism, communism, totalitarianism, authoritarianism, Nazism, or *whateverism,* is really unimportant.

What is important is this: the mark of Big Brother, the mark of the beast, the mark of the New World Order **are all synonymous terms.** They mean exactly the same thing; they are interchangeable. They are all describing the mark revealed in Revelation 13. If you choose to accept this mark, the consequences you may expect are described in Revelation 14: "If any man worship the beast . . . and receive his mark in his forehead or in his hand, the same shall drink of the wine of the wrath of God . . . and he shall be tormented with fire and brimstone."

Some Christians are reluctant to give up the idea that a tattooed barcode will be the mark described. I don't believe the facts support that conclusion. Personally, I am convinced that the syringe–implantable biochip (or some advanced form of the same technology) will be that mark. All the ramifications are spelled out clearly in the concluding section that follows: "The Bottom Line—A World in Disorder." Please consider it carefully.

CHAPTER NINE

THE BOTTOM LINE—
A WORLD IN DISORDER

Public speakers—and in particular, preachers—are taught to "tell them what you are going to tell them, then tell them, then tell them what you told them." In book parlance, that could be interpreted, "The Introduction" "The Chapters," and "The Summation." It is a proven technique that helps the listener or reader comprehend and remember a larger portion of the material being presented to them. Being a firm believer in a couple more clichés, i.e., "don't mess with success," and "if it ain't broke, don't fix it," I make it a practice to follow that time–proven formula in my books. Therefore, in wrapping up this book, it seems fitting to quote again Revelation 13:15–18; 14:9–11:

> . . . and cause that as many as would not **worship** the image of the beast should be killed. And he [Antichrist] **causeth** all, both small and great, rich and poor, free and bond, to receive a mark **in** their **right hand,** or **in** their foreheads: And that no man might buy or sell, save he that had the **mark,** or the name of the beast, or the number of his name. Here is wisdom. Let him that hath understanding count the number of the beast: for it is the number of a man; and his number is Six hundred threescore and six [666]. . . . If any man **worship** the beast and his image, and receive his mark **in** his forehead, or **in** his **hand,** The same shall drink of the wine of the wrath of God, which is poured out without mixture into the cup of his indignation; and he shall be tormented with fire and brim-

stone in the presence of the holy angels, and in the presence of the Lamb: And the smoke of their torment ascendeth up for ever and ever: and they have no rest day nor night, who **worship** the beast and his image, and whosoever receiveth the **mark** of his name.

In the previous chapters I have gone to great lengths to explain to you how the ID system and biochip technology work, as well as the ramifications of the use of this technology to electronically enslave us on a global scale.

I am firmly convinced that these things are leading us down the broad path of "convenience" toward the ultimate identification . . . the **mark** spoken of in the book of Revelation. And because the New World Order propagators don't want to "kick the sleeping dog," as it were, and create a rebellion to these methods, they are lulling us into a state of complacency about the long–term implications of what they are doing by giving us one little "convenience" after the next, each progressively more advanced than the one before . . . de-sensitizing us, if you will.

But these things are merely "technologies," they are not spiri-tual, nor can they send you to Hell. As described in the scriptures quoted above, receiving the mark of the beast *is not* something one will do unconsciously. With all their dire implications, neither the MARC card, the national ID card, nor the biochip are, in fact, **THE** mark referred to in Scripture, even though biochip implants seem to be the technology available which most closely matches that de-scribed in Revelation 13. Receiving the mark of the beast is going to be a matter of worship, not merely of economics. Notice, it does not say you will be *forced* to receive the mark, but you will be *caused* to receive it . . . in other words, by coercion you will *choose* to receive it because of the pressure brought to bear upon you, both economic pressure and peer pressure. Revelation 13:16 clearly specifies that those who reject the mark will be excluded from the world economic order the Antichrist is creating. No one will buy, or sell, or work, or eat, or receive government benefits (i.e., Social Security, medicare, welfare/food stamps, unemployment), or transact any business in a global cashless society without his mark.

No one will knock you out and inject an implant (mark) in your body (although you will remember the recommendation calling for babies to have an implant behind their ear before they left the maternity ward). That would defeat the purpose, namely, getting everyone to worship the Antichrist. Those who refuse to take the mark and worship the beast will be killed. How this will be done is described in Revelation 20:4: "... and I saw the souls of them that were *beheaded* for the witness of Jesus, and for the word of God, and which *had not worshipped* the beast, neither his image, *neither had received his mark upon their foreheads, or in their hands....*"

So, the punishment for rejecting the Antichrist is the loss of one's head—not a very pleasant thought! But as with all things prophesied in the Bible ... it will come to pass! This is a matter of your eternal destiny, and God created man with a free will—the ability and privilege of making the choice of whom he will serve. Therefore, you can't go to Hell by accident, nor can anyone else send you there (by forcibly injecting you with the mark; you would still have to choose to *worship* the beast). But it is a decision I strongly advise that you *not* postpone; it is *late* and the time for choices is *now*, before it is *too* late. At the end of this chapter, I have given you full instructions on how to make this choice and seal your eternal destiny with the Lord in Heaven, rather than in Hell with Satan and his demons. Accept Christ today.

Many places in the Bible we find the phrase, "I would not have you ignorant." My sentiments, exactly! And many other places in Scripture, especially in the words of Jesus Christ, we find the admonition, "Take heed that ye be not deceived." That is why this ministry exists—I want to warn you about deceptions lurking out there just waiting to ensnare us. We find that warning from Jesus in Matthew 24, Mark 13, and Luke 21. In Matthew 24, Jesus is educating His disciples about the end times. They were curious: "Tell us, when shall these things be? and what shall be the sign of thy coming, and of the end of the world?" (v. 3). Since Jesus didn't want them "ignorant," He spent nearly the entire chapter of Matthew 24 (and many other places in Scripture) telling them (and us) what could be expected to be seen by the generation that was alive upon earth when the "end" arrived. He began His reply by saying, ". . . Take heed that no man deceive you, For many shall come in my name, saying, I am Christ; and shall deceive many" (vv. 4–5). Then he tells about all the terrible events leading up to the end. But right in the middle of the chapter He returns to the warning not to be deceived. "For there shall arise false Christs, and false prophets, and shall shew great signs and wonders; insomuch that, if it were possible, they shall deceive the very elect. Behold, I have told you before" (vv. 24–25).

Then Jesus continues with other terrible events that will occur and tells us that even though we won't know the day nor hour (v. 36), we can know the season (v. 32) by recognizing that it is Scripture being fulfilled when we see these events happening all around us. "So likewise ye, when ye shall see all these things, know that it is near, even at the doors" (v. 33). Then Jesus tells us, ". . . This generation [the one that witnesses these events] shall not pass, till *all* these things be fulfilled" (v. 34).

Even though He tells us that no man can know the day nor hour, He does indicate that we can know the season, if we are careful to observe the signs occurring about us.

You may ask how this all ties in to our study of the New World Order and identification technology . . . read on.

THE REAL ORIGIN OF THE NEW WORLD ORDER

It is my opinion that we are that generation of which Christ spoke, and that all things found in Matthew 24 (and other related prophetic books, i.e., Daniel, Ezekiel, Revelation) will be fulfilled in our lifetime. Ever since the Tower of Babel, Satan has been attempting to create a New World Order where people would worship him as the god of this world. Scripture indicates that God, indeed, will permit this to occur at the end of the age. For the past two hundred years, specifically subsequent to May 1, 1776, the Luciferians, New Agers, witches, Satanists, socialists/communists, fascists/Nazis, liberals, *et al*, have all been using a new term to describe this final form of global enslavement under the Antichrist. The term they have been using is the New World Order.

Jesus warned us that deception would be rampant during this

time—so much so, He specifically warned us that even the elect of God would be deceived and believe the lie of this New World Order under the devil, if it were possible. He implied that only the elect *could not* be fooled, and this is why so few today are able to discern the truth of what's occurring. Most people—unfortunately, even most Christians—are blind to what's happening in terms of the prophetic scriptures, as they apply to the times in which we live. We are warned in 1 Thessalonians 5 to beware when people speak of peace and safety, and indeed George H. W. Bush promised us peace and "security" (safety) when he announced the beginning of the New World Order, then committed the U.S. to fight in the Iraqi war. The Lord tells Christians that they should not be asleep like the rest of the world; rather we should be awake, aware, and watchful regarding these end time events. Unfortunately, most *are* dead, asleep, or blind to what's happening. The signs of the Lord's second coming are all so visibly apparent, even in our secular news media, that no one should miss the signs of His soon return.

THE EPISTLE OF BARNABAS AND THE 6,000–YEAR PLAN

There is a little–known book called the *Epistle of Barnabas* included in a respected work by Lightfoot entitled *The Apostolic Fathers.* Although no one can attest for certain that this is the same Barnabas who accompanied Paul in the book of Acts, it is believed to be true. In chapter 15 of the Epistle of Barnabas, a six thousand–year plan is mentioned specifically as God's total plan from beginning to end. It says that at the conclusion of six thousand years, the sabbath millennium will begin.

Please understand that I am not setting dates for either the end of the age or the return of Jesus Christ (although the Bible definitely indicates, in Jesus' own words, that we should be able to see these events and know that the end is near), nor am I implying that the Epistle of Barnabas is some missing part of the Bible. As a matter of fact, there are many other extrabiblical historical books that indicate that six thousand years holds some special significance, and may indeed witness the conclusion of all human history. Revelation

20 implies this, because it mentions six times that there will be a thousand-year millennium of true peace, under the true God of this world, Jesus Christ, in a true "New World Order," of which this present New World Order is merely an evil counterfeit—just as Satan counterfeits other manifestations of God's power.

Matthew 24:36 only restricts us from knowing "that day and hour" of the end, but other scriptures (Matt. 24:33, *et al*) say we will know when it is very "near, even at the doors," because we will witness the events outlined in Matthew and other prophetic books. Therefore, be very clear—I am NOT saying that I know the day nor the hour nor the specific year . . . but I believe that the six thousand-year plan may hold prophetic significance; all signs seem to indicate that things are about to wrap up soon . . . and we were told to *watch the signs.* It appears that Lucifer's final hour is at hand and the Great Tribulation period is about to begin, being ushered in by the current New World Order.

PAT BUCHANAN'S DENOUNCEMENT OF THE NEW WORLD ORDER

Reference to the New World Order is turning up in literature of all types, but most significantly in articles and books dealing with politics, the military, and the United Nations. In a January 10, 1995, article in the *Charlotte Observer,* Patrick J. Buchanan liberally referred to the New World Order, though mostly in a derogatory context. No surprise, he says: "Dr. Kissinger is often invoked as our most insightful guide to the New World Order. . . ."

Of course, this article addresses, in particular, the situation of the U.S. bailout of the Mexican economy, of which Buchanan was in staunch opposition. He continues:

> As Wall Street is taken off the hook, U.S. taxpayers are put on. That's what the game is all about. The U.S. branch of the New World Order conscripts America to bail out its Enchilada Chapter in Mexico City. . . . Take away the smoke and mirrors, and what the "New World Order" comes down to is capturing America's wealth and squandering it all to prop up the dreams and designs of the globalists,

until the last dollar runs down the gutter....

Either America jumps ship from this doomed vessel, the New
World Order, or one day, we go down with it.

Mr. Buchanan is not just your ordinary newspaper reporter. He is a
former presidential advisor, a former presidential candidate, a 1996
presidential contender, a syndicated columnist, and host of "Cross-
fire" on CNN. He keeps tabs on the activities of the New World Order,
to which he is adamantly opposed, as you can see. His colleagues and
other politicians would do well to heed his advice.

BUSH'S DISARMAMENT PLAN FOR THE NEW WORLD ORDER

Buchanan addressed the New World Order from the economic viewpoint, but George Bush carried the implications of the New World
Order much further, into every area of our lives, but in particular into
the military, defense, and "police action" portion of our nation. In the
September 28, 1991, edition of the *Honolulu Advertiser,* in an article
titled "New (safer) world order," Bush's plans for the disarmament
of the U.S., following the end of Desert Storm, was announced. "...
The plan outlined by Bush yesterday calls for such weapons to be
dismantled and destroyed after they are withdrawn."

Then he stated his hopes that this would encourage the Sovi-
ets to do likewise. He called for the elimination of ground–launched,
short–range nuclear weapons; removal of all short–range nuclear
arms from submarines and ships worldwide; removal of all U.S. strategic bombers from day–to–day alert status and the return of their
weapons to storage areas; withdrawal from alert of all interconti-
nental ballistic missiles scheduled for deactivation under the yet–
unratified Strategic Arms Reduction Treaty (START); and abandon-
ment of the controversial rail–based system for the MX missile. And
all the while, our military forces are becoming increasingly subjugated to U.N. control.

Then there is the matter of our Air Force. Are you interested in
how a B–52 meets its end? I'm more interested in *why* it meets its
end! In he July 1995 edition of the Smithsonian publication *Air &*

Space, there is an article entitled "Death of the Beast." By the way, in this edition there are an unusual number of biblical terms used throughout the publication, e.g., their "Viewpoint" column is titled "Tower of Babel," this article refers to "the Beast," using a "guillotine" to "decapitate" the tails of the aircraft, and actually quotes the scripture found at Revelation 13:18, then the acronym AMARC [a mark of the beast? a MARC card?] is used for the name of the place where the aircraft came to be retired. Very curious!!

Anyway, about the loss of our B–52s . . . a veteran of 157 combat missions and a recipient of a Distinguished Flying Cross referred to this as an "execution." AMARC is the facility where the U.S. military stores aircraft and Titan II missiles it has removed from service. The article points out that AMARC also has the responsibility for destroying aircraft—often perfectly good ones. Our tax dollars at work!! In 1993, the center began carrying out the terms of the START treaty mentioned above, which called for the deactivation of so much of our military apparatus.

> . . . To disable the bombers visibly and permanently, as the treaty requires, AMARC personnel use a six–and–a–half ton steel blade deployed from a crane to chop them up. Afterwards, the remains are left in place for 90 days so that the treaty signatories can use satellite overflights to verify the destructions. . . .
>
> Today the guillotine would descend on tail number 666. Nicknamed "the Beast" because of the biblical reference to that number. . . .
>
> *Rolling Thunder,* its back broken and its wings severed, lay on its side like a dead fish. A junk dealer had paid 18 cents a pound for it. Nearby, an older bomber painted Air Force gray bore a blue stripe and the sun–bleached words "Peace Is Our Profession"—the motto of the Strategic Air Command, the now–defunct division then in charge of the Air Force's bombers and missiles.

Small wonder they referred to this as an execution. Even the caption under the photos tell of "the bombers crudely broken bodies [that] give the desert landscape at AMARC a post-apocalyptic look," but they stress that this signifies a more peaceful era of international relations. Oops ... don't forget about that "peace and safety" scripture.

Of course, the end of the cold war is the excuse that was used for the elimination of our protection. The headline of article, "New (safer) world order," expresses pretty accurately the intent of the scripture: "For when they shall say, Peace and safety; then sudden destruction cometh upon them. . . ."

However, as the well–known saying goes, men who forget their history are doomed to repeat it. See if some of the following quotations sound familiar—this is not a trick, I'll tell you in advance this was not written about any of our recent administrations. It is one of those things we should have learned from history, so we won't have to repeat it. But as with so many other things we should have learned, we obviously didn't learn this lesson either, because we are currently in the midst of repeating it!

"ANOTHER" NEW WORLD ORDER

... With amazing rapidity the whole standard of living fell throughout Europe to a level which had not been known for centuries. In less than a year, it seemed as if one hundred and fifty years of civilization had been wiped out. Near–famine in certain regions, want and scarcity everywhere became the norm. Culture receded. Only a few books were published. . . . The freedom of the Press disappeared. . . . Seldom had Europe as a whole been subjected to such physical and spiritual degradation. Seldom had a whole form of civilization been so quickly and radically menaced by the destructiveness of tyranny.

But no echo of this disaster can be found in [his] speeches. Quite the contrary; and if future historians had nothing to base their judgment on except these speeches, their conclusion would be that Europe had never been so close to the millennium nor so anxious to hasten the final triumph of its new Messiah [Sound familiar?]. . . . The messianic conception he had of himself is what enabled him so consistently to disregard the ruins and misery which his conquests spread and to assert that out of these ruins and sufferings, in spite of all evidence to the contrary, a New European Order was being born.

The *leit-motiv* of the New Order was not new.... The purpose of [it] was to transform radically the political, social, and spiritual complexion of Europe. The fundamental idea of the New Order was that all European nations should be integrated into one vast economic and political unit.... On the contrary, the picture offered an increasingly sharper contrast between [his] dream of a regenerated and peaceful world and the frightful reality. [Author's note: Remember what the Bible has to say about the "peace and safety" promises.] Europe was changed indeed, but what that change meant was a tragic regression, an accumulation of ruins and untold suffering.

... The plundering of these borderlands and the enslavement of the conquered nations were the basis of [his] New Order. And what this New Order actually meant in practice could now be seen: it was nothing but the system by which [his] armies could be maintained at the expense of the conquered.

The Order in fact was only an attractive word to designate the rule of military occupation.

... [This] New Order was indistinguishable from domination supported by force and that as long as other powerful groups of nations such as the Anglo–American bloc refused to recognize [his] rule, there could be no New Order and no peace.

See how important it is for the citizens of a nation to stand their ground—tyrants recognize that as long as they continue to do so, there can be no New (World) Order. Now, listen to this direct quote of some of his promises:

... The world shall open up for every one. Privileges for individuals, the tyranny of certain nations and their financial rulers shall fall. And last of all, this year will help to provide the foundations of a real understanding among peoples, and with it the certainty of conciliation among nations.

Sounds like he is just about to build the organization that will supersede the United Nations, doesn't it? But in the midst of (realistically) chaos, he talks like we're all headed for Utopia.

> ... [he] had to prophesy, as he had always done, that the end was near and that peace, order, and happiness would reign on earth ... [words] intended to deceive.
>
> There it little new in [this] strategy. .... One finds the same persistent effort to exonerate himself from all responsibility ... [even casting a] morbid spell produced by his oratory. His appeals for peace fall on deaf ears. ...

Although most of the similarities end here, there is one other to point out. Think back to the Oklahoma City bombing and President Clinton's remarks about purging the "forces of darkness," the compare them with the following:

> The third motive was the hope of spreading confusion all over the world. .... [They presented their] propaganda as the crusade of civilization and Christianity *against the forces of darkness*. ... [He], in his new role of champion of Christianity, was to lead the whole of Europe against Moscow and destroy Communism once and for all. This was a new war aim and a new and convenient ideological basis for the European World Order.

By now you have undoubtedly determined that the above excerpts refer to Adolf Hitler and the Nazis. The quotations are from the book *Adolf Hitler: My New Order*, edited with commentary by Raoul de Roussy de Sales (Angus and Robertson, Ltd., Sydney/London, 1942). Long out of print, this rare copy was located just this year. Coincidence? I think not. Isn't it amazing how well it fits with the New World Order being thrust upon us today? Even the terminology is similar—not just the philosophy.

In Ecclesiastes we learn that "there is nothing new under the sun," and this certainly proves the point. As I have explained before, the New World Order is really just an Old World Order that Satan has been unsuccessfully trying to foist on mankind since the Tower of Babel, and before. I'm sure he is dancing with glee to realize that it finally will come into existence in the near future; I'm also sure he is painfully aware that his time is short, and this New World Order is the final stage of his death grip on this earth. As I mentioned at the beginning of this chapter, when God's New World Order arrives, Jesus will be the King of Kings and Lord of Lords over this earth and its inhabitants. As I also warned you, if you are not prepared for that event, I recommend you get prepared at once—time is short. If you don't know how, continue reading . . .

RAMSEY CLARK'S DENOUNCEMENT OF BUSH'S NEW WORLD ORDER

I want to recommend a book to you. It contains much heretofore undivulged information and is written by "an extremely reliable source," to quote a favorite line of news reporters. The only difference is, this is not "an unnamed" source—this source is a very prominent figure, having served as U.S. Attorney General under three presidents (two Democrats and one Republican) and having been a most vocal opponent of the United States' participation in the Gulf War activities. I am referring to Ramsey Clark and his book, *The Fire This Time: U.S. War Crimes in the Gulf* (Thunder's Mouth Press, New York, 1992).

Let me make it clear that I don't necessarily agree with many of the notions espoused by Clark, as he is a liberal, pro–United Nations/world government man, and I am certainly the opposite (conservative, fundamentalist, anti–U.N., anti–world government, and anti–Antichrist), but the book is really interesting because it accuses George Bush of being a dictator who trashed the U.S. Constitution, and accuses him of committing high crimes, misdemeanors, and other gross international crimes in the pursuit of "George Bush's New World Order." However, the author must be somewhat confused, as he fails to recognize that the United Nations, which he supports, and the New World Order, to which he is opposed vehemently, are really one and the same, or, at best, the U.N. is the foundation upon which the New World Order will be established.

Much of the content of this book is reminiscent of the terminology and phrasing that appeared in Hitler's book, *My New Order,* quoted above. Match some of the comments below, from Clark's book, with the quotations above, from Hitler's book. The similarities are mind-boggling; the attitudes and actions of George Bush parallel Hitler's actions to an uncanny degree, and the naïve have believed "the lie" and been deceived. I will address the matter of the deception further in this chapter.

". . . The most powerful capacity for propaganda and the most sophisticated technology for death in history acted in concert [Author's note: read that "conspiracy"] to slaughter an army, cripple a nation, name it liberty, and call for a celebration."

Almost exactly what Hitler did. And remember when Hitler practically proclaimed himself the Messiah and said he was waging that campaign to promote the Christian faith? Well, following Desert Storm, January 27, 1992, Bush spoke at the annual convention of the National Religious Broadcasters. His address included the following comments: ". . . We fought for good versus evil. . . . And today I want to thank you for helping America, as Christ ordained it to be a light unto the world." They responded with an enthusiastic ovation. He promotes the occultic New World Order (and don't forget his Skull & Bones affiliation) and all it represents, then adds a few Christian "buzzwords," and everyone applauds! This was what Satan tried on Christ in the wilderness. Quote a few scriptures (usually incorrectly) and many will be deceived.

Whereas Hitler, for the most part, ended the free press, ours just chose to play the game, using the "party line" to brainwash us when it came to reporting on what Clark alleges as the atrocities of the Gulf War. Some of his stinging indictments follow:

> . . . The press rendered First Amendment protection meaningless, because its wealthy owners uncritically supported the government as it destroyed Iraq. It barely reported dissent; when it did, it ridiculed, misrepresented, or marginalized those who criticized U.S. intervention in the Gulf. TV coverage of the Gulf crisis . . . was more a long-running commercial for war . . . than news reporting.
>
> The media, owned by the wealthy, speaking for the plutocracy [Webster's definition: government by the wealthy/control by the

wealthy], has the dual role of anesthetizing the public to prevent serious consideration or debate of such staggering human issues . . . and emotionalizing the people for aggression. . . .

. . . The American media, guardian of the First Amendment, has abandoned its ward in favor of Mammon. [Author's note: the use of biblical terms is growing in popularity—I'm sure that is no accident.]

While receiving extensive coverage in the international press, the U.S. major media blackout of the [International War Crimes] Tribunal was almost complete. . . .

His allegations are not limited to the media; he has plenty to report on George Bush, as well, including attempts to impeach him based on a number of charges, not the least of which is conspiracy. First, I want you to read the letter from Mr. Clark to President Bush, dated March 4, 1992.

Dear Mr. Bush:

In May 1991, you were sent an initial complaint by the International Commission of Inquiry containing the 19 charges against you and others of crimes against peace, war crimes, and crimes against humanity. You were asked to submit any evidence you wished in your own defense and invited personally or by representative to attend any hearings and examine all evidence against you. The Commission has since conducted hearings in more than 20 countries with over 30 hearings in the United States alone.

On Saturday, February 29, 1992, in New York, the International War Crimes Tribunal, having considered the evidence gathered by the Commission, held the final hearing. At the conclusion of the hearing, you were found guilty of all 19 charges. The other defendants—Vice President Dan Quayle, Secretary of Defense Richard Cheney, Joint Chiefs of Staff Chairman Colin Powell, former CIA director William Webster, and General H. Norman Schwarzkopf—were also found guilty of the charges against them. Enclosed is a copy of the Final Judgment of the Tribunal, a copy of the charges, and a printed list of the Tribunal Judges.

The consequences of your criminal acts include the deaths of more than 250,000 children, women, and men, mostly civilians, and the crippling of an entire country. You are held accountable by hundreds of millions of people around the world, and you will be by history. You have placed another bloody stain on the honor of your country and its people.

You must not engage in further violence, murder, and militarism. You must not let your arrogance, falsity, and hostility for the poor and the weak—all of which were aided by the silence of the media—lead you to commit further crimes.

If you have anything to say for yourself, the Commission and the Tribunal will hear you and your representative.

Sincerely,

Ramsey Clark

Here are some of the accusations he makes against Bush, most of which are valid and heretofore publicly ignored, which is why I am bothering to include Clark's efforts in my book.

. . . The people of the United States watched in general silence or outright approval as *President Bush seized absolute power* [Author's note: prior to any congressional approval] to assault a defenseless people. . . . No dictator was ever less restrained.

Article I of the U.S. Constitution vests power over war and peace in the Congress. President Bush usurped these powers to wage his war. . . .

On January 9, President Bush reasserted his view that he needed no congressional authorization to attack Iraq. He reinforced his earlier claims to presidential power with responsibilities created by U.N. Resolution 678. . . .

Remember, in an earlier chapter I warned you about the U.N. Resolution 666 (and following) which gave away our sovereignty to the control of the United Nations. That's what Bush used to take this unprecedented action of going to war without congressional approval . . . he no longer needed it!—which he was quick to point out fervently in interviews covered on the national media when questioned about it. Clark is not the only one with this opinion of Bush's actions.

Congressman Calls for Impeachment of President Bush—January 16, 1991

On January 16, 1991, the day President Bush ordered the bombing to begin, Congressman Henry Gonzalez of Texas spoke to the House of Representatives in a great act of individual courage, conscience, and vision.

Then he quotes the entire impeachment speech, as reported in the *Texas Observer* on January 25. While corroborating this event, I spoke directly with personnel in the office of Congressman Gonzalez, who advised me that the facts are basically correct, but clarified one point: the Resolution as presented on January 16 contained some technical errors (primarily typos) which were corrected, whereupon the Resolution was resubmitted to the 102nd Congress in February. When I requested permission to duplicate the Resolution in my book, I was informed that there are no restrictions, as it is now a matter of public record.

I have paraphrased the speech below, as it was reported by Ramsey Clark:

Mr. Speaker, it is with great sadness, yet with great conviction, that I introduce today a resolution of impeachment for President Bush.

... The Iraqi people are as opposed to war as are the American people—the difference is that the Iraqi people have no choice but to support their country's leader, but the American people not only the right to oppose and speak out in disagreement with the President, but they have the responsibility to do so if our democracy is to be preserved.

... I swore to uphold the Constitution. The President's oath was the same—to uphold the Constitution of the United States. We did not pledge an oath of allegiance to the President, but to the Constitution, which is the highest law of the land. The Constitution provides for removal of the President when he has committed high crimes and misdemeanors, including violation of the principles of the Constitution. President Bush has violated these principles.

My resolution has five articles of impeachment. First, the President has violated the equal protection clause of the Constitution. Our soldiers in the Middle East are overwhelmingly poor white, black, and Mexican–American.

Article II states that the President has violated the Constitution, federal law, and the United States Charter by bribing, intimidating, and threatening others, including the members of the United Nations Security Council, to support belligerent acts against Iraq. It is clear that the President paid off members of the U.N. Security Council in return for their votes in support of war against Iraq. [Author's note: Although two acts of conspiracy are charged below, it seems to me that this would qualify as an act of conspiracy, as well.]

Article III states that the President has **conspired** to engage in a massive war against Iraq....

Article IV states that the President has committed the United States to act of war without Congressional consent and contrary to the United Nations Charter....

Article V states that the President has **conspired** to commit crimes against the peace by leading the United States into aggressive war ... in violation of ... the Constitution of the United States.

Do you remember seeing anywhere at that time that someone in Congress was calling for the impeachment of the president? Talk about your media blackouts!

I'm sure you have all heard the Marxist claim that religion is the opiate of the people. Well, here is what Clark believes: "... The belief that governments will solve our problems may be the *most dangerous* opiate of the people...."

Clark makes plenty of references to Bush's New World Order.

... Orwell's doublespeak has become the official language of the Pentagon....

The apparent popular approval by the American people of the destruction of Iraq is the greatest threat to the future.

Most dangerous of all, the United States is seeking a new world. . . . Even those with short memories can see the cynicism of this new world order. . . .

. . . Millions foresaw more U.S. military actions as a principal means to achieve the "new world order."

Yet only the morally blind will fail to see that U.S. political and military leadership has proven itself totally untrustworthy to lead the world to a new order.

. . . But this is hardly a new order.

DON'T BE DECEIVED—DON'T BELIEVE THE LIES OF THE NEW WORLD ORDER

To reiterate—the Bible says if it were possible, even the elect of God would be deceived in the last days. Read Matthew 24:24–27; Mark 13:5,22; Luke 21:8—all the words of Jesus. He talks much about false christs who would be coming in these final days, and when they do—don't follow after them, don't believe the signs and wonders they will perform, and other things. We must be on our guard; we need the renewed mind of Christ to avoid falling into the trap and believing the lie—even at that, Satan will attempt to ensnare us. Mr. Clark is a good example. He thinks he is right—he truly believes it—but he has been deceived. He has believed the lie. Study the following quotation, keeping in mind he has been firmly disavowing the New World Order (world government) throughout his book: ". . . a brutal and deadly future is inescapable. The threat of a new world order based on technological violence and designed to control the poor for the benefit of the rich *has made organized and spontaneous worldwide effort absolutely essential for human fulfillment.*"

In one sentence he has both decried the New World Order and called for it as "absolutely essential for human fulfillment." Now, I am not talking about the "uneducated masses" here; Mr. Clark is a man of prominence, well educated, highly intelligent, and influential worldwide, yet he still does not recognize that he himself is confused and deceived. Jesus warns us multiplied times throughout the New Testament *not* to be deceived. Of course, such warnings would not be necessary if it were not possible for us to actually be deceived.

I will deal more with Satan's deception as this chapter progresses, because the whole idea here is that the New World Order is a spiritual matter, and has been all along, but most have not yet recognized that fact.

Of course, there is a spiritual counterpart (or counterfeit) upon which the New World Order is founded—we call it the New Age movement. The New Age movement is the demonic world religion that ultimately will deceive the world into worshipping the leader of the New World Order as the messiah (Antichrist), which is specifically what Jesus warned us against in the scriptures referenced above. This book is designed to focus on the New World Order and the technological aspects that will be used to enslave us, therefore, I will not provide extensive discussion on the religion of the New Age. There presently is a wealth of material exposing the dangers of the New Age. Most Christian bookstores stock an abundance of books, videos, and CDs by extremely knowledgeable people on the subject of the New Age, as well as other satanic deceptions. I recommend you become familiar with their content, if you are not currently aware of the infiltration into our day-to-day lives.

WILL THE UNITED NATIONS BECOME THE NEW WORLD ORDER?

What about the United Nations? Is it going to evolve into the infrastructure of the New World Order? Only God knows for sure, but based on over six years of research into this matter, there is no doubt in my mind that it will. At present it couldn't accomplish the feat because it is still a collection of independently sovereign nations; whereas the New World Order eventually will relegate independent nations to the state of "world-states" or nation-states," only operating under the auspices of the head of world government (Antichrist). But I believe that it is the forerunner that is laying the groundwork for the New World Order.

PRESIDENT CLINTON CALLS FOR A REFORMED UNITED NATIONS

Whether you are a Republican or a Democrat, it makes no difference to those pushing for a New World Order. We've heard a lot about George Bush, but he was not alone in his promotion of the New World Order. President Bill Clinton spoke at the 50th Anniversary Celebration of the United Nations, in San Francisco's War Memorial Opera House where President Truman signed the Charter in 1946. President Clinton offered a number of telling and constructively critical remarks concerning the status of the United Nations at that time. He supports the organization, but believes a "reformed" U.N. would do more for the world. He urged reform of what he called a "bloated organization." "The new United Nations must peel off what doesn't work and get behind what will," Clinton said.

Writer Steve Komarow, in a June 27, 1995, issue of *USA Today*, reported that Clinton said the U.N. too often appears to be spending money on meetings instead of results, and that this pattern fuels U.S. critics, including some who might be supportive if they felt U.N. money was better spent. However, Clinton made it clear that he was not among those who consider the U.N. useless. Clinton recommitted the U.S. to continue to pay "its fair share" (whatever that means) of the cost of the U.N. and its so-called peacekeeping missions, and attacked those to whom he referred to as "new isolationists."

It is appropriate to remind you at this point that Bill Clinton is a member of the Council on Foreign Relations, the Trilateral Commission, and the Bilderbergers, as is George Bush, who is also a member of the Skull & Bones "Brotherhood of Death" Society. So is there really any difference between the Democrats and Republicans? Not much, since most of the top leaders of our government have joined and sworn allegiance to these New World Order clubs, irrespective of their political party—there is really only one political party in America . . . the global government New World Order party. Contrary to what Rush Limbaugh says on national "conservative" talk radio, there is no difference between the Republicans and the Democrats—it's all for one and one for all in the New World Order.

Is there a conspiracy? You figure it out!

OUR NEW CONSTITUTION?

As I write, there are numerous calls coming in nationally for a constitutional convention to rewrite our hard-won, time-honored guardian of freedom—the U.S. Constitution, which was purchased with the blood of the patriots from 1776 to 2009. One such recent call has been termed the "Philadelphia II Con-Con" (i.e., constitutional convention). Another effort to redraft the U.S. Constitution was called the "New States Constitution." There are others, as well. The unseen elite behind the scenes are pushing fervently to scrap our existing Constitution because they claim that it is outmoded, outdated, inefficient, and unable to deal with the demands of the New World Order. But their ulterior motive is clearly to eliminate the Constitution because it is our safeguard, a barrier to world government, and assures our nation's sovereignty, something they cannot tolerate.

The Constitution for the Federation of Earth essentially relegates the U.S. to a position of statehood in the world society of nations. This particular constitutional draft is being acclaimed globally as a viable solution to fill the alleged need for a world constitution. They have called for a fourth parliamentary meeting to ratify this global constitution, the gross fallacies of which I pointed out at length in an earlier chapter.

The World Constitution and Parliament Association happily concur with Clinton regarding the reformation of the United Nations. In fact, they are the ones who believe the U.N. won't work because it consists of a collection of as-yet sovereign nations. In June and July 1996, they summoned delegates from all over the world to the fourth session of the Provisional World Parliament. The stated purpose of which was to make "rapid progress towards the establishment of a functioning world federation and world government under the Constitution of the Federation of Earth."

This bunch would be laughable if it weren't for the fact that so many prominent people of influence take it seriously and are actively engaged in trying to bring about its program, including placing into effect the new world constitution. Apparently, they are feeling the heat from some of you out there, because they have included one rather paranoid paragraph in their letter of invitation. I quote:

But, please, the . . . meeting is only for persons who sincerely want to help, and not for detractors. In a country where armed militia and ultra right groups are rampant, some of those receiving this letter may be unfriendly to our purposes. We recognize this hazard. That is why the enclosed reply form is drawn with a commitment to support and assist the achievement of our defined objective. We must depend on your word of honor in this respect.

I feel compelled to quote some more of it here.

The importance of our global campaign may be judged in the following light: We aim to accomplish—

» What was not accomplished by World War One;
» What was not accomplished by World War Two;
» What was not accomplished by the League of Nations;
» What has not and cannot be accomplished by the United Nations;
» What has not been accomplished by 50 years of trying to amend or strengthen the U.N.;
» What has not been accomplished by thousands of protest demonstrations against the military system.

We aim to accomplish enduring world peace, total disarmament of war–making capabilities, a comprehensive program to save the environment and prevent impending catastrophes from climate changes, a new world economic order designed to give everybody equitable opportunities in life, and to establish those global institutions under federal world government by which the above mentioned problems and all problems which transcend national boundaries can be solved peacefully for the good of all by applied intelligence.

Our aim is to begin World Government soon *with more than 70% of Earth included at the start....*

What we are creating is an immediate and practical alternative to the present chaotic, destructive, unfair, life–threatening, and unsustainable course of human affairs on Earth, in which everybody is now trapped.

There is nothing covert about this organization—they openly pro-

mote one–world government with all power over all nations controlled by one central enforcement agency. Will this be the "baby"
that grows up to be the full–blown Antichrist–controlled New World
Order? Maybe—at this point there is no way to determine that, but
their goals certainly meet all the requirements. For more information or to purchase copies of their materials, write to: World Constitution and Parliament Association, Inc., 1480 Hoyt Street, Suite 31,
Lakewood, CO 80215. Of course, I do not advocate becoming associated with them or supporting their new constitution, but it is certainly interesting to gain insight into their plans for us in their New
World Order.

These aren't the only people who are meeting to form a "more
perfect" world government. Remember, I told you earlier about a
meeting in San Francisco in October of 1995, where Mikhail Gor-
bachev, George Bush, Margaret Thatcher, Al Gore, Bill Gates, *et al*,
met to discuss "the fundamental principles the world should embrace in a New World Order," as well as to formulate an international
braintrust and adoption of an "Earth Charter for an Environmental
Bill of Rights" dedicated to the preservation of Planet Earth.

INFORMATION WARFARE IN THE NEW WORLD ORDER

In spite of the philosophical ideas being espoused by the globalists, all the things I have discussed throughout this book are possible only in the new information superhighway that is being pushed
so strongly by Al Gore, Microsoft's Bill Gates, and other globalists,
especially for third–world countries that are currently outside the
system. You see, realistically, there can be no global government nor
cashless economic system without a computerized information infrastructure in place that can handle the massive transfer of digitized information globally to make it viable.

In a book published in 1994, New York author Winn Schwartau
warns us about chaos on the electronic superhighway, which is
somewhat ironic, considering he is a futurist and his book is distributed by the World Future Society, a New World Order think tank. The
futurists are firm believers in one–world government and liberally

promote the idea of global government. Mr. Schwartau, however, is intellectually honest enough to warn us about the disadvantages of the electronic control of the world in his book, *Information Warfare.* He addresses the assault on personal privacy, national economic security, industrial espionage, solutions in cyberspace, and much more.

Robert D. Steele, former deputy director, USMC Intelligence Center, says of this book: "Winn Schwartau is the most dangerous man in America—and the most valuable. His insights into our nation's vulnerabilities to information warfare, and his solutions, are the foundation for our survival. Computer sabotage will wipe out banks, and your savings, in two days, retailers in four, and factories in seven. Our national security is at risk, and the President has not acknowledged the problem. Winn Schwartau is the Nathan Hale of the 21st Century." These are more than just glowing accolades for Mr. Schwartau— these are alarming possible accidents going somewhere to happen.

Schwartau points out that currently, information warfare costs the United States an estimated $100 to $300 billion a year through industrial espionage, hackers and "cyberpunks," malicious software and "viruses," data eavesdropping, code breaking and "chipping," attacks on personal privacy, and other causes.

In his introduction to the second edition, he states, "*Information Warfare* was intended to be a prophetic warning about things to come . . . but . . . so soon?" Then continuing from his original introduction: "This book is about how we as citizens of both the United States and Cyberspace must come to terms with our electronic destiny, . . . the Information Age." Then he follows by referring to the "proposed National Information Infrastructure."

> As the specter of apocalyptic global warfare recedes into the history books (and stays there!), a collective sigh of complacency is replacing the bomb–shelter hysteria. . . . However, as equally dangerous international economic competition supplants megaton military intimidation, offensive pugnacity will be aimed at the informational and financial infrastructure upon which our Western economy depends.

The Cold War is over and has been replaced by economic war-fare....

The foundation of modern society is based on the availability of an access to information. . . . In today's electronically intercon-nected world, information moves at the speed of light, in intangi-ble, and is of immense value. Today's information is the equivalent of yesterday's factories, yet it is considerably more vulnerable.

Right now, the United States is leading the world into a glob-ally networked society, a true Information Age where informa-tion and economic value become nearly synonymous. With over 125 million computers inextricably tying us all together through complex land– and satellite–based communications systems. . . . Computers and other communications and information systems become attractive first–strike targets . . . an electronic Pearl Har-bor waiting to happen. As a result of inadequate security planning on the part of both the government and the private section, *the privacy of most Americans has virtually disappeared.*

In a recent study, two–thirds of Americans polled said that computer usage should be curtailed if their personal privacy was at risk.

Information Warfare is an integral component of the new eco-nomic and political world order.

In other words, my friends, the New World Order. He goes on to in-form us: "Cyberspace is a brave new world . . . a world where the power of knowledge and information usurp the strength of military might. A world totally dependent upon new high–tech tools that make information available instantaneously to anyone, anywhere, at any time. *A world where he who controls the information, controls the people. A world where electronic privacy no longer exists.* . . . A conflict which turns computers into highly offensive weapons [on] the elec-tronic financial highways. . . .

As with any profession, the computer industry has spawned numerous buzzwords, unique to the trade. Cyberspace is one such word. Schwartau defines it as: "that intangible place between com-puters where information momentarily exists on its route from one end of the global network to the other. If Cyberspace is 'that place in between' the phones or the computers, then there are no borders. As we electronically project our essences across the network, we become temporary citizens of Cyberspace, just like our fellow cyber-nauts."

Schartau says that in Information Warfare, Information Age weaponry (the age in which are now living) will replace bombs and bullets. However, these "cyber" weapons are no longer restricted to the government or the CIA or KGB—they are readily available from computer catalogs, retail stores, and trade shows. Many can be built at home from hobby parts. He continues: ". . . of course, the military is developing its own arsenal of weapons with which to wage Information Warfare."

As I mentioned briefly earlier, in the coming New World Order, we will be living in a cashless society, so the world economy will depend upon the successful and reliable operation of the worldwide information superhighway. For a worldwide society to function, the individual must be a citizen of the world . . . which means all information about each person must be in a database which can be accessed by all who need information on you (and many who don't)—again, relying upon the dependability of the worldwide computer link (information superhighway). And any other type of control over all aspects of life in that era will be accomplished by way of electronics, even to the extent of sorting and recording the trash that you discard.

Since our whole existence will depend upon the reliability of the hardware, software, and data input operators, you can imagine what kind of damage could be done to the world society if someone decided to intentionally (or even unintentionally) create havoc within the system. That's why Schwartau calls it *warfare.* He tells us in very specific terms what all this information warfare is about.

> *Information Warfare is about money.* It's about the acquisition of wealth, and the denial of wealth to competitors. It breeds Information Warriors who battle across the Global Network [Author's note: This is the global network which will support the infrastructure of the New World Order.] in a game of cyberrisk.

Information Warfare is about fear. He who controls the information can instill fear in those who want to keep their secrets a secret. It's the fear that the Bank of New York felt when it found itself $23 billion short of cash in only one day. [Author's note: Of course, this is the excuse businesses are using to promote use of the new ID system . . . e.g., you shouldn't mind giving them your fingerprint when you cash a check unless you have something to hide.]

Information Warfare is about arrogance, the arrogance that comes from the belief that one is committing the perfect crime.

Information Warfare is about politics. When the German government sponsors intelligence–agency hacking against U.S. computers, the concept of "ally" needs to be redefined. Or when Iran takes aim at the U.S. economy by state–sponsored counterfeiting, we should have a glimmer that *conflict* is not what it once was. [Author's note: It begins to appear that as much havoc and chaos can be inflicted using paper and electronics, as when you use the aforementioned bullets and bombs—without the bloodletting or the expense of the machinery and armies.]

Information Warfare is about survival. France and Israel developed their respective economies and based entire industries on stealing American secrets. Japan and Korea purloin American technology as it comes off the drawing boards with the help of their governments.

Information Warfare is about-defiance and disenfranchisement in both modern and Third World societies. From the inner cities of Cyberspace come fringe–element hackers with nothing to lose. Some will band together to form Cyberspace's gangs, Cyberspace's organized crime. They recognize the economic benefits of waging Information Warfare. [A New York bank recently lost $400,000 to a European team of hackers—who would have gotten away clean if they hadn't gotten greedy. They came back for another several million dollars and got caught in the act. They currently are fighting extradition to the U.S. for prosecution.]

Information Warfare is about the control of information. As a society we maintain less and less control as Cyberspace expands and *electronic anarchy reigns.* Given global conditions of the late

1980s and 1990s, *Information Warfare is inevitable.* Today's planet offers ripe conditions for Information Warfare, conditions which could not have been foreseen even a few short years ago.

The threat of a future computer Chernobyl is not an empty one. It is only a questions of who and when.

It is my opinion that such a "digital Chernobyl" is intentionally planned in order to create the necessary international "emergency" needed to force the reorganization required to initiate the new world economic order of electronic enslavement, or "cyberprison" under "cybersocialists."

Schwartau goes on to tell us that anyone with an agenda and an attitude can wage Information Warfare, at three distinct levels of intensity: personal, corporate, and global.

Can you guess what would happen if you suffered "Cyber-death"? Electronic murder in Cyberspace and you are *gone!* He has much to say about personal warfare, and *most of it is bad!* And he refers frequently to the "digital you," which is what we have become on the super information highway.

There is no such thing as electronic privacy. The essence of our very being is distributed across thousands of computers and databases over which we have little or no control. From credit reports to health records, from Department of Motor Vehicles computers to court records to video rentals, from law enforcement computers to school transcripts to debit card purchases, from insurance profiles to travel histories to our personal bank finances, everything we do and have done is recorded somewhere in a digital repository.

The sad fact is that these very records which define us as individuals remain unprotected, subject to malicious modification, unauthorized disclosure, or out–and–out destruction. Social Security Administration employees have sold our innermost secrets for twenty–five dollars per name. Worse yet, as of today, there is nothing you can do to protect the digital you. You are not given the option or the opportunity to keep yourself and your family protected from electronic invasions of your privacy.

Your life can be turned absolutely upside down if the digital you ceases to exist. Electronic murder in Cyberspace: You are just gone. Try proving you're alive; computers don't lie. Or if the picture of the digital you is electronically redrawn just the right way, a price can become a pauper in microseconds. In cyberspace, you are guilty until proven innocent.

The corporate information systems don't fare any better; in fact, they have much more at stake than individuals, on an economic level. Schwartau says: "Diligence in weighing the risks associated with placing our entire faith on a technical infrastructure remains in short supply. As we shall see, the federal government must shoulder much of the blame for our current posture. In fact, it is often not in the government's best interest to assist us in *protecting* our computer's and networks."

Now isn't that a surprise – I *wonder* why?! They claim they will protect our privacy rights . . . they know what is best for us. I am reminded of that priceless classic line from the musical, *The King and I*. When faced with the possibility of Siam becoming a British protectorate, the king exclaimed, "Might they not protect me out of all I own?!" Without a doubt! Schwartau continues:

> Their noncommittal attitudes have even harmed efforts now under way to enhance personal privacy and commercial national economic security.
>
> Nonetheless, inane antique policies continue unabated, and in some cases, overt attempts on the part of the federal government have further undermined the electronic privacy of every American citizen. Even President Clinton's proposal to address personal privacy and protect American businesses was met with nearly universal derision, suspicion, and doubt. No matter how hard they try, politicians just don't get it.

Since the subject of this book is the one–world government theme, presently called the New World Order, we should be interested particularly in what Schwartau has to say about information warfare on a global scale. He says that all branches of our government are missing the point—they have not yet realized that ". . . [information] is a vital national asset." He continues: ". . . They miss the fundamental concepts behind the New World Order, the National Information Infrastructure, and our place in the econotechnical Global Network. . . . Information . . . is intangible and does not have an immediately quantifiable monetary worth—unless you lose it. Then it costs a great deal more than you ever   thought. . . . We must take off the blinders and accept—not deny—that *the New World Order is full of bad guys* as well as good guys. . . ."

In much of his material, Schwartau refers to the "nation–states." It is very apparent that he believes we will be in a world–government situation . . . and soon. And since he refers to it frequently as the New World Order, I am inferring that he believes that's what it will be. He asks the questions: "Why will information warfare be fought?" and "Is it a foregone conclusion?" Then proceeds to tell us:

> The incredibly rapid proliferation of high–quality, high–performance electronic information systems have created the Global Network—Cyberspace—thus redefining how we conduct business. Not only did business and government buy into technology, but tens of millions of individuals were, within less than a decade, suddenly empowered with tools and capabilities previously limited to a select few. The comparatively simple technology required for Information Warfare is universally available. Technological anarchy is the result.
>
> The Global Network is a historically unprecedented highway system that defies nationalism and borders. *It places the keys to the kingdom, to our wealth, and our digital identity, within equal reach of everyone with a computer.*

Have I made my case? Can you envision how easily a global dictator could commandeer cyberspace and control every aspect of our lives, including our "buying and selling," as described in Revelation 13:16–18?

When Jesus told us about all those signs for which we should watch, signaling that the end of the age was near, one of them was that "knowledge would increase." However, knowledge has always increased, as one generation passes on to the next what it has learned, creating cumulative knowledge. So, how does that differ from the knowledge that will indicate the end of the age? I am told that taken in context, in the original Greek, it is implied that it really means *knowledge would increase exponentially*. In that case, this expansion of knowledge—just in the last decade—certainly would add to the other evidence of rapidly increasing knowledge in these days and fulfill at least that one prophecy.

I think by now you have grasped the importance of what is happening... everything about everything and everyone is in some computer, and the security stinks! Yet this is the infrastructure that will run the New World Order.

Please keep in mind that I don't agree with much of Mr. Schwartau's philosophy, as he is a futurist who supports one-world government and all that goes with it, and this book is distributed by the World Future Society. But as I told you earlier, he is intellectually honest enough to point out what is inherently wrong with the system, as it pertains to the Information Age. I recommend that you get this 432-page book and read it carefully all the way through.

THE NOAHIDE LAWS—COULD THESE BE THE FOUNDATION FOR CAPITOL PUNISHMENT IN THE NEW WORLD ORDER?

Revelation 13:15–18 (quoted in the beginning of this chapter) calls for capitol punishment for failure to **worship** the beat (Antichrist) or to accept his **mark**. Then in Revelation 20:4, we learned that the prescribed method of execution was decapitation/beheading.

I have spent this entire book laying the foundation for what I'm about to tell you, and giving you an overview of what the New World Order is politically, economically, and spiritually. I have attempted, hopefully successfully, to convey from a secular viewpoint (though I make no apology for the fact that I believe it fulfills prophecy in the Bible) how God's scripture is being fulfilled in our time. I have told you about electronic enslavement, biometrics, smart–card identification on a global scale, which it appears ultimately will evolve into use of biochip technology *in our right hands* to totally enslave us. I have given you scriptures to tie it all to the fulfillment of Bible prophecy, i.e., you cannot participate in any of the world's activities without the **mark,** once the Antichrist takes command of the New World Order. And I have told you what will happen if you decline the offer of this Satanic **mark** (probably a biochip).

By now it should be apparent that this is all adding up to a spiritual choice—you will be required to *worship* this world dictator as god. The punishment for rejection will be swift and final—execution by decapitation. Now, in recent years, this has not been the form of capitol punishment in practice, *but it will be*, if for no other reason than because the Bible says it will be. However, the Antichrist isn't likely to do anything recommended by the Bible—at least not intentionally. So we must have some foundation for switching back to this ancient form of execution, if the Bible prophecy is to be fulfilled as written. I believe we now may have such a foundation in place.

During Bush's administration, shortly before the Gulf War, an innocuous–sounding little piece of legislation was signed into law, allegedly to honor an old man on his ninetieth birthday. H.J. Resolution 104 was signed into law as a proclamation to designate March 26, 1991, as "Education Day, U.S.A." Sounds innocent enough, doesn't it? Not so! Written into all the "whereas" sections were a number of references calling for the return to the ethical values of the seven Noahide laws. Now, you won't find any call for decapitation in this seemingly harmless little document, but, beware; that's just a smoke screen. When one begins to dig into the historical documents of the ancient Jewish Talmud with reference to the Noahide laws, you will find the commandments they consider ethical values, and what they consider just punishment for breaking them . . . guess what, you lose your head!

Now, we don't want anyone to jump to any wild conclusion, because a law has no apparent "teeth" in it yet, as there is no prescribed punishment for violation of it—the government did not call for the establishment of capitol punishment by decapitation, but by joint resolution of the House and the Senate it did establish Public Law No. 102–14 (published in the United States Statutes at Large containing the laws and concurrent resolutions enacted during the first session of the 102nd Congress of the United States of America, 1991, and Proclamations, Vol. 105, Part 1, Public Laws 102–1 through 102–150), which calls for the return to the ethics of the Noahide laws. I don't think it's too much of a stretch to extrapolate this into fulfillment of Scripture, once the Antichrist comes into power. I believe the foundation has been placed into law.

However, once the Antichrist comes into power, whether or not a foundation has been laid will become a moot point . . . he will be an absolute dictator, and if you don't worship him and take **his mark**, you'll lose your head! Because one of the seven Noahide laws concerns blasphemy, Christians who refuse to worship the beast likely could be executed under the violation of the blasphemy law, as they will not acknowledge the Antichrist as God.

I want to cite the seven Noahide laws, as defined in *The New Standard Jewish Encyclopedia* (Doubleday and Co., Inc., New York, 1977).

> **LAWS OF NOAH**: Seven laws which the rabbis hold binding upon all mankind, derived from early chapters of Genesis (e.g. 9:4–7). Six of these laws are negative, prohibiting idolatry, blasphemy, murder, adultery, robbery, and the eating of flesh cut from a living animal. The single positive commandment is that requiring the establishment of courts of justice. The "Noahide Laws" were much discussed by European scholars in the 17th century in connection with the Law of Nations.

These seven laws are again defined in *The Jewish Encyclopedia* (KTAV Publishing House, Inc., p. 648–9), followed by the prescribed punishment.

> **LAWS, NOACHIAN:**
> (1) not to worship idols; (2) not to blaspheme the name of God; (3) to establish courts of justice; (4) not to kill; (5) not to commit

adultery; and (6) not to rob. . . .

. . . the prevalent opinion in the Talmud is that there are only seven laws which are binding upon all mankind. . . .

In the elaboration of these seven Noachian laws, and in assigning punishments for their transgressions, the Rabbis are sometimes more lenient and sometimes more rigorous with Noachidae [non–Jews] than with Israelites. But with a few exceptions, the punishment meted out to a Noachid for the transgression of any of the seven laws is **decapitation**, the least painful of the four modes of execution of criminals. The many formalities of procedure essential when the accused is an Israelite *need not be observed in the case of the Noachid*. The latter may be convicted on the testimony of *one witness*, even on that of relatives, but not on that of a woman. He need have had no warning from the witnesses; and a *single judge* may pass sentence on him. . . .

There are numerous other references to both the seven laws and their prescribed punishment in other works.

Under these laws, would Christians be considered guilty of violating the blasphemy law, because they believe that Jesus, the Christ, is God manifest in the flesh? (You may recall that Jesus was tried for blasphemy because He claimed to be the Son of God.) Who knows at this time what the real ulterior motive of these laws might be.

As we make a cursory examination of the laws, we don't see anything blatantly objectionable. In fact, we encourage efforts to improve the ethical conduct in our nation. But I must tell you . . . there is more to this than can be seen from a cursory examination.

In the July–August 1991, issue of *The Gap*, the newsletter published by the Noahide movement, the lead article revealed that there is pressure being applied for a worldwide recognition of the seven laws. Ernest Easterly, professor of international law at Southern University Law Center, said: "With further recognition by other nations and international courts, **the seven Noahide laws should become the cornerstone of a truly civilized international legal order.**" *Read that: New World Order!*

My main goal here is to bring your attention to something about which few Americans are aware. I don't profess to have any supernatural insight as to what unseen forces may have propelled George Bush and Congress to bring forth this kind of national law, but given my biblical insight regarding last days' prophetic events, I am extremely suspicious regarding why such a law may be useful at this time, other than furthering the agenda of the New World Order advocates. However, since the Bible says that anyone who refuses to take the Antichrist's mark will be beheaded, this very well could be the case. What do you think?

Legislation before the state of Georgia proposed that execution by guillotine be offered as an alternative option for convicts sentenced to the death penalty. The reason was strictly humanitarian, at least so they would have us believe. One article reads:

Guillotine Proposed as Means of Execution in Georgia

Georgia lawmaker Doug Teper (Democrat, 61st Dist.) has proposed a bill to replace the state's electric chair with the guillotine. Teper's reasoning? It would allow for death row inmates as organ donors, he says, since the "blade leaves a   clean cut and leaves vital organs intact. . . ."

The guillotine, invented by the French Dr. Guillotine, was mainly used in the 18th and 19th centuries and chops off a person's head. It hasn't been used for decades in any country in the world.

Excerpts from Georgia's H.B. No. 1274 follow:

BE IT ENACTED BY THE GENERAL ASSEMBLY OF GEORGIA:

SECTION 1: The General Assembly finds that while prisoners condemned to death may wish to donate one or more of their organs for transplant, any such desire is thwarted by the fact that electrocution makes all such organs unsuitable for transplant. The intent of the General Assembly in enacting this legislation is to provide for a method of execution which is compatible with the donation of organs by a condemned prisoner.

SECTION 2(a): All persons who have been convicted of a capitol offense and have imposed upon them a sentence of death shall, at the election of the condemned, suffer such punishment either by electrocution or by guillotine. If the condemned fails to make an election by the thirtieth day preceding the date scheduled for execution, punishment shall be by electrocution.

SECTION 3: The Department of Corrections shall provide a death chamber and all necessary apparatus, machinery, and appliances for inflicting the penalty of death by electrocution or by guillotine.

SECTION 4: This Act shall be applicable to all executions occurring on or after August 31, 1996.

Of course, it contains all the necessary legalese to change and/or replace old laws and initiate the new policy, but the above gives you the "nuts and bolts" of the act as proposed by "Doug 'Heads Will Roll' Teper," as he is called. Tabloids have had a field day with this bill. The legislation failed to pass, but rest assured, you have not seen the last of such attempts . . . *the Bible says so!*

CONSPIRACY THEORIES GROW

After the unfortunate 1995 Oklahoma City bombing tragedy, the government and liberal media began a barrage of propaganda against all fundamental Christians, conservatives, conservative talk-show hosts, patriots, *et al*, labeling them as extremists, ultra–right wing fanatics, "militia types," and/or armed–and–dangerous. It was as if they suddenly became "enemies of the state," as it were, for no other reason than their opposition to excessive government controls. Aren't you a little suspicious as to why one criminal (allegedly McVeigh) perpetrated an isolated event, and thereafter, the government began branding most conservatives and patriots as potential terrorists and/or fanatics who should be feared by the populace at large? Anyone (and anyone affiliated with them) who was opposed to the alleged conspiracy to subject the U.S. to a U.N.–controlled world government automatically was considered one of the above-mentioned radicals, and potentially dangerous. It almost seemed as though the government were waiting for the New World Order system. Suddenly, all who opposed global government became suspect in their minds. The dissenters were labeled as "anti-government" by President Bill Clinton.

The media joined right in with hundreds of articles maligning anyone who fit *their* description of **extremist!** One such media accusation on the front page of the *Detroit News and Free Press*, dates Saturday, April 29, 1995, conveys just such a message. This article reports the facts quite accurately; however, they inevitably put their own liberal spin on the material, apparently in an effort to defame or discredit anyone who believes the facts as stated. Unfortunately, even though McHugh's report technically was accurate, some of the people he quoted have made several incorrect assumptions regarding biochip technology.

Actually, this one article makes reference to George Bush's introduction of the term New World Order, which he subsequently used over two hundred times in public addresses. But even the media in general has admitted that no one fully understood what he meant by the use of that term. His frequent use of the term is what awakened many conservatives and patriots to its imminent approach.

This newspaper article also discussed Pat Robertson's 1991 book, *The New World Order*. In the article, reporter David McHugh accuses Robertson of "parroting the classic conspiracy theory, complete with Illuminati and Freemasons." McHugh says that Robertson claims the Gulf War was a ploy to get Americans to accept United Nations' rule. I fully agree with Pat Robertson and his view, and his book is excellent. I highly recommend you read it. Pat Robertson is no fool, and he is no religious extremist. In fact, he is a highly educated man with a law degree from Yale University, coincidentally Bush's alma mater. He is most articulate and an extremely reliable source of trustworthy research.

I will close my comments on conspiracies by pointing out that Clinton's remarks (above), labeling dissenters as "anti-government," are extremely hypocritical. Isn't it interesting that Bill Clinton himself started out as an anti-government "protester" of sorts in his youth. Rumor has it that he went to liberal/socialist colleges in England, avoiding participation in the Vietnam War, that he denounced the United States government, and that he visited Communist Russia for unknown reasons when it was still considered the "evil empire." He admittedly smoked marijuana (though he claimed he "never inhaled"—what a joke!), and now one of his ex-partners in adultery, Jennifer Flowers, has stated in a media interview that he used cocaine when they were together. Further, in 1994 (and following) the Clintons were under investigation for fraud and other crimes. And this man has the audacity to label Christians and conservatives "anti-government dark forces which may need to be purged." What hypocrisy! Government propaganda has turned the tables on us now; where they used to accuse us of seeing everything as a conspiracy, now they see us as the conspirators.

Possible Scenario to Usher in the New World Order

Based on over seven years' of research, having read over three hundred books, mountains of periodicals and technical product brochures, occultist newsletters, and various New Age and Masonic publications, I feel I have gained an incredibly good understanding into the mindset of Satan's people who wish to bring about this New World Order. I will attempt to convey to you a possible scenario that could occur in the next few years to bring about world government under the Antichrist. I want to make it absolutely clear that I am not prophesying—I do not consider myself a prophet in the biblical sense; however, the knowledge I have accrued during these seven years gives considerable credibility to my conjectures concerning these events.

The Luciferians, who desire a New World Order under the devil, often use a little-known Latin phrase that describes how they intended to bring it all about. That phrase is, *ordo ab chao*. *Ordo ab chao* means "order from chaos." In other words, they purposely plan to create more than enough chaos in the world to convince us that we need a New World Order to fix it. The book of Daniel says that the Antichrist will first come as a peacemaker, and "by peace he will destroy many." So even though many wars and rumors of wars are occurring around the world presently, it's going to get worse, because the devil has to terrify the world into needing a worldwide peacemaker to bring order out of chaos. Frankly, I believe that in the not-too-distant future Korea will present the Antichrist with the chaos he needs to pull this off. Korea could explode soon into a "horrifying quagmire" that will call for a complete mobilization of U.S. Armed Forces to help quell the planned disorder, under the command of the United Nations, of course! There even could be a limited nuclear war, utilizing small atomic weapons. Such nuclear conflagration—unheard of since World War II—would terrify the world into thinking that it was on the very precipice of Armageddon (even though *actual* Armageddon will be several years after the Antichrist comes to power). The world, then, would need a world government under a charismatic, global leader (the Antichrist) to restore order and create peace from chaos.

In addition to the war chaos scenario presented above, Satan's people could also create an international financial disaster—an economic cataclysm the likes of which the world never has seen—creating havoc around the globe that is unparalleled in history. Among other possibilities, additional chaos could be created as a result of an information "meltdown," created by either terrorists or others. As Winn Schwartau suggested in his book *Information Warfare*, an informational "Chernobyl" is inevitable—it's just a matter of where and when. As a result, virtually everyone's wealth will be wiped out overnight—not difficult in a cashless society! Banks will close and circumstances will be desperate, even worse than the Great Depression of the 1930s. People will be reduced to poverty and will be totally dependant upon the government for sustenance. Money, food, medical assistance, and other benefits will be used to make people gratefully submit to the government's plan to resolve this and other global crises.

Dr. Henry Kissinger, a New World Order "lieutenant," was quoted several years ago as saying that what the world really needed to make it realize that world government was necessary was an outside threat of some kind. He postulated that a UFO alien invasion might be such a world-unifying threat. He further stated that when confronted by this threat, the people of the world would gladly relinquish their national sovereignty and individual rights to receive protection from the U.N.–led world government against these "invaders." So, based on this insight from Mr. Kissinger, I surmise that in addition to war chaos, economic cataclysm, and other disastrous events, such as natural disasters, i.e. floods, hurricanes, earthquakes, volcanic eruptions, etc., we also may be confronted with a demonic manifestation in the form of a UFO invasion. New Agers contend that the "aliens" are poised and ready to make intervention into the affairs of mankind at just the right time to "save us from ourselves."

By this time, advanced technology will probably have moved us forward to the point that our smart cards already have been replaced by a more positive, unalterable means of permanent identification (biochip implants). But until then, we are being preconditioned to accept such technology by means of routine use of biochip identification of animals, as well as imminent national ID cards— probably based on the current military MARC card. Keep in mind that I described the function of the MARC card in chapter seven, and how it might possibly evolve first into a national citizen ID card, then eventually into a very personal, implantable ID biochip. Eventually, as citizens of the world we will be required to accept a new system of international identification, the MARK/MARC of the New World Order, which likely will be the mark of the beast described in the book of Revelation. Since Revelation 13:16 calls for this "mark" to be placed either in the right hand, or in the forehead, it is significant that we find the following in an article by Donald R. Richards, CPP, titled "ID technology Faces the Future," which appeared in the April 1994 edition of *Security Management* magazine, discussing biometric identification methods: "Since users are likely to be clothed from head to toe, the identification decision must be based on the hands or the head. . . ."

This is specifically what the Bible calls for; now we know why! This is the first time in history that such ideas are being postulated and the technology is available to carry them out.

THE ILLUMINATI GLOBALISTS ARE PREPARING A NEW WORLD ORDER OF SLAVERY AND DESTRUCTION!

It is an undeniable fact that we presently are being prepared in consciousness for a New World Order of satanically orchestrated communism, slavery, poverty, and destruction. They are in fact laying the final groundwork now with the phony so–called "war on terror," the "war on drugs," and the carefully engineered and executed global ECONOMIC CRASH and economic "BAILOUTS." All such strategically planned events are together a general "war on God's people." And this war is Satan's final "revolution against God," against anyone who's been purchased via Christ's sacrifice at the cross!

In the meantime, the mass media and Hollywood's sewage–pipe stream of movies, rock music, video games, and all other forms of TV–induced decadence, conditions us daily to sophisticated forms of anti–God perversion, homosexuality, general immorality, prostitution, drugs, lying, brutality, and violence. Indeed, there is an overriding repetitive and reductive obsession with degenerative sex, nudity, bodily functions, and homosexuality.

If the Illuminati's real purpose is to eliminate God, it then follows that we should make God the center of our consciousness. People ask me, "What should we do?" I tell them not to look for direction from others; look to God for direction. The best way to fight the darkness is to shine God's light.

Don't feel oppressed by the world. It hasn't changed any simply because you now are aware of it. Devote each new day to fulfilling God's purpose for you.

AN ENGINEERED ECONOMIC COLLAPSE CRISIS OBAMA WON'T WASTE

The 2009 economic crisis is much too "useful" for Obama to want to end it. When Rahm Emanuel, and later Hillary Clinton, spoke of never letting a good crisis "go to waste," many people were shocked. But now Obama seems to embody the corollary: that the crisis should continue until he has thoroughly milked it to reshape American politics, society, and the economy. Like Faust, he seems to wish that this "given moment" will "endure forever." Unlike Faust, however, he will not lose his "life and soul" to such a wish; rather, he'll sacrifice ours instead.

First came the "stimulus package." With only about $185 billion of its $800 billion in spending to be spent in 2009, Obama clearly never intended the spending to be about stimulus but wanted the need for a stimulus to trigger the spending he wanted anyway.

Then came the Troubled Asset Relief Program (TARP) funding, often forced down banks' throats. Now comes word that even as banks want to return the money, the Treasury is making them keep it. One source at a TARP bank reports that Treasury secretary Timothy Geithner is insisting that banks go through their "stress test" before refunding the TARP money. As Stuart Varney speculates in the *Wall Street Journal,* Obama wants the banks to keep the money so he can enforce his regulations on them.

Now comes Geithner's plea for extra regulatory powers and Obama's concession to global economic regulation at the G-20 summit. Both moves are game–changers for any major American business. Geithner wants the power to take over any business, presumably in any field, whose failure would imperil the national economy. Today it's banks, brokerage houses, car companies, and insurance firms. Tomorrow, who knows?

Moreover, Obama agreed to agree on international "high standards" for the regulation of all "systemically important" companies to be promulgated by the new global Financial Stability Board (FSB). The United States, occupying one of twenty chairs on the FSB board (twenty–one if we count the EU), will come to a consensus with other central bankers from the G–20 nations on what these regulations should say. Then the Securities and Exchange Commission, the Federal Reserve and the other regulatory arms of the U.S. government will impose them on our economy.

And, finally, there is Obama's delegation of a total overhaul of the tax code to a commission headed by Paul Volcker with a mandate to report back in December of this year.

Some have objected that Congress needs to be consulted, but as long as the agreements are "voluntary" and the U.S. agencies are merely "asked" to impose the regulations, no further grant of congressional authority is needed. Of course, there will be nothing voluntary about the administration's demand that the agencies implement the coming directives, no matter how intrusive they may be.

So with the tax code totally changing, Europe about to formulate regulations for our economy, the U.S. government empowered to take over any large company, the deficit and spending reaching unbelievable levels, and the feds insisting on continued control of banks, what businessman in his right mind is going to invest in anything? How could even the most foolish optimist pull the trigger on a business investment without knowing the tax consequences, the regulatory framework, and the policy of the banks on lending?

But Obama knows all this. He knows that his steps will delay economic recovery. But he wants these changes, not as means to an end, but as the end itself. And he is determined to get them passed and set in stone while the rubric of "crisis" justifies his doing so. He is not unlike a leader who takes his country into war, knowing that by "wagging the dog" he can reinforce his power. This is why Obama is deliberately NOT doing anything to solve our financial crisis! It serves his aims of creating a DICTATORSHIP to deplete out assets, drive us further into debt that can never be repaid, and lead his supporters to devastation as they cheer him on assuaging his narcissistic ego!

Indeed, Mr. Obama's obvious Communist purpose in doing such treasonous things is to gain lifelong power, promote Islam and Sharia law here, and turn America into an unspeakably horrifying dictatorship none of us want to even contemplate; i.e., the American branch of Satan's international New World Order!

AMERICA'S FUTURE: A NATION IN CRISIS!

The Apostle Paul wrote of just such a time as exists in America (and the world) today; a time when people would be lovers of themselves, covetous, boasters, proud, blasphemers, disobedient to parents, unthankful, unholy, without natural affection, trucebreakers, false accusers, uncontrollable, fierce, despisers of those that are good, traitors, heady, high–minded, and lovers of pleasures more than lovers of God.

In view of the fact that fifty million innocent babies have been murdered intentionally with premeditation and in the most heinous ways, I would add murderers to that list, which of course only highlights Paul's offering of "being without natural affection."

There does not exist a more apt description than this of the nature of the United States today, for it is a nation that consists, collectively, of a people led away from God by divers lusts; it is an ever-learning acculturation of those who are never able to come to a knowledge of the truth. It is in fact a nation of people who resist the truth, an irreverent fellowship of men of corrupt mind and reprobate faith.

The inimical indoctrination of the people of this nation begins in the public schools where the ungodly elements of communism, sexual perversion, deviancy, false doctrines and a rejection of biblical tenants are instilled in young minds and taught as gospel by an autocracy of Marxist persuasion. An open-minded and healthy examination of social issues is disallowed, and a narrow, subjective, and politically correct curriculum is rigidly enforced. The National Education Association, a radical, revolutionary, and powerful labor union, is using the political clout it purchases with the dues of its members, has eliminated the traditional approach to the training of young minds in the basics of education and concentrated on a radical program of mind control and brainwashing to shape the values— I should say lack of values—of America's children.

Parents, if you think that you have any input into the way that public schools educate your children, you need to put that thought out of your mind quickly. The majority of public school systems view your children as property of the state and therefore beyond your control. Moral relativism is promoted and ethical codes and morality based upon absolute standards is not a part of **their satanic bible.** "If it feels good do it" is their motto and their creed. You need to get your children out of the public schools and you need to do it now before any more of our children are corrupted and led down criminal paths to the point that many additional millions of dollars have to be spent on correctional facilities to incarcerate the emotional cripples turned into the streets by the public schools.

The United States has crossed a great divide and is now on a dizzying slide downward through an ever-quickening succession of events, both of the cosmos and of manmade induction, which are stepping this nation toward a now inevitable time of a complete and climactic destruction.

Prayers from an apostate people for deliverance from catastrophic events current and future will not be heard. In the parlance of the Bible, it is a time for sackcloth and ashes.

Those who believe that there is hope for a secular deliverance of this country from an increasingly inescapable terminal destiny at the hand of Almighty God, or that the government or its leaders possess the answers to the nearly total social and spiritual unraveling of this commonwealth, are barking up a wrong tree. Nowhere in the population of this nation or in the government or the institutions thereof exists a savior. Our Savior has come to this earth, and gone, and will return again; and it is He alone that we should look to for deliverance. It is Jesus Christ who is the true Savior, and if you have not accepted Him as such and taken advantage of His work upon the cross for the expiation of your sins past, present and future, you most surely would do well to do so now, and quickly!

The prophets of old who were sent to deliver hard messages unto God's people and to their kings, and religious leaders were censored and imprisoned, and those who speak the truth today can expect the same circumstances as even now we can see an unrighteous abridgement by a seemingly fascistic government—of individual rights and liberties. "When I say unto the wicked, Thou shall surely die; and thou gives him not warning, nor speaks to warn the wicked from his wicked way, to save his life; the same wicked man shall die in his iniquity; but his blood will I require at your hand" (Ezek. 3:18).

Clearly, those in the liberal "Aquarian" New Age ministry today who tickle the ears of their lost followers with various "New Age" doctrines of demons—such as the goodness of man, a lack of evil, that man is divine and therefore can create his own spiritual destiny, or that Satan is an imaginary being and there are many roads to salvation—have not read the above Scripture. And if they have and have rejected it, or any other of God's truths, they will stand and give an account for every lost soul that was in their charge.

Devastating natural events are being poured out upon this nation one upon another. Ten of millions of homes have been destroyed and hundreds of millions of people displaced and made homeless. Local economies have been wiped out and the U.S. economy, already a tottering shambles held together by chewing gum and duct tape, is being pushed to the edge. In truth, the economy of this nation is, for all intents, shot; fooled away by seeming halfwits.

Middle–income taxpayers cannot continually bail out one area after another from the costs of major catastrophic events, and it is with a certainty that the major corporations that are virtually completely exempt from taxation are not going to contribute to any recovery, as greed is the name of their game. Therefore, the soon coming tax burden the government will place upon the dwindling few working citizens will be crushing.

A wrecked car in such a dismal shape as our economy would be declared a total loss and scrapped. I think that this is exactly the plan of those who pursue a one–world order. They endeavor powerfully and vigorously to scrap the dollar and negate our sovereignty in order that this nation might be coalesced with Canada and Mexico in a North American Union and then integrated into a New World Order.

Our elected politicians have put into place a consortium of bureaucratic storm troops that control every facet of our lives. Thousands of decrees, edicts, and administrative rules with the force of law suppress our freedoms and curtail the guarantees of the Bill of Rights.

The courts have eviscerated the Constitution and bureaucratic storm troops carry out the orders and writs of judges issued all too often out of a subjective interpretation of the law rather than on constitutional principle. The first, second, fourth, and fifth amendments are routinely circumvented or ignored and bureaucratic agents and law enforcement agents on all governmental levels are coached in such circumvention. *Habeas corpus* has been nullified and the power of eminent domain is routinely savagely abused.

We have come to a point in this country where police death squads in coal scuttle helmets, black armor, and jackboots strike the same terror and fear into the hearts of innocent law–abiding citizens that their counterparts of the SA and SS did in Nazi Germany. All that is missing is a crooked cross upon their helmets. State and local law enforcement agents are increasingly being made a part of a federal police state. Local law enforcement officers are being sworn-in as federal U.S. Marshals and are being used to carry out the dictates of an increasingly totalitarian "American" government.

Here's a horrible thought: Just think about the widespread collapse of civil order and the collapse of emergency services that occurred in New Orleans after Hurricane Katrina—except on a national level. The implementation of gun confiscation laws, looters and thugs terrorizing the elderly with impunity, besieged hospitals without power, doctors, and medicine. People forcibly herded into "containment zones" and denied access to food, water, and medical attention. At least forty-five patients died in one city-run hospital after being abandoned by doctors and staff.

The recent collapse of the U.S. fuel infrastructure is a major warning sign that the energy supply chain is stretched dangerously thin, which combined with financial unrest, has the strong potential to create major disruptions in the food supply chain! Please note that most population centers have only a three-day supply of food available to the public through supermarkets! This means panic runs on food are a distinct possibility as the potential for social chaos continues to mount.

If you think these scenarios cannot happen in the United States of America, talk with anyone who has ever been in the path of a hurricane. They will confirm that by the time the general public catches on to the danger, getting everyday items such as gasoline, batteries, plywood, medicine, water, and food becomes next to impossible. Social services, police protection, public transportation, and highway systems will become next to useless during those times.

Who can know the evil that lurks in the minds of men? Well, God knows, and soon, so shall we, if we don't already know.

A virtual Trojan horse of monumental proportions has been rolled across our borders. Such an event could not have been accomplished without the ignorance, apathy, and complaisance of the people and the treasonous endeavors of the politicians who feed at trough of the corporate pirates who control the government and society with the monies that they have amassed by deceit, trickery, and larceny beyond imagination. To be subject to these is the fate of a people who have no knowledge of Almighty God. This horse carried the seeds of an invasive and pernicious evil that will render this nation completely impotent and cause it to lie prostrate before its enemies.

Out of this **Trojan horse** poured predators, malcontents, criminals of all stripe, disease carriers, freeloaders, mercenaries, and subversives who have molested, raped, and killed our children, disrupted and corrupted every facet of an amalgamate and orderly society, bankrupted our local governments and institutions, piled the people high with debt to sustain the invaders with perks beyond anything available to ordinary citizens, caused us to build an ever-increasing number of prisons to incarcerate alien invaders who kill, violate, and maim American citizens, and opened the country to the predations of clandestine enemy agents who have infiltrated via open borders and lax immigration policies and who are supported by enemy citadels that have been openly set up under the noses of the government and its security agencies in the guise of mosques and embassies!

The floods, the hurricanes, the tornadoes, the fires, the earthquakes, and the manmade disasters presage the time of the end. Soon—very soon—our cities will be host to civil strife such has never been experienced in the history of this nation. A pestilence of violence will roll across the land, cities will burn, and the carnage will be great. Our panicked fascist government will add to that carnage. The violence will exacerbate an already degraded situation and disease and famine will spread exponentially in the wake of the violence. There will be widespread panic brought about by the rolling and continuous collapse of services and social order.

When the nation has been sufficiently weakened by all of the foregoing, an utter annihilation will fall upon the land and it will be made desolate by nuclear fire. "In all your dwelling places the cities shall be laid waste, and the high places shall be desolate; that your altars may be laid waste and made desolate, and your idols may be broken and cease, and your images may be cut down, and your works may be abolished. And the slain shall fall in the midst of you, and ye shall know that I am the LORD" (Ezek. 6:6–7).

This Is Scary Enough, But What Else Could Happen?

Right after leaving office, Vice President Dick Cheney warned of the possible deaths of "perhaps hundreds of thousands of Americans" in a terror attack using nuclear or biological weapons. "I think there is a high probability of such an attempt," the straight–talking Cheney warned during a 2008 interview with *Politico* magazine.

An important item buried deeply in another 2008 article in the *Washington Post* noted there are already twenty thousand commercially–available labs in the world where a single person could synthesize any existing virus he wants! In those same labs, five people with $2 million can create an advanced pathogen—meaning a virus that would be able to infect several million people, killing perhaps a million of them.

Former Health and Human Services secretary Tommy Thompson confessed to a reporter that he "worries every single night" about a possible bioterror attack on the U.S. food supply. "For the life of me," he said, "I cannot understand why the terrorists have not attacked our food supply because it is the easiest thing to do".

Ramifications of Accepting the Mark of the New Word Order

Though I quoted it at the beginning of this chapter, it bears repeating here at the close of the chapter. In Revelation 14:9–11, we read:

> And the third angel followed them, saying with a loud voice, If any man worship the beast and his image, and receive his mark in his forehead, or in his hand, The same shall drink of the wine of the wrath of God, which is poured out without mixture into the cup of his indignation; and he shall be tormented with fire and brimstone in the presence of the holy angels, and in the presence of the Lamb: And the smoke of their torment ascendeth up for ever and ever: and they have no rest day or night, who worship the beast and his image, and whosoever recieveth the mark of his name.

It is also important to repeat that neither the smart card, MARC card, national ID card, nor implantable biochip, in and of themselves, are in fact THE mark of the beast, although some technically advanced form of biochip seems the most likely contender to meet the requirements. You can't go to Hell by accident, nor can someone send you there. Receiving this mark will be a conscious choice, as reiterated in the scripture above, because you must both worship the beast AND receive his mark. Acceptance or refusal of this economic mark of the beast will determine whether you may buy or sell (or receive government services and/or benefits) in the New World Order. It will be the economic coercion by which people will be forced to join Satan's Antichrist–led world system. In addition to preventing you from buying or selling, there will be severe punishment for refusing to worship the beast and rejecting his mark; as documented earlier, you will forfeit your head. The Antichrist will not physically force people to receive his mark, but he will "cause" them to receive the mark—because the consequences are extremely stringent—they will be excluded from transacting any business in his global cashless world economic order and ultimately be martyred if they continue to refuse to worship him. I know I've told you all this before, but it is so crucial that I must tell it again.

CHOOSING THE RIGHT NEW WORLD ORDER

The drive toward a New World Order continues. Jesus predicted a time of terrible judgment, so bad that if God did not intervene, there would be no flesh left on the earth (Matt. 24:22). Someday Jesus will return, and when He does, He will establish His reign on the earth for a thousand years (Rev. 20:6). This will be God's New World Order promised throughout the Bible. The time to choose which New World Order is for you is **now**, before the time for choices is past. Satan's counterfeit is near at hand and, according to Joel 3:9–12, millions will perish during his cruel reign; however, Jesus, the Savior, invites you to receive His grace and forgiveness instead, and rejoice in His New World order forever.

No one can serve two masters; that is biblical admonition, but you know it to be true from everyday experience. Two other scriptures warn us to "choose you this day whom you will serve" and that "today is the day of salvation." Those are easy to interpret—the choice is ours—don't wait until it is too late to make it. Today is the only day we have to accept the Lord's offer of salvation, since none of us have any guarantee of tomorrow.

In spite of New Age propaganda to the contrary, there are really only two choices: the Son of the one true God, the Lord Jesus Christ—or Satan, the fallen father of lies, the Antichrist, the false god, whose number (according to Scripture) is 666! God said in the Old Testament: "I set before you this day of life and death—choose life!" I also urge you to *choose life!* Not only are the rewards "out of this world," but you can escape God's judgment for rejecting his Son.

The Bible promises that all who have received Jesus Christ as their Savior and Lord will be saved from the coming wrath of God on a Christ–rejecting, God–hating world. Yes, you too can escape the coming New World Order horror by making Christ your Lord and Savior today. Don't procrastinate; do it now. Worship Jesus Christ, not the Antichrist. All it takes on your part is a sincere invitation (it's actually called a prayer), then Jesus does the part He promised: He washes you clean by His shed blood, welcomes you into God's family, and becomes your Savior. This is not religion; it's a relationship. Once you have established the relationship with Jesus by asking Him to become your Savior (an immediate transaction), then proceed to make Him the Lord of your life. Seek to pattern your life after His example, described in the Bible, and seek His direction for your life. He has promised never to leave us nor forsake us. Then tell someone about this new relationship. The Bible says that you must believe in your heart and confess with your mouth—you can think of it as confirming the transaction.

Of course, being spiritually prepared is the most important thing, but you might give consideration to preparing in the natural as well, i.e.—store extra food, acquire some precious metals, etc., because some very precarious times lay ahead of us.

Jesus said, "Surely I come quickly." To which we respond, **"Even so, come, Lord Jesus."**

*May God bless you
and keep you
in the days ahead.*

Other books by
Bible Belt Publishing
To order, call 1-800-652-1144

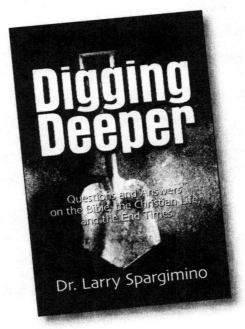

The central message of the Bible is so simple, that even a child can understand it.

Yet every reader of the Bible knows that God's Word is thought–provoking. Haven't you read the Bible and had questions about what you are reading pop into your mind and wish that you could dig a little deeper?

In this volume, Dr. Larry Spargimino raises and answers a number of relevant questions that every Christian has asked at one time or another. You will get the questions, the answers, and the scriptural reasons for the answers.

Digging Deeper will help you travel the road of personal Bible study and bring you the joy of discovery as you dig deeper into the unfathomable riches of God's Word.

ISBN 1-933641-29-0
Retail $14.95

This book is written about the life, times, and prophecies of Daniel, a man beloved of God.

Daniel prophesied the exact chronology for the rise and fall of nations and empires during the times of the Gentiles. He foretold the exact date of the crucifixion of Jesus Christ, and the nations that would be involved in the Middle East in the last days. Jesus referred to the prophecies of Daniel in the Olivet Discourse. Michael informed Daniel that in these days when the time drew near for God to set up a Kingdom on earth that would never pass away, the prophet's sealed book would be unsealed. NOW IS THAT TIME!

ISBN 1-933641-16-9
Retail $14.95

In *25 Messianic Signs in Israel Today* Dr. Hutchings outlines signs occurring in Israel that the Bible says will immediately precede the Great Tribulation and the coming of the Messiah.

To Christians, this means that Jesus Christ must be coming soon. God is now showing the Jews through these signs what is coming very shortly.

Dr. Hutchings and Mrs. Treibich have put these signs in chronological, documented order so that no Jew can doubt (if he believes the Torah) that before the Messiah comes, a time of great persecution and trouble must come first.

ISBN 1-933641-06-1
Retail $12.95

The book of Revelation is, beyond controversy, the most misunderstood of all the 66 books of the Bible. The reason is that the events prophesied in this book were not possible until the present generation.

The setting for this verse–by–verse commentary is centered on Revelation 11:18 where we find God's promise that Jesus is not coming to destroy this earth, but to "destroy them which destroy the earth." In view of the rising dangers to this world from new diseases, biological warfare, and nuclear destruction, without the promise of God in Revelation that Jesus is coming back, this world would have no hope.

The Bible reader will discover a new understanding of this exciting book. The unsaved will be challenged to accept Jesus Christ as Savior and Lord and miss the coming Great Tribulation.

ISBN 0-9744764-4-7
Retail $14.95